Economic Relations between East and West

OTHER INTERNATIONAL ECONOMIC ASSOCIATION PUBLICATIONS

MONOPOLY AND COMPETITION AND THEIR REGULATION
THE BUSINESS CYCLE IN THE POST-WAR WORLD
THE THEORY OF WAGE DETERMINATION
THE ECONOMICS OF INTERNATIONAL MIGRATION
STABILITY AND PROGRESS IN THE WORLD ECONOMY
THE ECONOMIC CONSEQUENCES OF THE SIZE OF NATIONS
ECONOMIC DEVELOPMENT FOR LATIN AMERICA
THE THEORY OF CAPITAL
INFLATION
THE ECONOMICS OF TAKE-OFF INTO SUSTAINED GROWTH
INTERNATIONAL TRADE THEORY IN A DEVELOPING WORLD
ECONOMIC DEVELOPMENT WITH SPECIAL REFERENCE TO EAST ASIA
ECONOMIC DEVELOPMENT FOR AFRICA SOUTH OF THE SAHARA
THE THEORY OF INTEREST RATES
THE ECONOMICS OF EDUCATION
PROBLEMS IN ECONOMIC DEVELOPMENT
THE ECONOMIC PROBLEMS OF HOUSING
PRICE FORMATION IN VARIOUS ECONOMIES
THE DISTRIBUTION OF NATIONAL INCOME
ECONOMIC DEVELOPMENT FOR EASTERN EUROPE
RISK AND UNCERTAINTY
ECONOMIC PROBLEMS OF AGRICULTURE IN INDUSTRIAL SOCIETIES
INTERNATIONAL ECONOMIC RELATIONS
BACKWARD AREAS IN ADVANCED COUNTRIES
PUBLIC ECONOMICS
ECONOMIC DEVELOPMENT IN SOUTH ASIA
NORTH AMERICAN AND WESTERN EUROPEAN ECONOMIC POLICIES
PLANNING AND MARKET RELATIONS
THE GAP BETWEEN RICH AND POOR NATIONS
LATIN AMERICA IN THE INTERNATIONAL ECONOMY
MODELS OF ECONOMIC GROWTH
SCIENCE AND TECHNOLOGY IN ECONOMIC GROWTH
ALLOCATION UNDER UNCERTAINTY
TRANSPORT AND THE URBAN ENVIRONMENT
THE ECONOMICS OF HEALTH AND MEDICAL CARE
THE MANAGEMENT OF WATER QUALITY AND THE ENVIRONMENT
AGRICULTURE POLICY IN DEVELOPING COUNTRIES
THE ECONOMIC DEVELOPMENT OF BANGLADESH
ECONOMIC FACTORS IN POPULATION GROWTH
CLASSICS IN THE THEORY OF PUBLIC FINANCE
METHODS OF LONG-TERM PLANNING AND FORECASTING
ECONOMIC INTEGRATION
THE ECONOMICS OF PUBLIC SERVICES
INFLATION THEORY AND ANTI-INFLATION POLICY
THE ORGANIZATION AND RETRIEVAL OF ECONOMIC KNOWLEDGE
THE MICROECONOMIC FOUNDATIONS OF MACROECONOMICS
ECONOMETRIC CONTRIBUTIONS TO PUBLIC POLICY

Economic Relations between East and West

Proceedings of a Conference held by the
International Economic Association at
Dresden, GDR

EDITED BY

NITA G. M. WATTS

05774

First published 1978 by
THE MACMILLAN PRESS LTD
London and Basingstoke
Associated companies in Delhi
Dublin Hong Kong Johannesburg Lagos
Melbourne New York Singapore Tokyo

Printed in Hong Kong

British Library Cataloguing in Publication Data

Economic relations between East and West
   1. East—West trade (1945—) — Congresses 2. Communist
countries — Foreign economic relations — Congresses
I. Watts, Nita G M II. International Economic
Association III. Title
382.1 '09171'7   HF1411

ISBN 0-333-24008-1

Contents

Tables and Figure

Acknowledgements

The International Economic Association wishes to express its thanks to those responsible for the planning and organisation of the 'Round Table' discussion reported in this volume.

The subject was proposed by Academician T. S. Khachaturov at the meeting of the IEA Council in Budapest in 1974 and it was decided to seek a venue for the meeting in the GDR. A Programme Committee was then formed, under Professor Oleg Bogomolov's chairmanship, and Professor Oelssner accepted the responsibilities of Chairman of the GDR Organising Committee.

The National Committee for Economics in the GDR of the GDR Academy of Sciences undertook the reproduction and circulation of the papers submitted by the participants at the Round Table and provided interpretation of the discussion into the working languages — English, French, German and Russian. It also provided most generous hospitality for the participants. At the closing session Professor Bogomolov thanked Professor Oelssner and the National Committee for their hospitality and their admirable servicing of the meeting — thanks which it is appropriate to repeat here.

Apart from those more special forms of assistance to this Conference, the International Economic Association was indebted, as always, to its two principal sponsors, UNESCO and the Ford Foundation, whose support made possible the invitation of many of the participants.

A record of the discussion was prepared by Mr Ivo Bićanić, who was greatly helped by the notes on their contributions kindly provided by many of the participants.

Programme Committee

Oleg Bogomolov (Chairman) Franz Nemschak
Abram Bergson F. Oelssner
Michael Kaser Josef Pajestka
Gunther Kohlmey

List of Participants

Mr Peter Abbam, Director of the Division of Centrally Planned Economies, Ministry of Foreign Affairs, Ghana

Mr Ivo Bićanić, Oxford University, UK

Professor Oleg T. Bogomolov, Institute of Economics of the World Socialist System, Academy of Sciences of the USSR, Moscow, USSR

Dr Leonid G. Chodov, Moscow University, USSR

Professor Nicolae N. Constantinescu, Academy of the Socialist Republic of Romania, Bucharest, Romania

Professor Béla Csikós-Nagy, Chairman of the Hungarian Economic Association; President of the Board of Prices and Materials, Budapest, Hungary

Professor Luu van Dat, Institut du Commerce Extérieur, Hanoi, Vietnam

Dr Mikhail Davydov, UNCTAD Secretariat, Geneva, Switzerland

Dr Diakin, International Institute for Economic Problems of the World Socialist System, CMEA, Moscow, USSR

Professor Antoni Fajferek, Academy of Economics, Kraków, Poland

Professor Luc Fauvel, University of Paris I, France; Secretary-General of the International Economic Association

Professor Zdzisław Fedorowicz, Warsaw School of Economics, Warsaw, Poland

Dr Marian Guzek, Academy of Economics, Poznan, Poland

Dr Philip Hanson, University of Birmingham, UK

Dr John P. Hardt, Library of Congress, Washington DC, USA

Professor Wolfgang Heinrichs, Zentralinstitut für Wirtschaftswissenschaften der Akademie der Wissenschaften der DDR, Berlin, GDR

Dr L. Albert Hernandez, University of Barcelona, Spain

Professor Franklyn D. Holzman, Tufts University, Medford, Massachusetts, USA

Dr Hanns-Dieter Jacobsen, Stiftung Wissenschaft und Politik Ebenhausen b. Münschen, FRG

Professor Werner Kalweit, Akademie der Wissenschaften der DDR, Berlin, GDR

Mr Michael Kaser, St Antony's College, Oxford, UK

Professor Etienne Kirschen, Université Libre de Bruxelles, Belgium

Professor Gunther Kohlmey, Zentralinstitut für Wirtschaftswissenschaften der Akademie der Wissenschaften der DDR, Berlin, GDR

Professor Helmut Kozialek, Zentralinstitut für sozialistische Wirtschaftsführung, Berlin, GDR

Dr Rafal Krawczyk, Institute of Economics, University of Warsaw, Poland

Professor Willi Kunz, Zentralinstitut für sozialistische Wirtschaftsführung, Berlin, GDR

Professor Marie Lavigne, University of Paris I, Panthéon-Sorbonne, France

Professor Detlef Lorenz, Free University, Berlin, BRD

Professor Carl H. McMillan, Carleton University, Ottawa, Canada

Professor Lutz Maier, Institut für internationale Politik und Wirtschaft der DDR, Berlin, GDR

Professor Evgeni Mateev, Karl Marx Higher Institute of Economics, Sofia, Bulgaria

Dr Aura Medina, University of Venezuela

Dr Vladimir Mshvenieradze, Division for International Development of the Social Sciences, UNESCO, Paris, France

Dr Natcho Natchev, Scientific Centre for Foreign Trade, Ministry of Foreign Trade, Sofia, Bulgaria

Professor Franz Nemschak, Vienna Institute for Comparative Economic Studies, Vienna, Austria

Professor Jüngen Nitz, Institut für Weltpolitik und Weltwirtschaft, Berlin, GDR

Professor F. Oelssner, Nationalkomitee für Wirtschaftswissenschaften der Akademie der Wissenschaften der DDR, Berlin, GDR

M. Pedro Calil Padis, University of Paris I, Panthéon-Sorbonne, France

M. José Anibal Perez de Pontes, IEDES, Paris, France

Professor Otto Reinhold, Institut für Gesellschaftswissenschaften beim ZK der SED, Berlin, GDR

Dr Philipp Rieger, Österreichische Nationalbank, Vienna, Austria

Dr Peter G. Rogge, PROGNOS AG, Basle, Switzerland

Professor Kurt W. Rothschild, University of Linz, Austria

Professor M. N. Savov, International Institute for Economic Problems of the World Socialist System, CMEA, Moscow, USSR

Professor Giuseppe Schiavone, University of Catania, Italy

Professor Max Schmidt, Institut für internationale Politik und Wirtschaft der DDR, Berlin, GDR

Mr Norman Scott, Graduate Institute for International Studies, Geneva, Switzerland

Dr Yuri Sdobnikov, Institute of Economics of the World Socialist System, Academy of Sciences of the USSR, Moscow, USSR

Professor M. V. Senin, International Institute for Economic Problems of the World Socialist System, CMEA, Moscow, USSR

Dr V. Shastitko, Institute of Economics of the World Socialist System, Academy of Sciences of the USSR, Moscow, USSR

Professor N. P. Shmelyov, Institute of Economics of the World Socialist System, Academy of Sciences of the USSR, Moscow, USSR

Dr August K. Tischlinger, Creditanstalt-Bankverein, Vienna, Austria

Professor Vaves, Brazil

Professor Vladimir Wacker, President of the Czechoslovak Economic Association, Prague, Czechoslovakia

Miss Nita Watts, Oxford University Institute of Economics and Statistics, UK

Professor Siegfried Wenger, Hochschule für Ökonomie, Berlin, GDR

Professor Thomas A. Wolf, Ohio State University, Columbus, Ohio, USA

Professor Noboru Yamamoto, Keio University, Tokyo, Japan

Professor Barbu Zaharescu, Academy of the Socialist Republic of Romania, Bucharest, Romania

Introduction

Nita G. M. Watts

The Executive Committee of the International Economic Association agreed in August 1974 to organise the Round Table Conference reported in this volume. Between that decision and the convening of the 'Round Table' at the end of June 1976, the Helsinki Conference on Security and Cooperation in Europe had been concluded, with the signing of a Final Act committing the signatory governments 'to promote . . . the expansion of their mutual trade . . . to encourage the expansion of trade on as broad a multilateral basis as possible . . . to encourage the development of industrial cooperation between the competent organisations, enterprises and firms of their countries' and to explore the possibilities of cooperation in a number of fields of science and technology, in environmental protection and in development of transport facilities and energy and raw material resources.* In February 1976 the Chairman of the CMEA Executive Committee sent to the Chairman of the Council of Ministers of the EEC a proposed Draft Agreement on basic relations between the two associations. Concurrently with the East—West negotiations on the intergovernmental level and the CMEA's framing of its proposals for an EEC—CMEA agreement, discussion and negotiation of course continued on the future of integration within each of these groupings, the IEA Round Table in Dresden coincidentally taking place only a week before the opening of a CMEA 'summit' meeting in Berlin, GDR. And in the background of such intra-Western, intra-Eastern and East—West discussion was the 'North—South' problem of trade relations and income distribution, and the proposals for a 'New International Economic Order' to meet the aspirations of the developing countries, discussed in several international forums including the UN General Assembly of September 1975.

The papers and discussions of the Dresden 'Round Table' were clearly influenced by these events, as they were by the exceptional (in the context of the last thirty years) conditions of the world economy in the mid-1970s — recession, heavy unemployment and rapid price inflation in the Western industrialised countries, marked fluctuations in national terms of trade (including the impact of a major revision of prices in intra-CMEA trade) and extreme disequilibrium of balances of payments, including the new pheno-menon of the accumulation of some $25—30 billion of debt to the West by the CMEA countries.

* *Conference on Security and Cooperation in Europe, Final Act,* Cmnd 6198 (London: HMSO, 1975).

While none of the economists gathered in Dresden contested the view of the Helsinki Final Act as an encouraging portent for future East—West relations, political and economic, the commitments and principles enshrined in it are sufficiently vague or qualified to leave ample scope for argument about what practical action by the signatory Governments they require. Professor Lavigne's paper elucidates those parts of the Final Act dealing with East—West economic relations, and draws attention to some of their ambiguities — also revealed, though less explicitly, by the passages chosen for reference in other papers and in some parts of the discussion. A number of participants from the CMEA countries took the Final Act, and in particular its signatories' undertaking to 'endeavour to reduce or progressively eliminate all kinds of obstacles to the development of trade' and reference to 'the beneficial effects which can result . . . from the application of most favoured nation treatment', as a text from which to argue their longstanding case for unconditional mfn treatment (unmodified by EEC preferences) for imports into Western countries from the CMEA area and for the abandonment of all restrictions on access to EEC markets, whether these arose from the Common Agricultural Policy or were imposed in other sectors of trade. Other participants noted the Final Act's reference to 'an equitable distribution of advantages and obligations of comparable scale', which led them to consider the appropriate response from the CMEA countries to any Western commercial-policy concessions.

In discussions of the desirability of modifications of existing policies and practices affecting international trade and payments, questions of the likely benefit to be derived by East or West from such modifications tend to become confused with questions of the 'balance' or 'equity' of the institutional arrangements or policies on the two sides. Dr Hanson's paper contributes to a lessening of such confusion by examining separately the two questions: (a) whether differences between the two economic systems tend to constrain the development of East—West trade; and (b) whether these differences produce any general bias in the distribution of the gains from trade in favour of the countries of one system or the other. Professor Wacker's paper, on the other hand, examines only Western tariff and other obstacles to the expansion of East—West trade, tacitly assuming that their removal must be beneficial to both sides; and similar references to such obstacles are to be found in the papers of Professors Schmidt and Mateev.

No member of the Conference showed any disposition to argue on economic grounds that such obstacles to trade expansion as exist in the West should not be lowered, subject to avoidance of 'market disruption'. But views diverged on the question whether there was a basis for an argument in 'equity' for a response from the CMEA countries — in the form of some modification of their trade plans or trading practices to give an effectively greater priority to trade with the West. Professor Nemschak's statement that 'what the Western side attempts to achieve with, for example, customs duties, import quotas, regulations on technical norms and standards, etc., is achieved much more thoroughly in the East through foreign trade planning and the state monopoly of foreign trade' (p. 33) contrasts with Professor Mateev's perception of the CMEA system as that which 'could least be considered an obstacle to the development of economic relations to the full extent of a world-wide division of labour' (p. 66); and the papers of Professors Schmidt and Senin stress the 'openness' of the CMEA trading system.

But if the degree and significance of 'effective protection' or 'effective discrimination' in East and West, respectively, remained matters of disagreement, it seemed nevertheless to be generally agreed that the full benefits of international division of labour were not being garnered in East—West economic relations; and in the view of several members of the Conference they were not being realised in intra-CMEA relations either. However, attempts to indicate the quantitative significance of trading opportunities forgone cannot be said to have taken the Conference very far, even towards assessing the likely expansion of East—West trade in more favourable conditions; and when it comes to assessing the probable economic benefits of trade expansion, and the likely distribution of benefits between the trading partners, the very concept of 'benefit' presents difficulties. As a number of participants pointed out, trade expansion is not an end in itself; any government will assess the relative economic benefits of alternative trading institutions and conditions, and their impacts on its country's trade, in terms of its own scale of economic objectives.

Differences between national economic systems, differing levels of economic development and differences in the relative priorities accorded to — often apparently common — national or regional economic policy objectives clearly complicate the problem of devising new 'rules of the game' of international trade, payments and development assistance adequately covering both 'East—West' and 'North—South' relations. This question is raised in the papers of Professors Schmidt, Nemschak, Lavigne and Kirschen and in the discussions in the first and fifth sessions, in particular. Professor Holzman's paper, though not directly addressed to this issue, is also very relevant to it; and it is even more relevant to the subsidiary question, given glancing attention by some participants, whether 'North—South' economic relations must inevitably continue in fact to be made up of 'West—South' and 'East—South' flows of trade and payments, separated by a virtually sealed barrier of 'East—South' currency inconvertibility and bilateral balancing of transactions.

The question whether either convertibility of the transferable rouble or the introduction of an externally convertible rouble could be compatible with the existing economic systems and the economic policy priorities of the CMEA countries is the main theme of Professor Holzman's paper. Most, though not all, participants in the Conference appeared to accept his negative conclusion; Professor Fedorowicz thought that the conditions of intra-CMEA trade already approximated to those in which the transferable rouble could become convertible. However, the discussion did suggest that 'convertibility' might soon produce as acute East—West differences of definition as has 'discrimination'.

Consideration of the current levels and patterns of East—West trade and payments, and the prospects for the immediate future, had naturally to take account of the impact of recession in the Western industrialised countries and price inflation in world markets. This is discussed particularly in the papers of Professors Nemschak and Fedorowicz and receives attention in other contributions also. Although Professor Holzman saw the nature of the economic systems and policy objectives of the CMEA countries as implying a persistent tendency to deficit with the West, the adverse effects on the economies of these countries of shrinking Western export markets and worsening terms of trade were no more in dispute that was the fact that these effects had been substantially mitigated by the ease with which credits had been raised in the West. Some concern was expressed at the strengthening of protectionist tendencies in Western industrialised countries, while other comments tended more to express satisfaction that no relapse into a spiral of trade restriction had occurred. But most participants from CMEA countries clearly shared Dr Hanson's view that 'the Eastern countries, especially the smaller ones, do seem to be more at risk from Western economic instability than vice versa' (p. 98); and recent experience probably explains in part the marked stress placed by some of them on the importance of both inter-governmental and inter-enterprise arrangements assuring stable medium-term or long-term markets. But this has been a familiar theme also in the past.

The rapid increase in the indebtedness of the CMEA countries to Western lenders naturally raised the question whether these countries were approaching a 'credit ceiling', either self-imposed in recognition of the danger of mortgaging future hard-currency earnings beyond a certain limit, or reflecting Western doubts of the CMEA countries' continuing creditworthiness. During the fifth session, Professor Wenger offered an estimate of these countries' ratios of debt service to export earnings in convertible currencies of some 20–30 per cent, which he regarded as still a 'safe' proportion. Others doubted the relevance of such a comparison and there were some conflicting views on the factors making for creditworthiness and the ability of the CMEA countries to control their hard-currency balances of payments. Professor Fedorowicz's paper, and other contributions, pointed out that much of the Western credit raised by these countries was directly linked with investment projects designed to increase their export and convertible-currency debt-servicing capacity; and attention was also drawn to the value of 'product-pay-back' agreements in assuring export markets for goods produced by externally-financed investment projects. However, the quantitative significance of such agreements, in relation to total debt-service commitments, must be relatively small and some anxiety was expressed about the absorptive capacity of Western markets for the increased flow of exports of manufactured products which the CMEA countries all appeared to be planning for the future.

The small shares of such goods in the trade flow from East to West was a matter of concern to a number of participants contemplating the present structure of East–West trade, and it receives attention in the papers of Nemschak, Mateev, Hanson, Holzman and Wacker. The explanations offered in the papers and discussion vary considerably, at least in emphasis. They include technology 'lags' (general or sectoral) in the CMEA countries; inflexibilities, distorted prices and lack of competitive pressures within those countries (limiting their ability to seize new market opportunities quickly and to achieve adequate standards of quality); restricted access to, or uncertainty of, Western markets (making it hardly worth while for some large Eastern enterprises to tailor their products to the precise needs of Western customers); marketing difficulties resulting from the need to deal with 'small' Western importers, and inappropriate patterns of diversification of Eastern exports (towards the less income-elastic products).

A number of contributors saw East—West industrial cooperation as a promising development in this context — tending to narrow technology gaps, ensure conformity with Western quality standards and tastes and give assurance of Western markets. Some, indeed, saw increasing industrial cooperation as an inevitable feature of future East—West economic relations or, at least, as essential if the full potential benefits are to be realised — a case argued vigorously in Professor Mateev's paper, among others. Professor McMillan contributed an analysis of possible inter-firm cooperation arrangements, essentially in terms of alternative distributions of property rights between the parties. His paper discusses the factors influencing the choice of form of cooperative arrangement, setting the question also in the specific East—West context; and Professor Csikós-Nagy's paper complements McMillan's more general analysis with a review of Hungarian experience in this field and of the way in which international industrial cooperation arrangements, and 'joint ventures' in particular, have been accommodated within the Hungarian 'economic mechanism'. More general reviews of past experience, and speculations on the probable nature and scope of industrial cooperation in the future and the possibilities of relaxing existing constraints on this development, are to be found in the papers of Professor Shmelyov and Mr Scott, both of whom foresee a considerable expansion of such relations.

The nature and the distribution of the benefits and the disadvantages of closer interdependence are likely to constitute the underlying theme of any discussion on economic relations between East and West; and virtually all the contributions to this Conference can be seen as variations on this theme. Views on the desirable institutional framework for these relations are likely to reflect assessments of the nature of the benefits and hazards of closer interdependence. Although there was not a clear East/West division of participants' views, there was a tendency for many of those from the CMEA countries to stress particularly the benefits of medium- to long-term certainty of sources of supply and of markets. Thus the desirable institutional framework became one of an EEC/CMEA agreement stabilising 'commercial policy' conditions, intergovernmental agreements confirming, and perhaps elaborating, stable bilateral relations on that level and then — in addition to 'normal' short-term trade deals, and advocated with varying emphasis — inter-enterprise links tending to stabilise and balance transactions. Although Professor Csikós-Nagy's conclusion that 'the factor overwhelmingly determining the volume of East—West trade, today and for the foreseeable future, is still the simple exchange of goods and services' received some support, there was also manifest enthusiasm for joint production arrangements and investment linked with 'product-pay-back', while some saw value also in barter deals.

The approaches of Western participants to the same question were not identical. But while it was taken for granted that stable medium-term inter-enterprise links might well be appropriate in many cases — being by now widespread in intra-Western trade — rather more emphasis was placed both on the benefits of short-term flexibility in trade relations and also on the problem of combining long-term stability of the commercial-policy framework with generally accepted 'rules of the game' of balance-of-payments adjustment (see the discussions in the third and fifth sessions in particular).

The feeling that the Conference was taking place at a moment of hiatus is apparent in a number of contributions — from Professor Nemschak's paper, presented to the first session, to the interventions of Professors Rothschild and Fedorowicz in the fifth session. The 'Bretton Woods system' which, while changing in detail over time, had yet provided the essential framework for 'intra-Western' (and 'North—South') economic relations for some twenty-five years, was now in disarray: if East—West economic relations were in future to be more closely integrated into a world-wide trade and payments system, what was that system to be? Directly or indirectly, the question was raised repeatedly. Not surprisingly, it remained unanswered.

1 East–West Economic Relations against the Background of New Trends in the World Economy

Max Schmidt

INSTITUT FUR INTERNATIONALE POLITIK UND WIRTSCHAFT DER DDR

We are at present witnessing a new phase in the development of economic relations between socialist and capitalist countries and quantitative changes in those relations now seem to be in prospect. This phase reflects processes leading towards a better articulated division of labour on an international scale as well as highly diversified approaches to the utilisation of the international division of labour for the benefit of national development.

Socialist economic integration and the rapid growth of the socialist countries' national economies have undoubtedly helped to produce the new situation. Factors of even greater importance providing favourable conditions for peaceful trade and cooperation, to the parties' common benefit, have included the turn from 'cold war' to détente in recent years, a more determined application of the principles of peaceful coexistence to relations between socialist and capitalist states, and the successful conclusion of the Conference on Security and Cooperation in Europe.

While, in recent years, the trade between capitalist industrial states has grown but little, or even stagnated, a sizeable expansion has been recorded of the economic relations between the member countries of the Council for Mutual Economic Assistance (CMEA) on the one hand, and the capitalist states on the other. The share of East–West trade in the capitalist world's total foreign trade has consequently greatly increased.

The considerable intensification of East–West economic relations is reflected in high growth rates for commodity trade, increasingly based on long-term governmental agreements, within which increasing consideration is being given to new forms and more efficient methods of economic cooperation. Cooperation is being undertaken in many fields, including science and technology, work on joint projects and the long-term organisation of production processes with shared responsibilities for management, finance and trade. With all that has been achieved, however, one cannot overlook the fact that neither the volume nor the structure of actual economic relations has so far reached the limits of the possibilities and the needs on either side. There are still obstacles to be removed and complicated problems to be solved.

I SOME NEW TRENDS IN THE INTERNATIONAL DIVISION OF LABOUR AND IN THE WORLD ECONOMY, AND THEIR IMPACT UPON EAST–WEST ECONOMIC RELATIONS

The reinforcement and expansion of economic and techno-scientific relations with the capitalist states is considered, and implemented, as a long-term policy by the member countries of the CMEA. It is not subject to sudden changes of tactics or limited by short-term interests. We do not see this expansion as a 'boom' phenomenon. It is rather assumed that favourable conditions exist for a continuing process of consolidation and expansion of economic relations and, consequently, the international division of labour between the socialist states and the capitalist industrial countries, and that those favourable conditions stem from a number of new trends in the world economy and in world politics.

The first trend to be noted justifies the expectation that continuing *political détente* will be the main characteristic of future relations between socialist and capitalist states, even though the international situation remains complicated. The recorded results of the most recent congresses of communist and workers' parties in the socialist countries give strong indications of those countries' continued commitment to détente. These developments are in accord with the implementation of the principles agreed at the Conference on Security and Cooperation in Europe and with more intensive efforts to give practical effect to the principles of peaceful coexistence in the relations between the USSR and the USA. Future steps towards *military détente* can also have only a favourable impact on economic relations. The continued competition between the systems will then be ever more clearly shifted to the areas of the national economy and of international economic relations.

My first reference has deliberately been to détente, since all experience, from both the period of 'cold war' and the developments of recent years, suggests that politics and the political climate play a major, or even primary, role in international economic relations, particularly between states of different social systems. And it must be noted that there is a positive feedback effect of long-term stable economic relations on the stability of the political situation. The acceptance of this argument demands that all economists should fully understand one requirement: the Final Act* of Helsinki must be perceived and treated as a coherent unity and implemented as such.

The second trend to which I would refer relates to the qualitative change in the role and influence of socialism in the world. Production and the physico-cultural living standard of the working people are both showing a considerable upswing in the socialist countries; and the process of gradual approximation of all the socialist countries to similar levels of economic development has come to appear as a law of nature. The effects of socialist economic integration are thus becoming increasingly relevant to any analysis of developments in the

* All references are to the English text, *Conference on Security and Cooperation in Europe, Final Act*, Cmnd 6198 (London: HMSO, 1975).

world economy, as industrial output in the countries affiliated to the Council for Mutual Economic Assistance accounts for a rapidly growing percentage of the world's total industrial production.

Both the possibilities and the desires of the CMEA countries to take advantage of international division of labour with countries outside the CMEA will grow, along with their planned development of up-to-date economic structures reflecting the techno-scientific revolution and with increasing success in CMEA economic integration. But allegations, sometimes heard from political and journalistic circles in the West, of the 'indispensability' of such economic relations for socialism and the 'unilateral' benefit to the socialist countries are completely mistaken. Such an idea not only contradicts contemporary and historical evidence, but it is also logically unfounded. Trade is based on mutual benefit and conducted for that purpose. Plenty of advantages are drawn by the Western side from diversification of raw material supplies, the availability of large and stable markets, the long-term nature of transactions, safeguarded jobs, and low-cost production – all of them being advantages offered by the international division of labour. Repeated reference has been made to these advantages by many businessmen and politicians. No capitalist businessman would undertake trade or cooperation if disadvantage to him was the result.

The socialist countries, naturally, try to draw the maximum benefit for their own development from all economic relations with capitalist industrial states. They are purchasers of, and partners in cooperative activities to produce, commodities and services they need; otherwise trade would make no sense to them. Their policies are geared to the consolidation of socialism and the material safeguarding of détente.

The member countries of CMEA over the past decades have produced evidence of their higher growth rates of production and national income, as well as of stability and absence of crises in their economic development. The stability and dynamism of economic development under socialism are, and will increasingly be, important guarantees for the expansion and reinforcement of economic cooperation between the countries of the two social systems.

The third trend to be noted is the growing internationalisation of economic life, with far-reaching effects on the mechanisms of the world economy. New developments in the organisation of productive forces have resulted from the progress of the techno-scientific revolution. Some new interdependent and interconnected tendencies, due to the techno-scientific revolution, are becoming apparent, and are conducive to more efficient production. They seem to foreshadow the development of more clearly and objectively beneficial relations between the socialist and capitalist countries, involving an accelerated internationalisation of economic activity and new forms of international division of labour. Some of those tendencies may be noted as follows:

(a) Research and development expenses in the most modern lines of production have increased tremendously under the impact of several factors, including accelerating obsolescence.

Today no country is any longer in the position to draw solely from its own research and development potential the know-how required for lowest-cost, competitive production in all industries. Techno-scientific progress calls for the concentration of efforts and resources on priority areas, among them those for which the country possesses the most favourable conditions in terms of history, geography or geology. Countries, in other words, need to get fully integrated into the international division of labour.

Cooperation between socialist and capitalist countries has something to offer in many fields of research-intensive production. Reference has been made to some of them in the Final Act of the Helsinki Conference. Countries of both economic systems may draw from such cooperation the means for more economic use of their natural resources and other assets; and a solid foundation for such cooperation has been created by the comprehensive promotion of research in the CMEA countries.

(b) The optimum sizes of companies and other enterprises have tended to increase, as has the scale of investments needed for competitive production.

(c) The needs for large sales volumes and for growth of markets similarly become more exacting. More exchange of commodities is becoming increasingly urgent since, under the conditions of the techno-scientific revolution, automation and mechanisation yield their full benefits only if long-series production is undertaken. This, in turn, requires successful development not only of the national market, or the common market of a group of countries, but also of exchange between countries of different social systems.

In this context, reference should also be made to the growing amounts of machinery and other heavy-duty equipment exported by many countries. Business of this kind is no longer merely a matter of sales to 'unknown markets' or anonymous clients. The high manufacturing cost and sophisticated design of such means of production, particularly those used in research-intensive industries, have added new dimensions to the economic relations between socialist and capitalist states. More elements are involved in a transaction — advance orders, negotiated modes of financing, cooperation of manufacturers in plant assembly as well as in maintenance and repair; and business contracts often include also the transfer of technology by sale of licences. It is well known that the GDR takes a positive interest in licence business. She is able and willing, both to sell and to buy licences and has signed many contracts in recent years for licence-export and import business. A licence catalogue for the GDR has been drafted by the country's authorities with information on the research results available, under licence, to potential clients abroad.

There are many international transactions which are becoming increasingly complicated as a result of the techno-scientific revolution, and this has reinforced the trend towards internationalisation of production proper. That trend has taken the form of industrial cooperation.

Various types of industrial cooperation have been increasingly accepted between countries of the two world systems since the late 1960s, although none have so far reached major dimensions. According to available documentation some 800 cooperation contracts have so far been put into effect or signed. Momentum has been added to those developments by several factors, among them the clearly visible over-capacity in advanced capitalist countries in recent years, as well as increasing absorptive possibilities and dynamic economic growth in the countries affiliated to the CMEA.

Industrial cooperation, by its very nature, is a form of long-term, continuing economic link. The socialist countries can thus be attractive partners to capitalist firms, since their national economies are based on long-term planning. Cooperation can be useful for the socialist countries also, providing them with additional potential for accelerated techno-scientific progress, to the benefit of higher living standards for their peoples.

The modern forms of international division of labour may well become essential for increasing the efficiency of production in both world systems. To be successful these new forms require, like the extension of economic cooperation in other forms, lasting political relations of peaceful cooperation; and last but not least, they should be reflected in long-term agreements.

The GDR, as is well-known has repeatedly underlined her willingness to undertake industrial cooperation projects for mutual benefit, with the aim of creating stable economic links and strengthening comprehensive, long-term economic cooperation. It is an established policy of the GDR that industrial cooperation should be encouraged between competent organisations, companies, and corporations and facilitated by bilateral and multilateral agreements at government level. The GDR, in her quest for more progress towards cooperation with capitalist industrial countries, has signed a number of agreements at government level on economic, industrial, and technological cooperation — for example, with France, Italy, The Netherlands, Belgium, Denmark, Great Britain, Austria, Finland, Norway and Sweden. The agreement concluded with France in 1973, for a period of ten years, provides for specific kinds of cooperation and is the framework within which more detailed contracts are negotiated between foreign trade companies of the GDR and leading French firms.

Joint-venture agreements have proved to be a highly efficient arrangement and have been concluded between GDR foreign trade companies and a number of Western corporations, such as VÖEST in Austria, Montedison of Italy and ICI in the United Kingdom. Various forms of industrial cooperation are covered by these agreements, among them mutual adjustment of manufacturing programmes, supplies of parts to complete plants, or joint action in selling goods to, or erecting plants in, third countries.

The fourth trend we must note, of extreme importance to the development of economic relations, is the continuing effort to find solutions for global and regional problems, including those of raw materials and energy resources, the environment, the eradication of the most dangerous and most common diseases, the utilisation of the treasures of the seas, space exploration and transport of all kinds.

Energy and raw materials are already of major importance in economic relations between socialist and capitalist countries, and they will assume even more importance in the longer-run future. The CMEA countries have demonstrated for many years that problems in this field can be successfully tackled if the economic, as well as techno-scientific, potentials of all countries involved are combined and expanded on the basis of joint long-range schemes for planned development of raw-material or energy resources; and the CMEA countries do have considerable techno-scientific potential in this field.

More and more agreements are being negotiated, and talks held, between socialist and Western states and firms on cooperation in the energy and raw materials fields. It has been shown that the problems of opening up the deposits which exist in quantity on the territories of the socialist states are not restricted to those of financing or technology. Rather, a new approach to shaping the economic relations between capitalist and socialist countries is required in the context of development of raw materials and energy resources, just as in other contexts.

Thus, certain forms of cooperation, going beyond the limits of conventional trade, have worked well. I have in mind, above all, barter transactions which are in the interest of all parties involved and provide favourable conditions for all. Industrial units which will completely or partially come under a socialist state's ownership may be erected in cooperation with Western firms under a barter agreement. The CMEA country may buy equipment and licences, receiving some of them on a credit basis. Repayment will then be through 'product-pay-back', that is, both the credit and accrued interest will be repaid through deliveries from the new unit's, or other factories', production. It may well be a useful task for the future to find wider applications for such kinds of transactions — for example, to find more scope for them in the processing or manufacturing industries.

The natural foundations for man's existence are increasingly affected by pollution and other problems of the environment. The environment is second to none in demonstrating the interdependence between nations and continents; and the change from 'cold war' to détente has already facilitated mutually beneficial cooperation in this area. The first attempts have been made at bilateral or multilateral joint action by socialist and capitalist countries to settled environmental problems. Joint efforts have been made, for example, to establish pollution thresholds. Other activities have included the assessment of environmental changes on the biosphere and man, the design of decontamination plant, and the development of closed circuits for dangerous substances on industrial premises.

The USSR, following on certain clauses in the Helsinki Final Act, has suggested at one of the recent ECE meetings the calling of all-European conferences on energy, transport and protection of the environment. Such meetings might contribute greatly to solving problems. They could undoubtedly be used to hammer out more measures of full East—West cooperation, with important beneficial consequences for the world economy. Such projects deserve both interest and encouraging action by economists in East and West.

The fifth trend to be noted is the development of a world-wide crisis of the capitalist economy, widely discussed by economists concerned with its causes and consequences as one of the new phenomena in the world economy having a major impact upon East—West economic relations. Even economists and political leaders in capitalist countries have made the point that this is not merely a cyclical crisis, but that it represents rather a major breakdown threatening the continued existence of the present economic structure in capitalist industrial states — a situation characterised not only by a grave decline in industrial output in the two most recent years, but also by reduced prospects for growth and the need for far-reaching processes of structural readjustment within the Western industrial countries and in economic relations within the capitalist world at large. Aggravation of antagonisms in society has entailed aggravation of social conflicts; and all this seems to be an eloquent reflection of the instability affecting the basic structures of the Western economic system. Major sectors of the world economy are exposed to inflation, with effects on world market prices, and are affected by the international currency and trade crises. The foreign trade volumes of the capitalist industrial countries have fallen for the first time in many years, and their trade balances have shown extreme instability. It is not surprising that such developments produce contradictory influences on the economic relations between states of different economic and social systems.

The interest of capitalist business circles in economic relations with socialist countries is stimulated by the crisis and the associated decline in demand on Western markets — in other words, by the growing imbalance between production capacity and market possibilities. This has been confirmed by recent developments. Exports and other business with CMEA countries have increased in 1973, 1974 and 1975; and trade union leaders and representatives of governments have made repeated reference to the stabilising role of such relations and to their social implications. Large orders placed by socialist countries have, indeed, helped to counter large-scale unemployment in the West.

The quest of capitalist business circles for an expansion of economic relations with socialist countries has also been motivated by the structural problems of the capitalist economy. In this context reference may be made, not only to raw materials and energy, but also to sectors such as mechanical engineering and heavy-duty investment goods.

Recent experience has strongly suggested, however, that the ups and downs of the capitalist economic crisis have also been producing negative effects on East—West economic relations. In particular:

(a) The pressure of demand in Western markets is subject to excessive

variation, and ambitions to export are not matched by desire to
import. This will further worsen the historically unfavourable
structure of commodity exchange (the ratio of raw materials to
finished products).

(b) Inflation, with its related instability of exchange rates, is likely to
aggravate the uncertainty factor in this area of international trade.

(c) The intensifying competition is likely to entail stronger trends towards
protectionism and resort to traditional, and invention of new, measures
of discrimination against socialist countries — such as opposition to full
application of the most-favoured-nation clause in trade with them.

These problems are not temporary. Economic experts in Western countries
have forecast a highly complicated and disturbed future for economic development in the capitalist part of the world; and our scientific discussions should,
therefore, focus strongly on such problems.

Steps so far taken by governments to support national levels of economic
activity have widely failed to be effective in resolving the problems and contradictions, with the result that obstacles to satisfactory international economic
relations have increased. Necessary changes in the Western international system
or trade policies are often delayed for months or even years, as a consequence
of the long-drawn process of decision-making in the leading circles of capitalist
countries; and this cannot be without adverse influence on the general atmosphere required for the type of relations the socialist countries wish to
develop with capitalist partners — long-term relationships of the greatest
possible stability. To find solutions in principle and to suggest ways of trans-
lating them into practice is another challenge that should be met by economic
research workers.

The sixth trend to be noted, is in the attitudes of the growing number of
developing countries who have been taking up stronger positions of opposition
to the present international economic system and to the outdated mechanisms
which regulate their own relations with the most important countries of the
capitalist world, and with the multinational corporations in these countries.
Such attitudes can be observed in many developing countries, notwithstanding
their sometimes acutely divergent positions on particular problems.

Demands are being made for the introduction of a 'new international
economic order' that accords with the new structure of relations in the world
economy and the changing weights of the countries in the different economic
and social categories. Democratisation of world-wide economic relations is
one of the major demands raised in this context, and this would help to pave
the road toward equality in, and mutual benefit from, international relations
in general. It would mean imposing effective limitations upon the neocolo-
nialist and restrictive business methods practised by multinationals; and in some
developing countries the planned development of the national economy has
been rendered extremely difficult by such practices. Multinationals have been
controlling these countries' foreign trade, and have drained enormous profits
from them.

The foreign trade policy pursued by the GDR, and all her external economic relations, on the other hand, are visibly oriented towards supporting the developing countries in building independent national economies with efficient economic structures. This policy of support is reflected in sizeable deliveries to them of complete plant, efficient industrial units, and modern agricultural equipment. With due consideration of her own economic requirements, the GDR has helped to create conditions under which the developing countries can boost their exports of local produce, as well as of semi-finished and finished manufactured items. Aid in terms of production technologies, provision and education of specialists, as well as construction of research and education centres, is characteristic of the GDR's relations with the Third World. There is a real chance for economic relations between socialist and capitalist countries to take a new shape, as another dynamic element in the drive towards a world-wide recasting of economic relationships.

While attention must be given to both the general development of the international division of labour and the specific interests of socialist and capitalist states, there are several interests which these two groups of states have in common and which should ensure their support for an expansion of economic cooperation. The most significant fact of the present situation appears to be that commitment to, and involvement in, the international division of labour have become imperative for any country – big or small, developing or industrially advanced, socialist or capitalist – against the background of the new developments in the world economy. No country in the world, not even one of those at the highest level of economic development, can continue to make satisfactory industrial progress without taking advantage of the international division of labour. This process – a growing utilisation of the international division of labour for national development – has been defined as a peculiarity of our time by Leonid Ilyich Brezhnev, General Secretary of the CPSU, at his Party's XXVth Congress.

The areas of common interest are supplemented and complemented by the specific motivations of both the socialist and the capitalist countries. The socialist states seek to use the international division of labour to open up additional resources with which to tackle the problems of the economy and society as a whole and to strengthen the basis for their policy of peaceful coexistence. Representatives of Western firms and governments have mentioned the following specific points of interest: the safeguarding of sales outlets for long periods to come, under the pressure of intensifying competition; diversification of the sources from which raw materials and energy resources may be drawn; the import of machines, equipment and licences from which techno-scientific insights may be obtained; the interest of small and medium-sized enterprises, or even complete industries, in cooperation with socialist countries with a view to securing their own viability and survival in a competitive world; the securing of jobs and the hopes to use the commercial links with the long-term-planned, socialist markets as a means of stabilising activity at high levels.

II PEACEFUL COEXISTENCE AND ECONOMIC COOPERATION

Economic cooperation and further progress in the division of labour between socialist and capitalist countries can be seen to have been tremendously stimulated by a number of new trends in the world economy; and particular emphasis should be laid, in this context, on the assumption that economic cooperation is now to take place under conditions of peaceful coexistence between states of different social systems.

Mutual recognition of the fact that the social systems involved are different appears to be an essential prerequisite for cooperation. Each of the systems develops on its own socio-economic foundations. In other words, even with much higher levels of cooperation the internal processes of each system will continue to function by their own inherent laws. Contest and competition between the two systems will not disappear. The nature of each systems's internal motive forces and laws will be unchanged, even with more intensive cooperation and improved economic relations between countries of the two systems, since those differing motive forces and operating mechanisms are intrinsically linked with each system's own structure of ownership and political power.

The socialist planned economy, including state monopoly of foreign trade, is an essential component of socialism. The Western side has sometimes argued that the socialist planned economy inhibits East—West economic relations, or that the unsatisfactory structure of commodity exchange is attributable to centralised planning. The socialist countries, however, consider their socialist planned economies an irreplaceable advantage for their own dynamic, yet stable, development and also as a stepping-stone for expanding economic relations with countries of the other social system. In this context, E. W. Mommsen has stated that: 'Foreign trade with the Eastern Bloc is of interest to the Federal Republic, since, unlike the industrial countries of the West, those countries are not exposed to pronounced cyclical variations in activity. An element of stability should be found in that trade to offset the excessive variation of our sales to the industrial countries.'[1] State planning, in fact, provides state guarantees of the implementation of agreements. Neither is planning on a CMEA scale an obstacle to cooperation with capitalist countries; it is rather an instrument for the further economic development of the socialist countries, who thus will become increasingly attractive as partners for industrial countries of the West. It is an essential condition for the flexible response of the socialist system to new stimuli or demands and for the invention of new, mutually acceptable forms of advantageous international cooperation.

Should not the economists of Western countries try to work out ways in which to improve specific mechanisms of cooperation — the working of mixed commissions at government level with the participation of leading economists, businessmen, technologists and other experts, or the working of joint chambers of commerce or joint economic councils? Such mechanisms, after all, will be set up only after due consideration of the fact that East–West economic relations mean cooperation between states of different social systems. A wide range of ideas on means of cooperation has been suggested in the Helsinki Final Act, and reference will doubtless be made to them under other items on the agenda of this Conference.

Another point that should be made, in this context, is that certain circles have not yet abandoned their ambitions to use expanded economic relations as a vehicle by which to interfere in the internal affairs of individual socialist states or of the socialist community at large. Attempts are still being made to abuse such relations, by using them as means of political and economic pressure or politico-ideological subversion. Some of those attempts are made under the pretext of wishing to facilitate East–West trade through some transformation of the socialist system, by means of 'radical reforms' or 'decentralisation of planning'. Such activities, however, are in plain contradiction to the principles of peaceful coexistence and have nothing in common with the letter and spirit of the Helsinki Final Act, in which the participating states commit themselves to 'respect each other's right freely to choose and develop its political, social, economic, and cultural systems as well as its right to determine its laws and regulations'.*

The Western-type market economy, which depends on the laws of the capitalist system, and the socialist planned economy cannot be integrated with one another. Economic cooperation cannot generate a 'third type' of economic system in which elements of both systems might be combined. Each of the two systems has had its own intrinsic genesis. Advocates of the convergency theory in Western countries are in error if they believe that economic cooperation will eventually lead to 'approximation' between the two social systems or the two integrated groups. It is a fallacy if they describe integration merely as an 'expansive' process with two dimensions, 'depth' and 'width' (expansion of the range of subjects of integration and incorporation of additional countries, including those with different political systems). The two social systems are different by virtue of their very nature, for which reason a 'common' socio-economic basis cannot be created even by the most advanced sharing of activities.

All efforts to develop economic relations between East and West should be undertaken with the fullest possible acceptance of the primary role of politics, with closest attention being given to the *correlation between political détente and economic cooperation.*

The step-by-step development of a system of security and cooperation in Europe will provide better conditions for continent-wide expansion of economic and techno-scientific cooperation. Expansion of economic relations, conversely, will add substance to a system of mutual security or carry us closer to the day when such a system will be reality. A network of economic and techno-

* Cmnd 6198, p. 3.

scientific relations with capitalist states will strengthen and widen the basis for peaceful coexistence. It is essential, in this context, that advanced economic relations, once achieved, should be used to reinforce those trends oriented primarily towards cooperation rather than confrontation.

It is our firm belief that the principles of peaceful coexistence should shape, and determine the substance of, economic relations. This implies, above all, that those economic relations should be relations between sovereign and independent states on an equal footing, with due respect for national law and order, no interference with internal affairs, and no damage to the interests of third countries.

The *principle of reciprocal benefit* is of utmost importance and must be stringently observed as a major condition for the development of economic relations between socialist and capitalist countries. This implies exchange of goods on terms customary in trade and at justifiable prices, with no disadvantage to anyone. Also implied is the requirement that the economic benefit resulting from the exchange of commodities and services between countries and business partners as a result of other transactions than simple commodity trade should be shared by all those involved in the transaction. This requirement is quite incompatible with the common practice of multinationals to use international trade to gain one-sided economic benefit at the expense of the partner.

Economic relations under conditions of peaceful coexistence should be free from any discrimination whatsoever and should conform fully with the principles of reciprocal benefit and unconditional most-favoured-nation treatment. Yet, there still are cases in the actual conduct of business today in which those principles are jeopardised by the political attitudes and practices of certain governments and influential political circles in the West. Economic relations of real equality cannot be established until discriminating and inhibitory factors are first reduced and eventually eliminated. Partners to a commercial transaction, consequently, should grant each other equal rights and privileges on their own national territories, and no difference in treatment should be permissible between the several countries and companies doing business on a foreign territory. This would be an efficient way to adapt the concept of most-favoured-nation treatment to the peculiar conditions of business between countries of different social systems. The Western countries must be invited, in this context, to open their markets more widely to the inflow of products from socialist countries in the interest of deepening the international division of labour.

Some comment seems to be justified also on the argument that the socialist states alone are responsible for the imbalance of East–West trade and for the inhibiting effect of that imbalance on further expansion of economic relations. This is a very complex problem; the competitiveness of CMEA products no doubt plays a certain role and an improvement of competitiveness is the aim of all CMEA countries. However, far more detrimental impacts upon the balance, and mutual benefit, of economic relations stem from discriminating and restrictive measures taken against many imports from socialist countries by a number of West European countries and the USA. These include special duties, quotas, the Common Market rules for agricultural commodities, and the residue of earlier embargo measures. Such policies are now being intensified as a consequence of the economic crisis affecting the countries concerned. More opening of Western markets would be conducive to a better balance of East–West trade.

Credit transactions are considered as something quite normal not only by the member countries of CMEA, but also by realists in Western business circles. The CMEA countries themselves have been granting an increasing volume of credits to non-socialist partners to whom sales have been made of, for example, heavy-duty equipment and complete plants. Credits are indispensable, if economic relations are to be expanded and intensified. They are important tools in competition for new markets and for larger shares in markets. They enable suppliers to use their own potentials to capacity.

Incidentally, the totals often quoted for outstanding credits – and often widely exaggerated – are not of magnitudes to create any general problem for the CMEA countries, in view of their economic potential and their dynamic growth. Moreover, specific repayment arrangements are linked to some credits, where joint ventures for the construction and assembly of new industrial units are accompanied by product-pay-back agreements.

The quality of economic relations will improve along with the stability and duration of the agreements negotiated which, in turn, will have to comply with terms agreed between the governments involved. The aim must be to create a system of economic relations within which each country is given a genuine chance to use not only its own national resources but also those provided by international division of labour for the most rational and effective encouragement and development of its own productive resources and improvement of its own living standards. These principles are relevant also to certain ideas for a reform of world-wide economic relations, whose democratisation is still being blocked by politically motivated obstacles put up by multinational corporations and by some governments of capitalist countries. Given the existence of two different social systems, we do not, of course, expect that the world market structure and the nature of world-wide economic relations can develop on the basis of conditions typical of the relations which exist between socialist states. Yet, if democratisation is desired, it would be better for world-wide economic relations to be less dependent upon the capitalist economic system, and its political and economic attitudes and actions which, to some extent, tend to inhibit any improvement of the international division of labour. Steps taken towards reform should be designed to reduce obstacles to the international division of labour, particularly between East and West. There should no longer be any discrimination nor any artificial barriers to international trade. All manifestations of inequality, dictatorship or exploitation in international economic relations should be eliminated.

III THE ROLE OF DEVELOPMENTS IN 'INTEGRATION' AND THEIR IMPACT ON EAST–WEST ECONOMIC RELATIONS

Contemporary developments are characterised by growing trends towards the internationalisation of production and more international division of labour by means of economic integration. In Europe, economic relations between socialist and capitalist countries develop against the background of two different types of integration – in the Council for Mutual Economic Assistance and in the 'European Communities'. The trade between countries of these two groupings accounts for approximately 60 per cent of all trade between 'East' and 'West'. The countries within each of these two groups are those between whom economic relations in all forms are most advanced.

The Conference on Security and Cooperation in Europe has had major implications for these links, now and in the future. Much will depend on how the two integrated groups in Europe are prepared to accommodate to the prospects of closer East–West economic cooperation. Will their policy concepts and practical actions, as well as their economic and political mechanisms, be conducive or counterproductive to further progress in the international division of labour between East and West?

A full-scale study of the fundamental differences between the two types of integration would exceed the limits of this paper. Yet, it is taken as generally accepted that the two types of integration differ in the nature of their socio-economic foundations as well as in their principles and objectives. The difference in social character between the CMEA and the EEC is just as great as that between their attitudes to third countries or, even more, to cooperation with countries affiliated to other integrated groups.

The CMEA has proved to be an association devoted to encouraging world trade and economic cooperation. Discrimination against any country is ruled out by its statutes and is not practised:

(a) The 'open-minded' nature of CMEA is most clearly underlined in Article II of its statutes, which reads: 'Membership in the Council shall be open to other countries that undertake to abide by the principles of the Council and its goals and accept to carry out the duties stipulated for members in these statutes.' The idea of developing economic as well as techno-scientific ties with other countries, notwithstanding their social and political systems, is also stressed in the *Comprehensive Programme for Socialist Economic Integration*, and is a principle which is honoured by the CMEA countries in practice. The CMEA countries' trade with capitalist countries increased from 20 per cent of their total external trade in 1965 to roughly 33 per cent in 1975. Thus, there is no quest for autarky in the CMEA.

(b) The above considerations are likely to disprove the views held by some politicians in the West that the advance of socialist economic integration is an obstacle to further cooperation with countries in the West.

The contrary is true: CMEA integration will be conducive to East—West cooperation. Integration strengthens the economic potential of all the countries involved and adds momentum to their industrialisation. And since it is no secret that industrially advanced countries have a greater potential for participation in the division of labour, it must be accepted that a straightforward correlation exists between the progress of CMEA integration and the expansion of economic relations with Western countries.

(c) Rising trends have also been recorded in the relations between the CMEA as a whole and other states and international organisations. The CMEA cooperates with the United Nations, UNCTAD and the ECE. Agreements have been concluded with a number of national governments, for example, those of Finland, Mexico and Iraq. The CMEA has not established any customs tariffs or other rules which discriminate against third countries.

(d) The CMEA is well able to modify its own working in line with changing needs — that is, to amend its institutions, legal foundations and practice as may be desirable.

However, the European Communities so far have shown a different character. They assumed the nature of a closed grouping from the very outset, and their policies have been clearly characterised by trends adverse to third states:

(a) While certain modifications in trade practices have been conceded to certain third countries, the EEC has continued to insist on discriminatory practices against the CMEA countries. The EEC continues to maintain import quotas and other quantitative restrictions. The embargo lists, once set up by the NATO Committee COCOM, have been reduced but not abolished. One may also recall the customs tariffs, which are directed against supplies of the CMEA countries' most promising export goods.

(b) The member countries of the CMEA are increasingly prejudiced by the EEC's zones of free trade and preferential treatment.

(c) Restrictions have been imposed even upon techno-scientific exchange and other forms of economic cooperation which are of growing urgency in view of the demands of the techno-scientific revolution. The EEC Commission has repeatedly stated its intention to extend trade discrimination, making it applicable to these areas of activity also.

(d) The EEC's decision on a 'joint trade policy' has marked another stage in its attempt to force the CMEA countries into a position of inequality.

These policies have proved an obstruction to world trade, and their continuation would be most detrimental to any expansion and intensification of economic relations between the countries of the two groupings.

All European states, as well as the USA and Canada, in the Helsinki Final

Act have declared their interest in wider ranging economic cooperation, including multilateral or even all-European projects. Appropriate relations between the CMEA and the EEC are essential to that purpose. It should be accepted as a point of departure that integration will go ahead inside each of the two economic groupings, and the fact that two different types of integration will be proceeding simultaneously should not be allowed to prevent the development of businesslike relations and economic cooperation between the CMEA and the EEC or between their individual member countries.

These are the considerations behind the proposal made by the Council for Mutual Economic Assistance in February 1976 for the conclusion of an agreement between the CMEA and its member countries, on the one hand, and the EEC and its member countries, on the other. The following principles and courses of action must, in the view of the countries in the socialist community, be emphasised as a basis for normalisation of relations between the organs of the two integrated groupings:

(a) Acceptance and application of general principles of cooperation between socialist and capitalist countries and between the CMEA and the EEC on the basis laid down in the Final Act of Helsinki.

(b) Reduction and eventual elimination of discriminatory practices; application of the principle of most-favoured-nation treatment and implementation of customs and trade policies in accord with the principles of European cooperation.

(c) Modification of trade procedures in each grouping, including the introduction of a system of mutual preferences, with a view to encouraging cooperation for reciprocal benefit.

(d) Action to expand and stimulate industrial, financial and techno-scientific cooperation between the socialist and capitalist countries of Europe.

(e) Utilisation of all possibilities of combined efforts by the member countries of both groupings in getting to grips with problems of all-European concern in the fields of energy, the extractive industries, transport, telecommunications, environmental research and control, and in the setting up of specific projects of all-European cooperation.

It would be of the greatest significance for future cooperation, if the EEC was in a position to accept that each grouping should take appropriate action to ensure full reciprocal most-favoured-nation treatment, as a means of stimulating the expansion of trade between their respective member countries, on the basis of non-discrimination and reciprocal benefit, and that acceptance of the mfn principle should be the basis for studying or settling other problems relating to economic relations between them. Included in the problems to be settled on this basis should be those relating to trade in agricultural commodities, which should not be impeded by artificial barriers. Attention should be given to questions of standardisation, statistics, forecasting of production and of consumption demand and exchange of information, as well as to the promotion of conferences, seminars and similar events. Joint studies of currency and monetary problems might also be useful in the search for means to improve the stability of trade flows.

An agreement on the lines suggested above, which would best serve its purpose if concluded between the CMEA and its member countries, on the one hand, and the EEC and its member countries, on the other, should not rule out possibilities of more specific bilateral or multilateral agreements between individual CMEA member countries, on the one hand, and EEC organs, on the other, or between individual EEC member countries and CMEA organs, or between competent economic institutions of the two groupings.

Such an agreement would be a joint and positive contribution by the two organisations to an expansion and consolidation of economic relations on an equal footing and to their members' mutual benefit. It would be a step towards giving a material content to détente, towards consolidation of peace in Europe and towards the implementation of the aim of all-European cooperation.

Despite all the present obstacles to, and problems affecting, satisfactory economic relations between East and West, it is the accepted objective of the member countries of CMEA to promote in future, as in the past, economic cooperation between states of different social systems. These efforts will be continued in compliance with the letter and the spirit of the Final Act of the Conference on Security and Cooperation in Europe. A further deepening of the international division of labour between East and West may be expected in the second half of the 1970s. It will be reflected in a further expansion of mutual trade in commodities and of industrial cooperation, as well as in the development of new forms and methods of economic cooperation. To promote that process, to translate the potentialities already existing into practical effect, opens up a field of common interest and possibilities of complementary activity by economists in countries of both social systems.

NOTE

1 *Blätter für Deutsche und Internationale Politik,* No. 11/1975, p. 1225.

2 Economic Relations between East and West in the Light of Recent World Economic Trends*

Franz Nemschak

VIENNA INSTITUTE FOR COMPARATIVE ECONOMIC STUDIES

Economic relations between East and West — both developments up till now and the future prospects for, and problems of, East—West trade — have to be considered in the light of the international economic situation.

I THE BACKGROUND OF THE WORLD ECONOMY

The foremost question is: How was it possible for the international economy — after a period of striking progress lasting for almost a quarter of a century and interrupted by only relatively moderate setbacks — to drift into the most serious crisis since the 1930s?

One of the immediate causes of the recent world-wide recession was the boom of 1972—3, when there was a real growth in world production of almost 6 per cent and 7 per cent in successive years. This boom was very dangerous because, in contrast with all previous periods of economic expansion, it affected practically all economic sectors in all Western industrial countries — in Europe, America and Japan — as well as in most developing countries, *at the same time*. Since industrial capacities and labour supplies were more than fully utilised everywhere, significant price increases occurred as early as 1972 and the upward trend accelerated in 1973, especially for raw materials. Poor harvests in various parts of the world increased inflationary trends on an international scale. Attempts to slow down inflation by restrictive economic measures were unsuccessful, their only immediate effect being a dampening of real economic growth.

In this already extremely precarious and unstable situation oil prices were dramatically increased in October 1973, and consequently the rate of international inflation.

In 1974, uncertainty about future developments prompted employers to cut their investment plans drastically, while many consumers, concerned for their jobs, reduced their spending as far as possible and saved a relatively high proportion of their incomes. A sharp drop in the demand for cars, one of the

* The author would like to thank his colleagues B. Askanas, G. Fink, F. Levcik and J. Stankovsky of the Vienna Institute for Comparative Economic Studies, for providing information and ideas.

major economic indicators of the Western world, was characteristic of the situation at this time.

The oil crisis — for some time intensified by a partial embargo — combined with rising raw material prices, led many employers in the West to stockpile, somewhat hurriedly, oil and raw materials. With the fast-developing recession these stockpiles proved too big, and towards the end of 1974 they were reduced. This process at first led to a brief improvement in international trade but by the new year it served only to speed up recession.

The coincidence of world-wide recession, high unemployment and rapid inflation cannot be explained by any of the established economic theories, and the results of what the International Monetary Fund has described as a most complicated and dangerous combination of economic problems cannot be overcome by traditional economic measures.

It can be stated with a fair degree of accuracy, however, that in recent years both the structure of world trade and the international political balance of power have moved in favour of the oil producing countries and, to a lesser extent, of those developing countries with considerable raw material resources. Indeed, the leap in oil prices has radically altered the terms of trade between oil exporting and oil importing countries in favour of the former, presumably for a long time to come, and has started a *transfer of income on a world scale.* In figures, this can be estimated at some US $60—70 thousand million annually, leading to a total cumulative balance of payments surplus of the OPEC countries of some US $200—250 thousand million by 1980. This means that oil importers will be faced with the repayment of considerable debts plus interest, while their creditors gain international economic and political power. But in the long term it also means that there will be a close interrelationship between the economic interests of both debtors and creditors.

The situation with other raw materials is somewhat different. The changes in the terms of trade in favour of raw material producing countries did not last long. As a result of the recession, raw material prices dropped again somewhat while the prices for industrial goods rose as a result of inflation (see Tables 1 and 2). The major fluctuations on the international raw materials markets in recent years show that the prices of raw materials continue to be dependent to a great degree on current economic developments; and it is therefore understandable that the developing countries which export raw materials have been pressing, for some time, for an international agreement providing a long-term guarantee of adequate raw material prices. The countries involved would like to see such an agreement as an integral part of a 'New World Economic Order'.

In my paper, I can deal only briefly with this important subject, which has been occupying experts in all parts of the world for some time, and for which the developing countries and the Western industrialised countries have offered conflicting solutions.*

* The subject was closely examined by the 7th Special Session of the United Nations General Assembly on Development and International Economic Cooperation in New York (1—16 September 1975), which followed up the findings of the 6th Special Session on Raw Materials and Development Problems (9 April—2 May 1974).

The developing countries would like to see the establishment of an international raw materials authority, which would subject the most important raw materials markets to special regulations. With the help of internationally supervised raw materials stockpiles, and a common financial fund, minimum prices for several raw materials would be determined and adjusted in relation to appropriate price indices. Finally, by supervising and regulating deliveries

TABLE 1 WORLD EXPORT PRICES BY COMMODITY CLASSES
(index numbers, 1963 = 100)

	1970	1971	1972	1973	1974	1975
Manufactured goods	117	124	134	156	186	210
Primary commodities:						
Food	111	117	132	191	248	233
Agricultural non-food	101	105	120	184	219	192
Minerals	122	126	134	161	216	227
Fuels	108	127	143	188	553	568
All primary commodities	108	115	130	188	295	289
All commodities	113	119	130	158	223	242

Source: UN, *Monthly Bulletin of Statistics* (December 1975 and June 1976).

TABLE 2 WORLD EXPORT PRICES BY COMMODITY CLASSES
(annual percentage rates of growth, 1963–75)

	1963–70	1970–1	1971–2	1972–3	1973–4	1974–5
Manufactured goods	+2·3	+6·0	+8·1	+16·4	+19·2	+12·3
Primary commodities:						
Food	+1·5	+5·4	+12·8	+44·7	+29·8	−6·0
Agricultural non-food	+0·1	+4·0	+14·3	+53·3	+19·0	−12·5
Minerals	+2·9	+3·3	+6·3	+20·1	+34·2	+4·9
Fuels	+1·1	+17·6	+12·6	+31·5	+194·1	+2·8
All primary commodities	+1·1	+6·5	+13·0	+44·6	+56·9	−2·0
All commodities	+1·8	+5·3	+9·2	+21·5	+41·1	+8·5

Source: As for Table 1.

and purchases of raw materials by individual nations, the international authority would also assist in starting a transfer of wealth from the industrialised to the developing countries.

The Western industrialised nations reject this proposal as leading to 'a centrally planned world economy' and suggest reforming the world economy while maintaining market mechanisms. This would involve measures to stabilise the revenue from exports of raw materials in the event of a drop in the price or the quantity of exports. Furthermore, raw material agreements would prevent disproportionate short-term price fluctuations.*

Another major problem is that of the *balance of payments difficulties* faced by a number of industrialised and developing countries. These not only affect the current economic recovery, but may also impair the development of the world economy in the medium term. Even so, some of the worst fears felt for some time past have proved to be unfounded. Those industrialised countries which were suddenly confronted with unusually high trade deficits have not – so far at least – resorted to protectionist trade measures, nor have the oil producers' huge surpluses dislocated the international monetary system. By and large, the liberalisation of world trade has not been reversed, and the problem of 're-cycling' – the question how to bring foreign currency credited to the oil producers back to the industrialised countries – has been quietly solved by the international banking system, partly with the help of international organisations such as the International Monetary Fund.

In 1975 the balance-of-payments situation of the Western industrialised countries improved for various reasons, primarily because most of them combated boom and inflation with restrictive economic policies and, as a result of recession, imported much less oil and raw materials. Also, prices for industrial goods recovered and regained a good deal of the ground earlier lost to foodstuffs and raw materials (Tables 1 and 2). Furthermore, exports to the OPEC countries and to the credit-worthy developing countries could be significantly increased. Thanks to these developments, the balance-of-payments deficits of the Western industrial countries did not reach the astronomical levels which had originally been feared. Of course, the price which had to be paid for overcoming the international balance-of-payments problem was a sharp drop in production and a high rate of unemployment. By the end of 1975, unemployment in the industrialised countries of the West had reached a record total of 16 million persons. World trade in 1975 suffered its heaviest fall since the War (a fall in real terms of 6 per cent).

Although a new economic recovery has started, the world economy will no longer be able to continue on its old tracks in the future. But the question of where the world economy is going cannot be definitely answered at present. In this review, I have deliberately limited myself to a few phenomena which appear to point towards new, irreversible tendencies in the world economy.

I am thinking in particular of the change in the terms of trade in favour of the oil and raw material exporting countries. This has led to an increase not only in the economic, but also in the political, importance of these countries. The reverse side of the coin is the loss of prosperity and political power by those industrialised countries with a high degree of dependence on imports of oil and raw materials. These countries will have to contend with balance-of-payments difficulties as long as they are either unable or unwilling to adapt

---

* At the 4th UNCTAD Conference in Nairobi (3–31 May 1976), which ended with declarations not binding on the parties and conciliatory formulations, the real differences could not be reconciled.

their socio-economic structures and their expectations to the changed
circumstances.

This development has also affected those developing countries which have
no reserves of oil or raw materials worth speaking of, and which are industrially
underdeveloped and have major problems in feeding their rapidly increasing
populations. This is the desperate situation at present confronting almost two-
thirds of the member states of the United Nations (including India), in various
continents and with more than 2000 million people. These countries, in
particular, believe that a New World Economic Order would provide a new
international division of labour and thus more effective exploitation of the
world's resources; they are also convinced that it would take greater account
than does the present system of the needs of the less prosperous countries.

Various factors indicate that the new world economic order is likely to tend
towards dirigism and a planned economy rather than free world markets. It is
true that the interplay of forces in a completely free market economy cannot
be expected to solve the global problems facing modern civilisation – the
population explosion, widespread hunger, disease and illiteracy, the development of new sources of energy and raw materials, traffic chaos, the concentration of people in vast conurbations, environmental pollution and noise
nuisance.

A solution of these problems requires a high degree of planning and
channelling of productive forces – the careful coordination of a wide range
of economic measures at both national and international levels. But this does
not mean, in my opinion, that the future world economy can do without the
guiding and coordinating functions of the market. The market economy of the
Western world – despite various weaknesses which give rise to justified
criticism – has shown itself on the whole to be an efficient, adaptable
economic system which works with a minimum of bureaucracy. Its adaptability
has been demonstrated once again in the measures to overcome the recent oil
crisis. The present high rates of unemployment and inflation in a number of
Western countries should be seen as signals warning that, for too long, the
countries concerned have been living above their means, persistently spending
more for various purposes (consumption and investment) than they are willing
or able to produce. Of course, the market economy is capable of correcting
undesirable developments only partially and often at excessive social cost: to
take more efficient corrective measures is the task of the economic and social
policies of governments. As I have said, the market-economy system has major
weaknesses as well as singular advantages; it is far from perfect. Private and
state monopolies often insist on unjustifiably high prices or prevent possible
price reductions even if demand declines. On the other hand, strong trade
unions often push through unrealistic wage demands.

For these reasons, I do not plead for a free-market economy which, in any
case, has long since gone; but, rather, I am thinking of a market economy
with numerous elements of economic planning which, based on a workable
system of international law, would lead to a better division of labour and to an

increase in world trade.

In this economic panorama, in which the difficult structural problems of the highly developed industrial countries have been only briefly outlined, the place of economic relations between East and West now has to be seen.

II THE RELATIVE IMPORTANCE OF EAST—WEST TRADE

Though East—West trade has developed fairly favourably in the last twenty years since the end of the Cold War in the mid-1950s — expanding in most years at a higher rate than the rapidly increasing world trade — it still accounts at present for only 3·5 per cent of world trade (Table 3).

This percentage is remarkably low and is quite unrelated to the economic potential of the two areas. In 1975 the industrialised countries of the West accounted for some 60 per cent of world industrial production and 6 per cent of world trade. The Eastern European CMEA countries accounted for some 30 per cent of world industrial production, but only for some 9 per cent of world trade (Tables 3 and 4).

East—West trade is of relatively greater importance for the Eastern European industrial countries than for those in the West. Trade with the West accounts for between 20 per cent and 45 per cent of the former countries' foreign trade (Table 5) whereas only 5 per cent of the Western industrialised countries' foreign trade is accounted for by trade with the East.

III EAST—WEST TRADE DURING THE BOOM OF 1972/73 AND THE RECESSION OF 1974/75

The rapidly changing pattern of development of the world economy in recent years has inevitably affected the economic relations between East and West.

During the boom of 1972/73, a period during which trade liberalisation in the West was already far advanced, the Socialist countries, in particular the Soviet Union, were able to increase their exports to the Western industrialised nations considerably. At the same time, the Eastern European countries also increased their imports from the Western industrial countries — mainly of high-grade capital goods — with the help of Western credits.

The large-scale deliveries of grain and other agricultural products from the United States to the Soviet Union (and to a lesser extent to other CMEA countries) in 1972, 1973 and 1975 are a special case in the trade relations between East and West. They had little to do with the business cycle, although they did affect the world market prices of these products.

In 1974, when the recession was already making itself felt and oil prices had risen rapidly and raw material prices had also increased appreciably (Tables 1 and 2), the Soviet Union, thanks primarily to its oil sales, was the only Eastern country which registered a marked increase in its exports to the Western industrialised countries. The other CMEA countries had to be content with considerably smaller export growth rates.

TABLE 3 WORLD TRADE BY MAIN REGIONS, 1938–75

(percentage distributions)

	1938	1948	1950	1955	1960	1965	1970	1973	1974	1975
Developed market economies of which trade with:	68·0	64·0	63·1	64·8	66·0	68·6	71·5	71·6	67·8	66·1
developed market economies	45·0	41·4	40·9	44·8	47·5	51·7	55·5	54·9	47·7	46·0
developing market economies	16·7	20·0	20·5	18·3	16·1	14·3	13·2	13·5	17·0	16·6
centrally planned economies	6·3	2·6	1·7	1·7	2·5	2·6	2·8	3·2	3·1	3·5
Developing market economies of which trade with:	23·4	29·8	28·9	25·4	22·1	19·9	18·1	18·5	23·7	24·0
developed market economies	16·7	20·0	20·5	18·3	16·2	14·3	13·2	13·5	17·0	16·6
developing market economies	5·6	9·0	7·6	6·4	4·9	4·2	3·5	3·8	5·6	5·9
centrally planned economies	1·1	0·8	0·8	0·7	1·0	1·4	1·3	1·1	1·2	1·5
Centrally planned economies of which trade with:	8·7	6·2	8·0	9·9	12·0	11·5	10·4	10·0	8·5	9·9
developed market economies	6·3	2·6	1·7	1·7	2·5	2·6	2·8	3·2	3·1	3·5
developing market economies	1·1	0·8	0·8	0·7	1·0	1·4	1·3	1·1	1·2	1·5
centrally planned economies	1·3	2·8	5·4	7·6	8·5	7·5	6·3	5·7	4·3	4·9
Total world trade	100	100	100	100	100	100	100	100	100	100

Sources: UN, *Yearbook of International Trade Statistics*, and *Monthly Bulletin of Statistics* (December 1975 and June 1976); GATT, *International Trade 1974/75* (Geneva 1975).

In contrast, the imports of all CMEA countries from the West were still rising strongly in 1974 – mainly imports of high-grade investment goods – and, since foreign currency earnings from exports were not sufficient, their foreign debt increased. According to estimates by the Chase Manhattan Bank, New York, the CMEA countries' debts to the West rose from approximately US $15 thousand million in 1972 to some US $30 thousand million in 1975.

TABLE 4 WORLD TRADE BY MAIN REGIONS, 1972–5
(percentage distribution)

	1972	1973	1974	1975
Developed market economies	71·7	71·4	67·6	66·1
of which: European Economic Community	36·6	36·4	33·7	33·9
Developing market economies	18·0	18·5	23·8	24·0
of which: OPEC countries	5·2	5·4	10·0	13·0
Centrally planned economies	10·3	10·0	8·5	9·9
of which: European CMEA countries	9·5	9·1	7·7	9·0
Total world trade	100	100	100	100

Sources: As for Table 3.

TABLE 5 TRADE OF CMEA COUNTRIES WITH THE DEVELOPED MARKET ECONOMIES (percentage shares in country's total trade)

	Exports			Imports		
	1960	1970	1974	1960	1970	1974
Bulgaria	12·5	14·2	11·7	13·7	19·1	22·5
Czechoslovakia	16·7	20·4	24·0	18·9	24·5	27·7
GDR	20·2	21·9	27·4	22·0	26·7	34·1
Hungary	21·9	28·0	26·1	24·7	28·8	34·6
Poland	29·9	28·4	36·3	29·7	25·8	50·8
Romania	21·3	31·9	42·1	23·4	39·5	48·6
Soviet Union	18·2	18·7	30·2	19·8	24·0	32·6
CMEA total	19·7	21·7	29·4	21·4	25·8	35·8

Source: *Rocznik statystyczny handlu zagranicznego 1975* (GUS, Warsaw, 1975).

The Western industrialised countries, where the main domestic economic supports – investment and consumption demand – decreased, tried to support their economies with exports to Eastern Europe.

By 1975, the recession had affected virtually all sectors in the industrialised countries of the West, including foreign trade; and it became clear that East–

West trade would not remain unaffected. As a consequence of the general Western recession, the exports of the Socialist countries to the West stagnated in real terms. But, in contrast, their imports from the West increased in real terms by 10 per cent and in value even by 36 per cent. As a result the debt of the CMEA countries again rose considerably, and this trend probably continued in the first quarter of 1976.

An analysis of economic developments over the past four years leads to the conclusion that East—West trade is highly dependent upon the trade cycle in the West.

The same is true — perhaps even more true — for the developing countries, who conduct 72 per cent of their foreign trade with the industrial West. The oil and/or raw materials exporting countries were affected by the decline in demand in the Western countries, in that they were left with goods on their hands. The OPEC found it difficult to keep oil prices at their previous levels; and various raw material prices dropped during the recession, showing no convincing signs of recovery until the beginning of 1976 when the Western economy began to improve.

Iran is a good example of the interdependence of industrialised and developing countries. Iran is both one of the world's biggest oil producers and at the same time one of the most promising developing countries. As a result of the recession in the Western industrialised countries, Iran's oil sales were substantially reduced, thus forcing the country to limit investment in large industrial projects, to defer important infrastructure investments, and to raise credits in the Euro-currency markets in order to meet her most pressing commitments.

Based on these experiences, recovery from the current recession must be the most pressing objective of all countries — in East and West, in North and South — and, at the same time, the basic precondition for the solution of all other economic problems.

IV PRESENT ECONOMIC PROSPECTS

By the end of 1975, most of the national and international institutes which specialise in economic forecasts inclined to the view that a new recovery would come in 1976. In the United States, this recovery had already started in 1975 and it has gained momentum in 1976. The economic recovery in Western Germany has been stronger than expected and accompanied by a remarkably modest increase in prices. In France, economic growth similar to that in Western Germany is expected. The strong economic upswing in the leading Western industrial countries will, without doubt, stimulate the economies of other Western countries. However, in some Western European countries with serious internal difficulties, such as Italy and Britain, there is as yet little sign of recovery.

At the beginning of 1976, some voices warned against excessive optimism. In spite of these sceptical overtones, it can be assumed that the recovery of the Western industrialised economies will develop on a broader basis in the course of the next few years, and in turn exert a favourable influence on East—West trade. However, even if this is so, there are still various problems impeding a further extension of East—West trade; and I should like to deal with these difficulties in the final part of my paper.

V PROBLEMS OF EAST—WEST TRADE

The difference between the two foreign trading systems means that each side is employing different means to achieve certain desired effects and aims. What the Western side attempts to achieve with, for example, customs duties, import quotas, regulations on technical norms and standards, etc., is achieved much more thoroughly in the East through foreign trade planning and the state monopoly of foreign trade.

If the East requests the West to remove its trade barriers — which is a demand with which I am very much in favour — then it must also be prepared, *inter alia,* to grant imports from the West a higher priority in its foreign trade plans, and to inform Western business quicker and more fully of specific requirements of the Eastern economies, than has been the case in the past.

In my opinion, this reciprocity would also be in accordance with the basic principles laid down in the preamble of the chapter on Cooperation in the Field of Economics, of Science and Technology, and of the Environment in the Final Act of the Conference on Security and Cooperation in Europe (CSCE):* cooperation, with due regard for the different levels of economic development; reciprocity permitting an equitable distribution of advantages and obligations of comparable scale; respect for existing bilateral and multilateral agreements; special attention to the least developed countries. In the light of these constructive basic principles, it must be possible to find solutions that are satisfactory to both sides for the various problems arising in the economic relations between East and West.

One of the questions might be the application of *most-favoured nation* (mfn) tariff treatment to trade with Eastern Europe. I am very much in favour of mfn being granted without exception to all CMEA states without political preconditions. However, the mfn concept, in the context of the multilateral GATT treaty and of some intergovernmental bilateral treaties, recognises customs unions and free trade areas as exceptions. The concessions and rights which member states of regional integration areas mutually grant to one another apply only to these states. To this extent, all outsiders are in fact 'discriminated against'; but this 'discrimination' follows the logic of the situation and is a characteristic feature of regional integration areas. For the same reason, the CMEA countries cannot be accused of discrimination because

---

* All references are to the English text, *Conference on Security and Cooperation in Europe, Final Act*, Cmnd 6198 (London: HMSO, 1975) p. 13.

they grant themselves mutual rights and concessions which are not granted to all other states.

There should also be no differences of opinion over the *customs duty preferences* which practically all Western industrialised countries grant to developing countries, including some of the less-developed socialist countries. In this connection, I should like to suggest that the CMEA countries might also open their markets for specific products of the developing countries — such as coffee, cocoa, subtropical fruits, and similar items — instead of subjecting them to prohibitive taxes as at present. Such a policy could help to increase the trade between the CMEA countries and the developing countries, which in 1975 accounted for only some 2·5 per cent of total world trade (Table 3), to the advantage of both partners. Consumers in Eastern Europe would greatly enjoy a rich selection of these products at low prices, whilst the developing countries would be greatly assisted with investment goods which can be produced without difficulty in the CMEA countries.

In view of the heterogeneous situations in various parts of the world, it is not likely that a further general reduction of customs duties will be one of the objects of the coming world-wide tariff negotiations. It is more likely that selective measures will be envisaged to relieve the precarious economic situation of the poorest developing countries.

The *removal of quantitative trade restrictions* is already far advanced in the West. Further liberalisation has been stopped only temporarily by the recession.

I believe that it is also possible that the Western industrialised countries will make further tariff reductions in favour of the highly developed Eastern European industrial states, provided that *equivalent concessions* are made in return or, in the words of the above-mentioned preamble in the Helsinki Final Act, upon consideration of 'an equitable distribution of advantages and obligations of comparable scale'. I could imagine these concessions taking the form of an extension of the third commodity group foreseen in the 'Comprehensive Programme' of the CMEA countries. In this commodity group (mainly consumer goods) for which the CMEA trading partners are not obliged to fix delivery quotas in terms of quantity or value in their mutual trade agreements, Western suppliers may at present find it easier to get into the market than in the first two, much more important, commodity groups for which Western suppliers are considered only if the goods cannot be produced within the CMEA area.

A further problem is the *asymmetry of the commodity structure* in East— West trade. The proportion of industrial goods in the total exports of Eastern European countries to the Western industrialised countries is at present, on average, barely 40 per cent and only slowly rising, while the share of industrial goods in the exports of the West to the European CMEA countries is more than 80 per cent (Table 6). Exceptions are the Soviet Union, of whose Western exports only some 25 per cent are industrial goods and, at the other extreme, Czechoslovakia and the GDR, of whose Western exports some 65 per cent and 80 per cent are industrial products. Taking no account of Czechoslo-vakia and the GDR, two countries with export structures similar to those of the Western industrialised states, the extreme differences in the export structures of East and West become even more pronounced. The long-term prospects for exporting crude materials and agricultural products to Western Europe are not as good as those for manufactures. At the same time, the increasing domestic demand in the CMEA area will reduce the amount of raw materials, fuels and food available for export.

The reasons why most Eastern European countries are unable to increase their exports of industrial products quickly enough are many and various.

TABLE 6 COMMODITY COMPOSITION OF CMEA EXPORTS TO AND IMPORTS FROM DEVELOPED MARKET ECONOMIES, 1974 (percentages)

Commodity Groups	Exports		Imports	
	CMEA total	Soviet Union	CMEA total	Soviet Union
Agricultural products	11·6	3·7	9·5	9·0
Crude materials	17·8	26·0	5·2	2·8
Mineral fuels	29·5	43·3	0·8	0·3
Chemicals	5·8	3·8	14·5	11·0
Basic manufactures	20·6	19·1	33·5	38·7
Machinery	7·5	3·1	30·8	31·2
Other products	7·2	1·0	5·7	7·0
Total	100	100	100	100

Source: UN *Economic Bulletin for Europe,* vol. 27 (New York, 1975).

They range from the technical backwardness of many goods offered for sale, to inefficient marketing and service, or to unattractive packaging and presenta-tion. On the other hand, it cannot be overlooked that since the end of the 1960s the industrial structure in all CMEA countries has gradually changed in favour of high quality industrial products. Thanks to this development the CMEA countries will be increasingly able to offer more competitive manu-factured goods — capital goods, equipment, machines, instruments, chemical products — to the West and thus to help to the expansion of East—West trade.

In this connection, *industrial cooperation between East and West* could also serve useful purposes. Industrial cooperation offers Eastern European enter-prises the possibility of using Western know-how and also of producing, at competitive prices, goods which satisfy Western standards and tastes. Further-more, long term cooperation agreements have the advantage that, from the beginning, they provide a steady flow of goods and services in both directions.

Although the last three or four years have brought a considerable increase in the number of East—West cooperation agreements at enterprise level, I believe that deliveries of goods in the framework of such agreements will always only complement the traditional foreign trade, and not replace it. Even so, the advantages of industrial cooperation should not be underestimated.

Apart from the immediate economic benefits which both sides enjoy from their cooperation, they can profit from the process of learning which is inevitably brought about. The Western partner receives important information on decision-making processes in the centrally planned economies, as well as on any institutional changes in the mechanism and organisation of foreign trade, which might prove advantageous to him in the course of normal foreign trading business. The Eastern partner, on the other hand, gains experience of Western marketing methods, quality standards and service facilities, and also learns during the implementation of the cooperation agreement to adapt rapidly to changes in demand in the West. Here too, the experiences gained are not limited to the cooperation agreements but can be used in the course of normal foreign trading. Finally, some forms of inter-firm cooperation, especially the formation of joint marketing companies in the West, can open the door to new markets.[1]

It is understandable that CMEA partners who wish to develop cooperation relations with Western companies often prefer financially strong multinational companies who play an important role as pioneers of technical progress in modern industrial society. I would, however, point out that also medium-sized and even small companies in Western countries can be very useful cooperation partners, as can be demonstrated with numerous examples from various industries.

VI SUMMARY AND CONCLUSIONS

I believe the most important finding of my analysis of the economic relations between East and West, against the background of the world economic scene, is that East—West trade is dependent both on the phase of the business cycle and long-term growth in the Western industrialised countries and also on the economic efficiency of the CMEA countries.

During the boom period, the socialist countries were able to increase their exports to the Western industrialised nations considerably, and therefore could import on a larger scale important products — mainly high quality investment goods. During the recession, the fall in demand in the industrialised countries led to a considerable reduction of the socialist countries' exports to the West, due not least to the fact that the quality of the commodities offered was not up to Western standards. This meant that the socialist countries were forced to reduce their imports from the Western countries, since their ability to increase foreign indebtedness is limited.

The Western industrialised countries and the developing countries are economically interdependent on an even larger scale, as more than 70 per cent of the foreign trade of the developing countries falls to the Western industrialised countries.

It was only during the boom that the oil producing countries could succeed with their dramatic move which started a redistribution of income on a world scale; and it was also due to the heavy demand in the Western industrialised countries that the prices of various raw materials rose steeply. In the recession, however, raw material prices sank again, and even the OPEC has difficulty in maintaining the position which it won during the boom.

This economic interdependence exists not only during isolated periods, but is almost equally apparent if one considers the long-term development of the world economy. It becomes obvious that all three large regions of the world economy have a vital interest not only in their own economy flourishing, but also in the economy in all other countries of the world developing as favourably and smoothly as possible. These conditions would also best favour East–West trade.

For this reason, in my view, all speculations about the collapse of the 'capitalist system' are just as short-sighted and pointless as malicious pleasure on the Western side over difficulties and shortages in the socialist countries.

I do not wish to forecast here the growth-rates for the next five, ten, or twenty years. There are, however, some indications that the average annual rate of economic growth in the coming decades will be lower than during the past twenty-five years.

The gloomy forecasts drawn up by the Club of Rome's experts – according to which mankind is inevitably approaching 'the limits to growth' and should thus adapt itself as soon as possible to a 'zero-growth' – are of no use as working hypotheses. I am more inclined to believe those authors who remind us that in the course of its history mankind has found itself confronted with critical situations which were at least as difficult as the present one, and that Man has always found ways and means to overcome these difficulties.

As for me, I am convinced that the formidable economic and social problems of our time, which confront all countries regardless of their economic and social systems, can best, by far, be solved through constructive and trust-ful cooperation on a world-wide level. Indeed, this is perhaps the only way.

NOTE

1 The topic of inter-firm cooperation is dealt with in a book in the series 'Studien über Wirtschaftsund Systemvergleiche' of the Vienna Institute for Comparative Economic Studies: F. Levcik and J. Stankovsky, *Industrielle Kooperation zwischen Ost und West* (Vienna and New York: Springer-Verlag, 1976). (An English translation will be published in autumn 1976 by International Arts and Sciences Press, Inc., White Plains, New York.)

Discussion of the Papers by Professor Schmidt and Professor Nemschak

Introducing the papers, *Mr Kaser* noted that both took as their starting point the recent growth of East—West trade in conditions of economic stagnation in the West and decline in intra-Western trade. Professor Schmidt saw both conditions as stimulating the interest of Western firms in trade with the East; but as Professor Nemschak's Table 3 showed, a rise of 0·2 per cent in East—West trade had only very slightly offset the 8·2 per cent fall in the intra-trade of the developed Western countries. Much of the structural change in the latter countries' trade was a consequence of the faster rise in prices of oil, minerals and foodstuffs than in prices of manufactures (Nemschak's Table 1); and this had led both authors to consider the question of commodity prices in the context of the proposals for a New World Economic Order. But their assessments of the place of East—West economic relations in such an Order reflected widely divergent views on the desirability of planning; Professor Nemschak appeared to share the general Western rejection of the idea of an international raw materials authority as leading to 'a centrally-planned world economy' (p. 26), while Professor Schmidt's paper suggested (p. 14) that he would support such a counter to what he saw as exploitation of the developing countries by multinational corporations. Mr Kaser hoped that Professor Schmidt would elaborate on the actual mechanisms of a New World Economic Order which he believed could dynamise East—West economic relations; meanwhile he suggested that the rigours of trade between the CMEA countries and developing countries in two sets of inconvertible currencies might be eased by some form of agreed Western participation in clearing arrangements between socialist and developing countries. Possibly Mr Abbam — who had first-hand experience of the constraint on his country's trade with the socialist countries resulting from the inconvertibility among themselves of CMEA currencies — could contribute some ideas on this problem.

Mr Kaser drew attention to the possible fields for East—West collaboration mentioned in the Helsinki Final Act which the two papers stressed, and noted that Professor Schmidt appeared to see this complex of agreements on particular aims or principles as a unity, whereas the Western signatories tended to evaluate each mutual concession separately: Professor Nemschak attempted to interpret the reference to 'reciprocity' in trade relations, and thereby explored a question of major importance discussed in both papers — discrimination and the consequent sacrifice of some of the potential gains from trade. It was common ground that such gains were not being realised in East—West relations to the extent that they were in trade among Western Countries. The papers by Professor Holzman and Dr Hanson pointed to characteristics of planned economies which, in their view, also inhibited the realisation of those gains among CMEA members.

1 Mr Kaser wondered whether Professor Schmidt really intended to imply –
by his argument on p. 9* and his references to the primacy of political
factors in the correlation of détente and economic co-operation (pp. 8 and
17) – a contrast between economic gain as the determinant of interest in
trade in the West and a willingness of the planned economies to tolerate
economically disadvantageous trade in pursuit of some overall politico–
economic maximand; Professor Schmidt had also insisted that no 'third type'
of economic mechanism would be generated by deeper or wider exchanges.
Mr Kaser noted that Dr Hanson's paper also suggested that the CMEA countries
maximised national rather than enterprise advantage, and that Professor
Holzman saw intra-CMEA trade as 'an instance of gigantic barter' (p. 157).

On the question of discrimination, Mr Kaser thought that Professor Schmidt
went rather far in insisting that 'Partners to a commercial transaction . . .
should grant each other equal rights and privileges on their own national
territories, and no difference in treatment should be permissible between the
several countries and companies doing business on a foreign territory' (p. 18).
The first clause implied the same rights for foreign firms as for domestic ones;
the second that Western firms should have the same access to enterprises in a
CMEA country as do those from CMEA countries. The two papers expressed
widely differing views on the 'closed' or discriminatory natures of the EEC
and CMEA. He thought that Professor Schmidt's evidence of a sharp fall in the
degree of CMEA reliance on intra-trade was weakened by the fact of rising
prices in trade with the West while prices in intra-CMEA trade remained stable.
He noted that Professor Nemschak and Professor Holzman interpreted the
CMEA as a tightly knit preferential trading area, just as Professor Schmidt
spoke of the EEC as 'closed'. The relations of the EEC with developing
countries were characterised, however, by tariff concessions under the Lomé
Convention, by association arrangements for Greece and Turkey and by the
extension of preferences to Romania and Yugoslavia; and it had also made
tariff concessions to ex-EFTA states. Noting Professor Nemschak's suggestion
that one piece of 'reciprocity' for extension of more than formal mfn treatment (i.e. as defined in the GATT) by the EEC to CMEA countries could be
'to accord imports from the West a higher priority in foreign trade plans and
to inform Western business quicker and more fully of specific requirements of
the Eastern economies' (p. 33), he suggested that the first point indicated an
assumption that CMEA countries still pursued an 'imports first' policy; this
was less true today, as had been shown in a recent symposium.[†] The value of
the second element – advance documentation on import needs (and export
possibilities) – was underscored by Professor Schmidt's assurance that Eastern

---

* 'No capitalist businessman would undertake trade or cooperation if disadvantage to
him was the result. The socialist countries, naturally, try to draw the maximum benefit
for their own development from all economic relations with capitalist industrial states.'

[†] H. Matejka in H. H. Höhmann, M. C. Kaser and K. C. Thalheim (eds), *The New
Economic Systems of Eastern Europe* (London and Berkeley, California, 1975).

plans offer Western firms the prospect of long-term, lower-cost, contractual deliveries.

Finally, Mr Kaser drew attention to the range of statistics in the papers before the conference seeking to quantify the unrealised potential for East—West trade. The question that he hoped the conference would explore was whether the market or decentralised planning evoked more international trade that did central planning for an economy otherwise similarly endowed.

Subsequent discussion revolved around (i) East—West relations *per se* and (ii) the need for, and possible nature of, a New World Economic Order.

Dr Jacobsen regretted that Professor Schmidt's politico-economic approach did not deal fully with the question of the hindrances to expansion of East—West trade on the Eastern side. An analysis of present attitudes to East—West economic relations had to take into account that only a few years earlier some East European scientists (like Professor Wenger in 1970)* had described the goals of the Western countries as imperialistic, aiming to split the Socialist World System, to blackmail particular countries and to restore the capitalist system. One therefore had to ask what had changed in the meantime, since current Eastern analysis of East—West-economic relations seemed much more moderate in tone. It should also be noted that some of the small CMEA countries had clearly found the CMEA system too confining and were asserting their right to determine independently their economic policies and the forms of their international relations. More information was needed on the extent and forms of East—West cooperation acceptable to each country. In contrast, *Professor Wenger* saw Western attitudes as crucial. Western governments had been forced by experience to accept both coexistence — making détente possible — and the fact of the benefits to be derived from economic cooperation, all of which favoured trade expansion. Realists within these countries were trying to promote trade, but reactionary forces opposed this and 'liberals' were trying to use trade as a lever to bring about changes in the economic and social systems of the socialist countries.

The significance of political conditions was stressed also by *Professor Maier*, who also contested Professor Nemschak's analysis of the interaction of cyclical developments in the capitalist economies with the development of East—West trade. He accepted that recession in the West encouraged a search for new, Eastern, markets and also encouraged socialist countries to seize new import, credit-raising, etc., opportunities; but the negative side of the picture was the decreased absorptive capacity of Western markets, the associated balance-of-payments difficulties for partner countries and the marked increase in protectionist tendencies in the West. He interpreted Dr Hanson's paper as advocacy of a cyclical pattern for East—West trade, countering the Western

* S. Wenger, 'Aussenwirtschaftsbeziehungen sozialistischer Staaten mit kapitalistischen Industrieländern und die Hauptprozesse in der Entwicklung der Bedingungen auf dem kapitalistischen Weltmarkt' (Berlin, DDR: Hochschule für Ökonomie, Internationale ökonomische Beziehungen, 1970) Lehrbrief No. 8, p. 24.

trade cycle, and objected that this would be neither possible nor desirable. The aim should be to reduce the negative impact of cycles in activity in the West by developing the stable East—West trade relations made possible by the continuous rhythm of planned growth in the socialist countries. The scientific-technical revolution strengthened the argument for structural adaptations in national economies of a kind implying reliance on long-term, stable East—West division of labour. Methods of realising possibilities of international cooperation immune to cyclical disturbance included industrial cooperation in large-scale projects, and barter arrangements. *Professor Mateev* generally agreed with this argument, whereas *Dr Rogge* distinguished the desirability of long-run stable conditions of East—West trade from the need for short-run flexibility in levels and patterns of exchanges if maximum benefit was to be reaped. However, some actual fluctuations were of no benefit to either side, but these could be averted only by policies leading to the accumulation of adequate international reserves.

The question of the difference between national and enterprise gains from trade raised by Mr Kaser (and in the papers of Dr Hanson and Professor Holzman) was taken up by *Professor Rothschild*, who suggested that a neo-classical economist could hardly take the view that the efforts of the enter-prise to maximise its gains would conflict with the pursuit of national welfare. Apart from this, each economic system determined its economic institutions and practices according to its own idea of what best promoted the national advantage. Neither mutual reproaches on this account nor attempts to measure relative gains from East—West trade seemed likely to get us very far.

The need for a 'new international economic order' based on planned economic relations, and equity in such relations, was emphasised by *Professor Kohlmey*. Many Western industrial countries had been living beyond their means for years, and there was a transfer of national wealth and income from poor countries to rich capitalist economies. The labour of developing countries was being exploited through (i) a brain drain, (ii) other long-term migration to developed capitalist countries, (iii) *gastarbeiter* systems, (iv) a 'profit drain' by multinational companies, reflecting the greater discrepancy between the real wages of their employees in the developed and the developing countries than between the productivity of the two groups, and (v) a wealth drain, as the developed countries exploited the non-reproducible natural resources of the developing countries and neglected to develop substitutes for them.

But *Professor Lorenz* saw this exposition of the forces determining North—South income distribution as hardly up-to-date. Today's international strategy of trade expansion for the developing countries emphasised a new horizontal division of labour with the developed countries through 'substitutive exchange' — the encouragement of exports of more or less simple industrial goods to the latter, including, it was to be hoped, the socialist countries; but terms-of-trade problems could arise here similar to those which, it used to be asserted, applied to the 'complementary' raw materials/industrial equipment exchange. Secondly, as put into practice by OPEC, the strategy advocated by UNCTAD of enforcing 'fair' raw material prices had affected international income distribution to the benefit of the OPEC countries and the USSR and to the disadvantage of almost all other CMEA countries and the 'fourth' world. An appropriate balance of these two strategies had to be struck, not only in the light of income-distribution objectives — surely an issue in intra-Eastern as well as East—West and North—South relations — but also so as to avoid overburdening substitutive exchange, since complementary exchange could still contribute to expansion and to the solution of balance-of-payments problems in both North—South and East—West trade.

Professor Yamamoto was struck by the conflict between Professor Schmidt's denial of the possibility that cooperation could generate a 'third type' of economic system, combining features of the socialist planned and the Western-type market economies, and Professor Nemschak's expectation that such a system would have to be devised by international agreement as part of a more equitable new international economic order. Japan was in fact introducing strong economic-planning elements into its 'market' economy and it seemed to him that such a 'third type' of system might well suit many countries in both East and West.

Replying to the discussion, *Professor Schmidt* stressed the importance of the opportunity now to extend détente from political to economic relations. Increasing possibilities of economies of scale and rising costs of research and development, together with the rapid economic development of the socialist countries increased the potential benefits of closer cooperation; but their realisation depended on the removal of the trade barriers erected by the EEC and mutual agreement by East and West not to attempt to change each other's economic and social systems. He agreed with Professor Maier's assessment of the impact of crisis in the West on East—West relations. He believed East—West cooperation to be necessary in a global approach to the solution of the problems of developing countries.

Professor Nemschak suggested that all reasonable people in the West agreed that the internal economic systems of the socialist countries were their own concern. Mixed systems were developing in many countries and many markets were now managed, at least in part. An extension of planning and management was needed to deal with the problems of the developing countries and the Western systems were flexible enough to make the necessary adaptations, which could well amount to suspension of the market mechanism in some areas.

He doubted whether East—West trade could soon grow to very large dimensions, whatever the good-will on both sides. Difficulties to be overcome included the CMEA countries' difficulties in offering goods acceptable to Western markets, balance-of-payments problems and the large indebtedness to the West of some of the Eastern countries. There was also a need to develop new forms of cooperation, and his Institute was actively promoting exploratory conferences in this field.

He was convinced that difficulties retarding progress in one economic and social system were no cause for satisfaction to anybody. The interdependence of national economies, demonstrated during the recent experience of recession in the West and world-wide inflation, should encourage East–West cooperation in devising a better world economic order.

3 Motivations for Mutual Cooperation between Countries with Different Economic Systems

Marie Lavigne
UNIVERSITY OF PARIS I, PANTHEON-SORBONNE

There is widespread agreement on the general benefits to be gained by all partners from the promotion and diversification of trade and cooperation between countries with different economic systems, in Europe and in the world as a whole. The aims, the difficulties and suggested ways of dealing with them, the possible strategies of East–West trade, have all been discussed at length, and with growing intensity, in seminars, workshops and conferences during the past few years. The practical issues will be discussed here under other headings of our Agenda; and this is why I shall focus rather on the new context of this question, emerging from the Final Act of the Conference on Security and Cooperation in Europe, signed in Helsinki on 1 August 1975.*

If this text is to be taken seriously, we have a general agreement on the principles of economic relations between different socio-economic systems, the divergence between these systems being forthrightly acknowledged. Of course the Final Act is not a treaty with binding force; and we must hope that it is not 'final' – in the sense that we hope that there will be concrete results from the Conference. Especially in the West we may regret that too little attention has been paid to this historic event; and we may now suggest some possible developments from it.

It would be highly artificial to separate political and economic motivations for the agreement. In fact, the basic aim which is the reinforcement of 'peace and security in Europe and in the world as a whole' is closely linked with the desire to promote economic growth, social progress and the well-being of people through trade and cooperation. Although the political motive was the strongest when the first proposals for a Conference on Security and Cooperation in Europe were made by the socialist states ten years ago (Bucharest, July 1966; Karlovy-Vary, April 1967), the concern with economic relations soon appeared most prominently (Prague Declaration on Peace, Security and Cooperation, January 1972). Indeed, the consolidation of economic relations is seen as providing the most stable basis for cooperation throughout all Europe.[1]

* All references are to the English text, *Conference on Security and Cooperation in Europe, Final Act,* Cmnd 6198 (London: HMSO, 1975).

The Final Act of the Helsinki Conference sets out the objectives of co-operation in a strictly defined framework: these objectives are accepted by states belonging to different (diverse) economic systems and which have world-wide responsibilities beyond the continent of Europe. We may now analyse some of the issues inseparable from attempts to intensify economic relations under the following three headings: the intergovernmental context; the diversity of economic and social systems; world-wide interdependence.

I THE INTERGOVERNMENTAL CONTEXT

The motivations for the development of international economic cooperation are of a political nature, not only because such cooperation tends to foster peace and security, but also because independent, sovereign states are involved. And the fact cannot be ignored that these states belong to international organisations of various natures, where similar issues have already been discussed for a long time.

In the realm of international organisations, the text of the Final Act makes frequent reference to the United Nations and its specialised agencies and, in particular, to the Economic Commission for Europe. Not surprisingly, the concrete forms of industrial cooperation are described in exactly the same terms as in the analytical reports of the ECE on the subject in 1970 and 1973 (e.g. joint production, specialisation, cooperation in the setting up of complete installations, mixed companies, joint industrial research, etc.); and the ECE appears also as one of the best frameworks for study of the possibilities of statistical harmonisation or of improving sources of information about laws and regulations concerning foreign trade.

From the foregoing we may conclude that such organisations as the UN–ECE, or in other fields UNESCO, reflect the same underlying motivations as those of the Helsinki Conference. However, other international organisations, also, have among their main objectives the development of mutual economic relations.

Among these we have, first of all, the General Agreement on Tariffs and Trade. A major purpose of GATT is to encourage non-discrimination in trade and the lowering of all trade barriers, so as to increase foreign trade on the basis of reciprocal advantage. In fact, it is not an unambiguous purpose, as past GATT negotiations have shown, especially since growing numbers of the socialist countries have become members of the organisation.[2] Without encroaching upon Point 3 of our Programme, we must note here that although some GATT principles are embodied in the Helsinki Final Act, they are mentioned in a somewhat different and restrictive form.

The socialist states are currently asking to be granted the benefit of the most-favoured-nation clause. Some of them already benefit from it, but not always in all markets; others do not. A particular difficulty arises from the common trade policy of the European Economic Community towards Eastern countries. Since all the bilateral trade agreements entered into by EEC

countries with Eastern European partners expired at the end of 1974 or
1975 and none of them have yet been renewed — and cannot be on the EEC
side — there is, in effect, a sort of legal void so far as the mfn clause is
concerned; and mfn treatment can, in principle, from now on be granted only
through a Community agreement with an Eastern European country (or with
the Council for Mutual Economic Assistance itself, as seems to be expected
since the renewal of negotiations between the EEC and CMEA in February
1976). In fact, some bilateral cooperation agreements have already included
oblique references to a renewal of the mfn clause.

The recognition in the Final Act, even in a conditional form of 'the beneficial effects which can result for the development of trade from the application
of most-favoured-nation treatment (*Final Act* p. 14) may be considered as a
positive move towards a 'normalisation' of trade. Nevertheless, this recognition
of beneficial effects might well remain quite ineffectual. Beneficial effects
'can' result from mfn. However, they will not result automatically unless other
measures, additional to reduction of tariffs, are taken to eliminate various
forms of discrimination — among which export controls still play a large role.[3]

Mention of mfn treatment is matched, in the Final Act, by that of 'reciprocity', which expresses a political as well as an economic requirement of
the Western countries in their trade with the socialist world. Insistence on 'reciprocity' is currently interpreted by the East as an attempt on the part of the
West to deny the full effect of the mfn clause to the socialist states.[4] Because
of the 'specificities' of trade under conditions of a state monopoly of foreign
trade, Eastern countries are suspected by their Western partners of not granting
sufficiently substantial advantages just by lowering their tariffs (as in the case
of Hungary) or, if they have no tariffs when becoming members of GATT, by
agreeing to expand their imports from the West (Poland, Romania). The 'rules
of the game' are not meant to be the same for East and West; hence the demand
for 'reciprocity permitting, as a whole, an equitable distribution of advantages
and obligations of comparable scale' (*Final Act*, p. 13).

Quite obviously, some previously conflicting desiderata on the two sides
have thus been incorporated into the Final Act. To reconcile these conflicts,
we have the very general formula according to which the participant states
'are resolved to promote, on the basis of the modalities of their economic
cooperation, the expansion of mutual trade in goods and services' (*ibid.*, p. 14).
This uniform determination, and common willingness to cooperate, has undoubtedly influenced post-Helsinki relations between the EEC and CMEA.

The effects of these two international entities on East—West relations will
be examined later in our discussions. For the time being we will just assume
that there is a firm desire on the part of both the EEC and the CMEA to
develop trade and cooperation with states belonging to the other community;
and we may note that in the CMEA — even when account is taken of the fact
that world prices have risen more rapidly than intra-CMEA prices — the
propensity to trade with the West appears to remain constantly stronger than
the propensity to trade inside the socialist system.[5] However, both 'integra-

tions' do exist, with definite consequences for the patterns of trade and, for the EEC countries, for the modalities of foreign trade relations; and this is especially true if we assume that the EEC's 'common foreign trade policy' will one day actually be implemented. Consequently, the political-economic motivations to develop mutual cooperation might be expected not just to appear *per se*, but to be related to the facts of Eastern and Western 'integration'.

But when we look at the Helsinki Final Act, we find that the CMEA is not mentioned at all, and the EEC is mentioned at the very end, under Mr Aldo Moro's signature, which sanctions the active part played by the EEC semi-official representation during the Conference. The question may therefore be asked, are there motivations for long-term development of trade on the basis of agreements between the CMEA and the EEC?

If we simply look at the text of the Final Act we are bound to answer this question in a rather guarded way. The Preamble of the second 'Basket' mentions 'bilateral and multilateral agreements' (p. 13), which are later qualified to read 'intergovernmental' in the preamble to the section relating to foreign trade (p. 14). The only reference to anything which might not be simply inter-governmental is the mention in the same sentence of 'other agreements' which are apparently meant to play a subsidiary role.

The renewed contacts between the EEC and CMEA in 1976 stem from the general motivations for expansion of trade, and the communiqué published by the CMEA on this occasion (16 February) explicitly refers to the Helsinki spirit. With this open reference, we must perhaps admit that past approaches to EEC–CMEA relations are no longer relevant. On the side of the EEC, even though the Community authorites' willingness to implement not only a common foreign trade policy with the East, but also a common cooperation policy, has been expressed more than once, it has encountered the reluctance of member states. The CMEA, on the other hand, was said to be without either the willingness or the legal capacity to develop anything like a 'Western foreign economic relations policy'. But the issue of CMEA's willingness now seems to be settled, since the *Comprehensive Programme* of 1971 has already stated that member states would coordinate their foreign economic policy so as 'to ensure a normalisation of international trade and economic relations and above all the elimination of discrimination in this field' (Chapter I, section 1.3); and the amended (1974) CMEA Charter provides for the possibility, though not the necessity, of relations between the CMEA and either states (Article 11) or international organisations (Article 12).

Consequently, the question is no longer one of conflicts between inter-state relations and inter-community arrangements; the need for both types of relations has been stressed. As a result we may envisage a whole new series of relations — EEC – CMEA, EEC–CMEA member states, CMEA–EEC member states, inter-state relations and, finally, lower-level relations between firms or other organisations.

As reported by the ECE Committee on the development of trade,[6] the network of long-term economic, industrial and technical cooperation agreements in East—West trade (including Canada and the United States as well as Western European countries) consisted at the end of September 1975 of 118 accords, including the programmes and agreements which have the purpose of 'replacing' all the earlier trade agreements concluded by the EEC members and terminated at the end of 1974 or 1975. The usefulness of such agreements has been underlined since the Helsinki Conference by both Eastern and Western officials. Furthermore, according to the last point of the Final Act — on the follow-ups to the Conference — the participating states expressed their readiness to apply the resolutions of the Act, through bilateral inter-state negotiations in particular.

But intergovernmental or other agreements offer only a framework for trade and cooperation. To fill this framework with concrete action is possible only through contacts at a lower level, where the diversity of the different social and economic systems has to be taken into account.

II THE DIVERSITY OF ECONOMIC AND SOCIAL SYSTEMS

East—West relations still account for only a small part of the international division of labour. East—West trade represents at most 5 per cent of the foreign trade of developed market economies, although in the foreign trade of European socialist countries it amounts to about 30 per cent. Consequently, it is obvious that the motivations for trade will not only be different, but also of unequal intensity on each side. The point common to both is the primacy of intra-system foreign relations, particularly those within the two existing integrated communities.

Even taking into account this primacy, it is admitted (*Final Act*, p. 14) that 'the volume and structure of trade among the participating states does not in all cases correspond to the possibilities . . .' We might almost say: the volume, *because* of the unsatisfactory structure of trade does not correspond . . . It is in the best interest of all parties to develop further both commercial exchanges and industrial cooperation.

The great advantage for market economies lies in the benefits of expanded exports, especially during a period of recession and slackening internal demand. Recently there have been examples of East—West industrial cooperation contracts which have actually saved a big capitalist firm from collapse. On the side of the socialist countries, there is the frequently mentioned 'technology gap' and their efforts to accelerate the process of 'intensive growth', in which they have been engaged for more than a decade.[7]

However, these advantages must not be over-dramatised, as they sometimes are. For the Western partners, East—West trade will not solve the problems of reduced growth rates, inflation and unemployment. For socialist states, the import of Western technology plays a limited role in overall growth, although, of course, this import of technology might be very important for such industries as the motor industry and chemicals.[8] However, what seems true for the Soviet Union does not necessarily apply to smaller socialist states, where trade represents a larger percentage of national income.

Even more than their general interest in expanding reciprocal trade, however, it seems that all the parties have a particular interest in the stabilisation and diversification of East–West relations. Here again it is enlightening to consider the Final Act. The participating states have agreed to 'foster a steady growth of trade while avoiding as far as possible abrupt fluctuations' (p. 14). Through industrial cooperation they hope to 'create lasting ties thus strengthening long-term overall economic cooperation' (p. 16), and in general to promote stable relations. As for diversification, this term applies both to trade partners and to the fields of trade and cooperation. In particular the participation of small states and, in the West, of 'small and medium-sized firms' (p. 18) must be encouraged – as has not been the case in the past.

Diversification of products may have two consequences. The first is a progressive change in the structure of trade, which would enable the socialist states, especially through industrial cooperation and joint ventures, to develop their exports of manufactured goods and thus to evolve from their present situation as exporters mainly of primary products. The second consequence would be an improvement in general well-being and the quality of life for the consumer through an increase in 'the possibilities of choice of products' (p. 14).

But diversification must be well organised; and a common definition of products of mutual interest is of outstanding importance in this respect. Up to the present, industrial cooperation has developed rather erratically, through *ad hoc* agreements between big Western firms and state organisations in the socialist countries. In its Final Act the Helsinki Conference defined several fields of common interest – exploitation of energy and raw material resources, development of road networks and cooperation in transport; and scientific and technological cooperation is supposed to be developed particularly along these lines. There are the beginnings here of a general strategy, aimed at mutual advantage and satisfaction and channelling efforts for expansion and diversification of relations in the directions promising the greatest gains in efficiency.

The strategy of 'diversification' of inter-country trade flows implies that 'diversity', in the sense of differences between national economies, can be clearly defined. Do we mean only diversity of economic and social systems?

East–West relations are expanding between countries of 'different levels of development'. How can we measure these levels? To do so is a task for the follow-up to the Conference, as the Final Act insists on the publication and dissemination of as complete and detailed economic information as it is possible to obtain. For the time being, absolute figures of national income or consumption are hardly a basis for comparison; and we must judge differences in levels of development essentially by considering the differences in economic structures – the percentage of agricultural output in the GNP or, better, the share of agriculture in total employment, the structure of industrial production, etc.

Such comparisons suggest that there are differences not only between East

and West, but also within both areas. This is implicit in such extracts from the
text of the Final Act as: 'taking into account the interests of the developing
countries throughout the world, including those among the participating
countries as long as they are developing from the economic point of view'
(p. 13). That levels of development are unequal is already taken into account
in relations within each of the integrated communities. One of the aims of the
CMEA is the progressive equalisation of development levels, and the EEC has
long since tried to implement a regional development policy supported (not
too successfully) by the European Investment Bank and more recently by a
special Fund. Thus, although there might, in the future, be more opportunities
for promoting detailed intra-industry specialisation through trade and cooperation, today agreements based on economic complementarities still seem
more promising.

But of course the main element of 'diversity' among states is systemic.
East–West relations link socialist and capitalist systems. That is, these relations link one system based on the collective ownership of means of production with another based on private property.

Currently, in the West, this situation is seen as an 'obstacle' or an 'impedi-
ment' to the expansion of trade; and such a view may generate serious mis-
understandings. Some Western officials or businessmen suggest, in effect, that

could bring about complete decentralisation, and thus allow free access by all
suppliers to the end-users on socialist markets and freedom for socialist enterprises to decide for themselves what and where to export or import. But this
would abolish the socialist system itself. I quite agree with J. Szita when he
writes that such an approach 'does not seem to be realistic';[9] there is no sense
in suggesting the elimination of foreign trade planning (which brings about
what authors such as P. Wiles or F. Holzman call 'commodity inconvertibility'),[10] or of the foreign trade monopoly. As for the greater recourse to
'market categories' inside the socialist countries – and particularly the linking
of foreign and domestic prices with which Hungary and Poland began to
experiment in 1968 and 1971, respectively – this has now been almost abandoned or, more correctly, suspended. It would be difficult to blame these
countries for being unwilling to import inflation from the capitalist world,
especially since in their systems stability of internal prices is one of the most
important goals of economic policy.

The Final Act of the Conference on Security and Cooperation in Europe
takes into account these 'systemic' realities. Serious efforts are to be made by
the socialist states and foreign trade organisations to improve business facilities
– which means improving negotiating conditions, arrangements for representation, the availability of commercial information and marketing methods. Some
steps have already been taken in directions explicitly commended by the
Conference – in Czechoslovakia, for example, foreign companies are now
authorised to maintain representations in Prague. In the same spirit, the concept of 'market disruption' has been codified in such a way as to remove the

danger of damaging effects of trade on the market economies.

The same concern for expanding economic intercourse while continuing to take into account systemic diversity leads to an increased stress on – or at least a reaffirmation of – the role of joint bodies at the governmental, or macroeconomic professional, level – joint commissions, joint chambers of commerce, etc. However, industrial cooperation has to be conducted at a microeconomic level, between enterprises. For the East, this means that the activity of cooperating firms must be consistent with national plans; for the West, the protection of private property, when involved in joint ventures, must be guaranteed. Experience has proved that both kinds of interests can be safe-guarded in the various forms taken by cooperation so far.

III WORLD-WIDE ECONOMIC INTERDEPENDENCE

Economic relations between East and West are only one field in the whole area of the international division of labour, which is why the Final Act insists on Europe's contribution to the solution of major world economic problems. Among these problems is included environmental protection, to which a whole section of 'Basket 2' is devoted. However, the two main issues are undoubtedly the monetary problem and 'North–South' cooperation. This leads us to consideration of the new international order to be achieved.

The 'monetary and financial questions' are dealt with very briefly and the Final Act leaves us with an unresolved problem. Under Point 5 of our Agenda we shall deal extensively with this, and today we are concerned with the general economic motivations to develop mutual cooperation. If we agree that such motivations exist, how are they affected by monetary and financial problems?

The first point to consider is the hard-currency deficit of all the socialist countries in transactions with the West. This deficit is growing, even though the USSR had a small surplus in 1974. We should note in this regard that the question of bilateralism in East–West trade is no longer of interest.[11] Even if the Eastern countries are supposed to try to reach bilateral balances with their Western partners, so long as almost every one of them has a global deficit with the West and almost every Western country a global surplus with the East, the main problem for each socialist country is to reach an overall equilibrium in its 'Western' balance of payments. This means obtaining not only bilateral commercial credits but also, and increasingly, financial credits. The recent appearance of large loans raised on the Euro-currency market with the intervention of bank consortia is significant of a growing multilateralisation of such transactions.

Is there an upper limit to the indebtedness of the socialist countries? This question has raised a great deal of controversy. It must be admitted (a) that up to now these countries have always scrupulously respected their commitments, and (b) that their real indebtedness is unknown, and will remain so –

information about balances of payments is excluded from the provisions of
the Final Act.

The second aspect of the monetary problem is the question of the possible
integration of the socialist countries into the international monetary system.
The question is not merely theoretical. Romania is already a member of the
International Monetary Fund. As early as 1972, at a conference on East–West
cooperation held in Moscow, a Soviet participant suggested that the International
Investment Bank of the CMEA might form a joint bank with some Western
investment banks, and that the socialist states might find some way of cooperating with the IMF. It was even suggested that they might join the Special
Drawing Right system, on condition that the SDR be based upon a gold
standard[12] – a possibility which is now, since the Jamaica Agreements of
January 1976, definitely excluded.

Under present conditions, one may well ask whether economic and political
motivations for an expansion of East–West trade relations must imply strong
motivations for convertibility of the currencies of the socialist countries. At
least earlier arguments for convertibility might now be modified (I am referring
to such proposals as those made by R. Nyers in a study on intra-CMEA
economic integration, suggesting that the transferable rouble and the currencies
of the CMEA countries 'should possess realistic exchange rates relative to each
other, as well as to gold or the dollar, or to the paper-gold (SDR) issued by
the IMF').[13] With so shaky a basis for the SDR as resulted from the Jamaica
Agreements, is it reasonable for the CMEA countries to go further than intra-
regional convertibility, limited in scope though this is?

Even without any integration of the socialist countries into the international
monetary system, common action in favour of less developed countries might
appear as a motive for further East–West cooperation. The Final Act reaffirms
the desire of the participant states 'to cooperate for the achievement of the
aims and objectives established by the appropriate bodies of the United
Nations . . . it being understood that each participant State maintains the
positions it has taken on them' (p. 13). But, in fact, the participant states
have taken substantially different positions. The United States' thesis, as
expressed in the speech of Patrick Moynihan at the opening of the United
Nations VIIth Special Session on Development in 1975, is not identical
with those of Western European countries; on the same occasion, Romania
differed from most of the socialist states in not rejecting the principle of an
opposition between rich and poor countries. For the time being at least, the
socialist world is left outside the great 'North–South' debate.

Thus the only form of East–West cooperation consistent with a common
concern for the development of developing countries would seem to be the
promotion of tripartite cooperation, associating developing countries with
specific projects of common interest, especially projects to exploit raw material
resources. Detailed patterns of possible collaboration are to be found in
UNCTAD documents;[14] and such cooperation might be a modest but realistic
contribution to the establishment of a new international order.

NOTES

1 See for instance O. Bogomolov, 'The CMEA's Comprehensive Program and the Possibilities of Economic Cooperation with West European Countries', *Acta Oeconomica,* vol. 12 (1), (Budapest, 1974) p. 37.
2 UN Economic Commission for Europe, 'A Review of East—West Commercial Policy Developments, 1968 to 1973', *Economic Bulletin for Europe* (Geneva, 1974) vol. 25, pp. 49—50.
3 T. Wolf, 'The Impact of Formal Western Restraints on East—West-Trade: An Assessment of Existing Quantitative Research', in J. P. Hardt (ed.), *Tariff, Legal and Credit Constraints on East—West Commercial Relations,* (Ottawa, 1975) pp. 27—55.
4 On the socialist position, see G. Veliaminov, 'Les principes juridiques de la coopération économique européene', in O. Bogomolov (ed.) *Coopération economique européene* (Moscow, 1973) p. 81; J. Szita, 'On Intra-European Economic Cooperation and East—West Trade', *Acta Oeconomica,* vol. 13 (3—4), (Budapest, 1974) p. 285; a Western comment is to be found in G. Schiavone, 'The Most Favored Nation Clause and East—West Trade: Limitations and Prospects', *La Communità Internazionale, vol. 29* (4) (1974) pp. 641—52.
5 Gatt, *International Trade* 1974—5, (Geneva) p. 208; Iu. Kormnov and I. Petrov, 'Razriadka napriazhennosti i khoziaistvennoe sotrudnichestvo', *Voprosy Ekonomiki,* No. 2, (Moscow, 1976) p. 59.
6 UN-ECE 'Practical Measures to Remove Obstacles to Intra-regional Trade and to Promote and Diversify Trade,' *Trade* R/317/Add. 1/Corr. 1 (20 November 1975).
7 On the technological level and policy of socialist countries, see *Nauchno-tekhnicheskaia revoliutsiia i integratsiia stran SEV* (Moscow, 1974) especially Chapters III and XI.
8 P. Hanson, 'The Import of Western Technology', in A. Brown and M. Kaser (eds.), *The Soviet Union since the Fall of Khrushchev* (London, 1975) pp. 31, 41, 43.
9 J. Szita, *op. cit.,* p. 283. For a Western view, see F. Holzman and R. Legvold, 'The Economics and Politics of East—West Relations', *International Organization,* vol. 29 (1) (1975) pp. 275—320.
10 F. Holzman, *Foreign Trade Under Central Planning,* (Cambridge, USA, 1974) p. 22; P. Wiles *Communist International Economics,* (Oxford, 1968) Chapter X.
11 UN—ECE, 'Recent Changes in Europe's Trade', *Economic Bulletin for Europe,* vol. 27 (Geneva 1975) p. 92.
12 O. S. Bogdanov, 'Nekotorye voprosy kreditnoi politiki stran SEV', in *Problemy ekonomicheskogo sotrudnichestva mezhdu vostokom i zapadom Evropy* (Moscow, 1973) p. 22.
13 R. Nyers, 'The CMEA Countries on the Road to Economic Integration', *Trends in World Economy,* no. 16 (Hungarian Scientific Council for World Economy, 1975) p. 20.
14 UNCTAD, *The Scope of Trade-Creating Industrial Cooperation at Enterprise Level between Countries having different Economic and Social Systems,* (New York, 1975) Chapter III.

4 Motivations for Countries with Different Economic Systems to Develop Mutual Cooperation

Evgeni Mateev
KARL MARX HIGHER INSTITUTE OF ECONOMICS, SOFIA

I INTRODUCTION

The problems of cooperation between countries of different economic systems — cooperation in the fields of economics, science, ecology, etc. — have long been the object of lively discussion in the literature and at scientific congresses, symposiums and round-table conferences. There is a growing conviction that many issues, primarily those of the underlying possibility for cooperation, have by now been sufficiently clarified and that the time has come for the problems of principle to give place to the pragmatic problems — the forms of cooperation, the mechanisms by which it can be rendered most effective, etc.

Of particular significance is the fact that the problems of principle related to international cooperation have become the object of a document of such enormous significance for international relations as the Final Act of the Conference on Security and Cooperation in Europe. It is stated on p. 6 of this document that the participating governments* will

> endeavour, in developing their cooperation as equals, to promote mutual understanding and confidence, friendly and good-neighbourly relations among themselves, international peace, security and justice. They will equally endeavour, in developing their cooperation, to improve the well-being of peoples and contribute to the fulfilment of their aspirations through, *inter alia*, the benefits resulting from increased mutual knowledge and from progress and achievement in the economic, scientific, technological, social, cultural and humanitarian fields.

The course of recent discussions has indicated, however, that parallel with the pragmatic approach to the problems of cooperation — which really does become more urgent and necessary — there is still a growing interest in related problems of principle. It sometimes happens that, under the form of pragmatic interest, there arise disputes in the domain of principles which had earlier been considered to be no longer of topical interest.

* All references are to the English text, *Conference on Security and Cooperation in Europe, Final Act*, Cmnd 6198 (London: HMSO, 1975).

This paper will attempt to deal with those questions which still appear to be urgent and important; but it does not aim to produce on each of them a systematic, academic statement strictly confining the argument within the boundaries of the individual problem.

I IS THE INTEREST IN COOPERATION BILATERAL OR UNILATERAL?

The first problem to be resolved is whether the interest in cooperation between countries with different economic systems is bilateral – an interest common to both sides – or unilateral.

The bearing this question has on the motivation of the one or the other group of countries participating in the cooperation is all too obvious. The Final Act of the Conference on European Security and Cooperation contains a preamble to the section on cooperation in the fields of the economy, science and the protection of the environment, which treats the motives and the conditions of that cooperation and emphasises that it 'can be developed, on the basis of equality and mutual satisfaction of the partners, and of reciprocity' (p. 13).

If we limit ourselves to a narrow and purely businesslike approach to the problem of cooperation, the question just raised readily finds a simple answer. It stands to reason that when a firm in a Western European country decides to sign a contract with an economic organisation in some socialist country, it is prompted by no other consideration than an immediate and direct interest in (expectation of benefit from) the transaction; and the same is naturally true also of the organisation in the socialist country, which is its partner. With such a formulation of the problem there is little sense in philosophising about whether the interest is common or unilateral. Some ten years ago the author of this paper took part in a symposium in Brussels in which business executives exchanged, concretely and clearly, their experiences of the practical economic relations which they had begun building with the socialist countries. The aim was to find, through empirical investigation, the answer to the question whether these contacts promised real prospects of future development. The underlying idea was that only economic relations of bilateral interest could hold out real long-term prospects.

But these clear and simple findings give way to a problem warranting discussion when we pass from the multitude of individual transactions to that complex of measures of economic policy which defines the general framework of economic relations. The question whether there is unilateral or common interest in the development of economic cooperation between countries of different economic systems takes on a new dimension when we consider the motives which may inspire policies which change the 'economic climate' as a whole – the climate which will determine the nature and balance of the 'interests' of the parties to hundreds and thousands of actual or potential concrete transactions. Should the economic policy of one or the other of the two groups of countries be to create favourable conditions for economic ties or not? It is obvious that in the context of this question the problem of the bilateral or unilateral character of the interest in such ties acquires quite another meaning from that in the case of individual transactions alone.

The problem of the motivation of economic cooperation becomes further complicated by the fact that political considerations and political criteria frequently come into play under the guise of economic considerations and criteria. For the rather influential political circles which are opposed to the development of economic, or any other, links between the West and the socialist countries, to support their stand by direct political arguments alone becomes difficult or insufficiently persuasive. It is much easier for them to assert that it is only, or mainly, the socialist countries which have any real interest in these economic relations, and not their partners in the West.

It should be pointed out that the mass media in the West, certain leading news agencies included, discuss the motives for cooperation extensively and take great pains to present each step by the socialist countries aimed at intensification of economic ties as little short of a call for aid. True enough, the ever-repeated motif of such propaganda is not always successful in halting the development of cooperation, particularly since different theories leading to the same conclusion are put forward, for different purposes, in different contexts, and by different circles. Nevertheless, the mass media are largely responsible for the limited results obtained so far.

The need to proceed further with the international division of labour and with the internationalisation of economic life, not merely within the two individual spheres of the European Economic Community and the Council for Mutual Economic Assistance, but also between them and on a world scale, stems not from the one-sided interests of any particular grouping, but, much more fundamentally, from the trends of development of science and technology.

At the present stage of such development, particularly in the industrialised countries of America and Western Europe and in Japan, the conditions for maintaining a relatively satisfactory dynamism in the economy depend not so much on an extensive acquisition or expansion of markets for existing and traditional products, but on an *intensive* process — the continuing introduction of new types and qualities of goods, both means of production and consumer goods. This process of innovation has most significant economic implications.

Under today's conditions, almost every new manufactured product is the result of the devising, financing and organised implementation of complex programmes of scientific and technological research, personnel training and other activities, which mark the path from the initial discoveries made by the fundamental sciences to their practical utilisation. These programmes are themselves extremely complex in that they involve not only work in a direct line of development from the initial scientific discovery, but also many other research activities on, frequently rather distant, sidelines.

When speaking of such programmes we usually think first of such examples as space and thermonuclear research, the development of supersonic aircraft, and the like. However, similar problems arise with increasing frequency, and in varying degree, in connection with quite ordinary innovations in the industrial field which do not appeal to the imagination as do the programmes just mentioned. This is the more so as the systems approach becomes increasingly significant, even in provision of the most ordinary needs of life (furniture, kitchen equipment, fashions, etc.). The proving of a sufficiently broad range of uses for a new material likewise tends to large-scale and complex programmes of research and development, etc.

One characteristic feature of all such cases is that preparatory costs, largely unrelated to the amount of eventual output, bulk large in relation to the costs related to output levels. Thus the decisive condition for realisation of manufacturing projects of this kind is cooperation in ensuring both a sufficient scope of the preparatory work – which becomes increasingly expensive – and also that the scale of the market for which the product is intended should be such as to justify it. The classical type of competition in price and quality is increasingly being transformed into competition in the field of technology – that is, in programmes of the type described above. But the main condition for success in such competition becomes the scale of the possible production – that is, the size of the market. The trends in the automobile industry in Western Europe, in the field of computing equipment, and to some extent in the chemical industry, are sufficiently illustrative of this finding.

These tendencies mean that each new development in manufacturing tends to create a definite interest in the expansion of cooperation. One need hardly mention the fact that the national boundaries of small and medium-sized states are too narrow to provide sufficient scope for these new processes. We know that many US corporations have attained proportions which give them advantages over competitors who cannot rely on similar volumes of output. And if development up till now has pushed Western European firms towards integration within the narrow regional framework of the EEC, the same trend of development in the future will undoubtedly compel them to look for further advance into a still wider field of industrial cooperation.

The possibilities for such an advance are at hand. There is a community numbering 350 million stretching from the very centre of the small European continent to the Pacific Ocean and Central Asia. The highly dynamic economy of the socialist system creates a sufficient potential for industrial cooperation, in the sense both of participation in joint research and of undertaking parts of a complex production process, and also in the sense of providing a market for part of the output produced by the cooperating partner. Thus economic development in the West – in the conditions for industrial advance which now apply on a world scale – will itself intensify interest in industrial cooperation with the socialist world. And it can safely be expected that if real interests in cooperation are sufficiently strong they will lead to the gradual elimination of obstacles accumulated in the past, political prejudice included.

It would be proper for us now to look at these same tendencies from the viewpoint of the other partner in the process of cooperation – the countries of the CMEA.

Most of these countries — those accounting for the greater part of the population within this grouping — embarked on their road of socialist economic development from a relatively low level. Their paramount task at that time was to traverse, as quickly as possible, the distance separating them from the economically advanced countries. In a number of economic fields this task was accomplished by a process of introduction of already existing technological achievements; and this made it possible for the, initially quite modest, funds and personnel available for creative scientific and technological work to be concentrated on those sectors which were decisive for further development, while economising on funds and personnel in the fields which offered scope for extensive introduction of existing technologies. For example, in the presence of a vast unsatisfied market for cars it would have been irrational to invest heavily in research and design work to turn out new models every year — or even to invest in non-essential technical improvements — while the funds and personnel were needed for much more important tasks.

But this stage of development is now past; and this is true both of those socialist countries which have been in the lead in terms of economic development and of countries like Bulgaria which have had to make the longest journeys from their initial positions to the levels of today. None of the member countries of the CMEA any longer has reserves of manpower, or even labour which can easily be transferred from one sphere to another, as has been the case until recently for those working in the rural economy.

Under these conditions it becomes necessary for the sphere in which the socialist countries had from the beginning to forge ahead through the adoption of novel techniques now to expand to embrace the entire national economy, including those areas which, given the insufficient potential in the earlier stages, had then to remain outside the circle of priorities. It was also perfectly possible to leave them outside at that time, but today technological innovation has become the only source — or almost the only source — of economic dynamism throughout the economy.

This is why the XXVth Congress of the Communist Party of the Soviet Union and the congresses in the other member-countries of the CMEA, have brought to the fore the problems of quality and of economic efficiency.

It has already been pointed out that the need for creative work in the fields of science and technology, and the entire process of innovation underlying the dynamics of the modern economies of the developed West, are factors calling for enlarged production complexes and, in general, for a rapid internationalisation of economic life. Naturally, this argument is valid for the analogous process of development in the socialist countries also; and these countries today see the internationalisation of their economies as a condition for their continuing dynamism. The socialist countries are interested in a broad international division of labour both in the scientific and technological fields and also in establishing up-to-date production processes and products, since only this will permit the necessary concentration of their innovative resources and allow them to make the most rational use of the possibilities offered by modern technology. Vast though the resources and markets of the CMEA system may be – with correspondingly vast possibilities for cooperation and division of labour, both in research and design work and in production – the current scientific and technological revolution imposes the need for cooperation and internationalisation on a world scale; it is imposed on both the EEC and the CMEA.

The fact that interest in continuing economic advance today implies interest in cooperation on a very broad international scale is the essential basis for the common interest of countries belonging to different economic systems in the intensification of economic ties between them.

II THE STAGE OF DEVELOPMENT OF RELATIONS

It is necessary to examine the problem of intensifying cooperation between countries of different economic systems not only by considering what is in principle possible and desirable, but also the stage of development reached so far in relations between the two groups of countries.

If we look at the present state of East–West trade and, specifically, at the composition of the commodity flows, we shall discover that raw materials and certain traditional products predominate in the flow from East to West, whereas the commodity flow from West to East is dominated by finished products and particularly those incorporating new technologies. And if we look for an explanation of the relatively small volume of trade between the two parts of Europe, it is precisely this composition of the commodity flows that points to the immediate cause.

It is perfectly possible for the socialist countries to increase their imports from the West – their purchases of machines, of other finished goods, and of semi-finished goods also. They are a market of large potential capacity, particularly in view of their very high rates of economic growth – almost twice as high as those of Western Europe. Under such dynamic conditions the sole factor preventing their high import potential being fully realised is, precisely, the structure of their exports to the West. On the basis of foodstuffs – which in any case face import restrictions in the EEC – and of raw materials, it is not possible to obtain a sufficiently high rate of growth of exports or, consequently, of the foreign currency resources of the socialist countries. This fact compels them to pursue a policy of strict selection of their imports, hence the almost complete predominance of machinery and the limitations on rate of the increase of their imports in general.

The sharp difference that has so far existed in the composition of the two counterflows of commodities between East and West has provided the main argument for the theory of the unilateral nature of interest in economic cooperation.

The first objection to such a deduction from the disparate natures of the two commodity flows stems from the fact that the socialist countries are striving to attain such conditions of cooperation as will remedy this abnormal situation. Neither in considering future possibilities of cooperation nor in interpreting the actual development so far can the composition of the commodity flows be seen as reflecting the actual capacities of the socialist countries.

It is true that the socialist countries cannot, at this stage, compete with the Western European countries in all kinds of machinery. Their machine-building industry still lags behind that of Western Europe in respect of a number of specialised products, and for that reason they are compelled constantly to increase the import of such goods, despite insufficient foreign currency resources and the unfavourable terms on which they obtain these products. However, a growth in the export of machinery and other finished products from the socialist countries, to match the growing imports of such items, does not necessarily require the attainment of superiority over, or even equality to, Western standards in all kinds of finished products. It would be sufficient if equal or superior quality were attained in those categories in which the particular socialist country chooses to specialise. Therein lies the scope for international cooperation. But in actual fact, even in the case of those items for which the socialist countries have already attained the requisite quality standards, their exports to the West are low.

Furthermore, the failure to meet the requirements of the Western market is, in a number of cases, not so much a reason for the small share of finished products in the commodity flow from East to West, as it is a consequence of this small share. Under the conditions of a rather high degree of industrial concentration and large-scale manufacturing processes – which is increasingly the trend of development of our machine-building industries – it is hardly profitable to engage in a process of adaptation to other standards and requirements, and to maintain sufficiently extensive technical servicing facilities, when 'economic cooperation' means no more than unstable – almost accidental – exports of small amounts of any given product. Regular ties of a well-established, promising character are the principal condition justifying adaptation to the requirements of the Western buyer, particularly in view of the broad opportunities offered by industrial concentration in the socialist countries.

Thus, export volume, quality, standards and service facilities constitute a vicious circle, rather than the last three factors offering an adequate explanation of the small share of finished goods in the East–West commodity flow.

The economic policy of the countries of Western Europe – a policy connected with the EEC – plays an essential, though not an exclusive, role in determining the divergent composition of the two commodity flows between East and West. Tariff rates for the raw materials and sources of energy needed by the EEC have been fixed at very low levels, if they are not even duty-free. But the policy in the case of finished products, machinery in particular, is quite different – as it is also towards a number of important agricultural products. The general tendency is for the rates of duty on imports from countries outside this economic bloc to rise with the increase in the degree of processing of the imported product.

The United States is outside the EEC system, but the economic ties of that country with the EEC are far stronger than the ties of the socialist countries. Moreover, when the position of the USA is compared with that of the socialist countries, it must be borne in mind that the United States is to a large extent a party to the EEC bloc, entering it not through the door but through the window — via the multinational corporations, which constitute a channel closed to the socialist countries.

Thus, the present state of economic relations can be interpreted as indicating what must be done to provide for, and to strengthen, the interests of both parties in the further, and rapid, development of economic cooperation, rather than as indicating the capacity of either party for such cooperation.

There is another misconception to be dispelled when we attempt to assess the prospects for East—West economic cooperation in the immediate or more distant future, and particularly, the capacities of the socialist countries to alter the composition of the flow of goods from East to West — to supply not only exports of raw materials, but also finished goods incorporating new technologies. It is a misconception persistently encouraged by the mass media.

It was maintained in the past that a system based on public ownership and comprehensive planning was an impossibility which, if established, must inevitably collapse. Nowadays, it is admitted that such a system is possible; and there is also growing acknowledgement of the fact that, because of the possibility offered for the concentration of productive forces on a well-conceived complex of development priorities, this system has proved most appropriate for rapidly eliminating an inherited lag in economic development. However, this is all past. The prospects now are for a purely intensive pattern of development — through large-scale innovation; and the new version of the old theory is that an economic system based on public ownership and comprehensive planning lacks the institutional apparatus for this type of dynamic, and that the socialist countries would be incapable of further development if the West were not to supply them with the new equipment they need. The theory continues to explain that it is precisely because the socialist countries realise this, that they are so insistently looking for means to expand their economic cooperation with the West. Hence the political conclusions — which, in point of fact, are also the origin of the whole theory: let whoever wants to help the socialist countries engage in economic cooperation, while whoever does not want to play such a role must prudently oppose this policy.

Before examining the essence of this theory of unilateral interest in cooperation we must note the fact that the sale of licence rights, or of goods which incorporate new technology, is of interest to both buyer and seller; the recipient ensures its technological development while economising on expenses which it would otherwise have to incur in duplicating the research work done in the particular field, while the supplier obtains the benefit of a market ensuring a scale of production sufficient to provide economic justification of the research costs and the expenditure on new equipment. Thus this form of

economic relation also represents not a transfer of aid but 'bilateral interest' —
benefit to both parties.

However, the essential point is that the socialist countries are determined
to change the trade structure which has been typical of their relations with
the West until now. Common interest is strongest when each group of countries
is both supplier and receiver of products incorporating new technology. That
is why the socialist countries are ready to participate in economic cooperation,
both as consumers of products from the West incorporating new technologies
and as suppliers of such products.

The fact that in many industrial fields the socialist countries have been able
to do without any systematic or frequent innovation — which is why these areas
have so far been left without research and design resources — does not constitute
proof that they will carry out their new tasks in this field any less successfully
than they have their no less complex, though different, tasks during their past
stages of development. Of course, like any other economy, the economy based
on public ownership must constantly improve its complex of institutions and
mechanisms and adapt them to the specific demands of the problems to be
solved at a particular moment. It is precisely such an improvement and
adaptation of forms of organisation, incentives and methods of planning that is
currently taking place in all socialist countries to meet the needs of the new
intensive road of development.

We must also remember that in those fields in which the socialist countries
were able to concentrate a sufficient research potential, they most convincingly
demonstrated their capacities for rapid development of technology and its
practical utilisation. As regards modern methods of management requiring
coordination of a large complex of creative efforts to reach a particular goal —
which is needed for the objectives of contemporary technology — it can
hardly be doubted that the socialist countries possess the capacity, resulting
from the scale of their planning, sufficient experience in the field and a
sufficiently streamlined organisational and technical apparatus.

III THE NEED FOR A MORE COMPLEX FRAMEWORK TO HANDLE MORE COMPLEX MANUFACTURES

In the case of mass-produced and homogeneous goods based on traditional
technology, the nature of price competition and other forms of competition
in the contemporary market is little different from that of the past. But the
new manufactures are the creations of a long-term strategy and increasingly
demand a new organisational framework. They demand new and complex
forms of industrial cooperation between large organisations, as the activities
of today's corporations demonstrate.

Thus we read in the Helsinki Final Act that the participating states

recognize further that, if it is in their mutual interest, concrete forms such
as the following may be useful for the development of industrial cooperation: joint production and sale, specialization in production and sale,

construction, adaptation and modernisation of industrial plants, cooperation for the setting up of complete industrial installations with a view to thus obtaining part of the resultant products, mixed companies, exchanges of 'know-how', of technical information, of patents and of licences, and joint industrial research within the framework of specific cooperation projects (p. 17).

Industrial cooperation, unlike the classical forms of trade, implies a complex of lasting interrelations among the organisations involved. Within this complex, trade is only the final result, preceded by much more complex relations connected with design work, production processes, the exchange of 'know-how', specialisation, the securing of markets, and other activities.

Recognition of the possibilities for expanding industrial cooperation, in the sense in which the term has been defined here, can help to settle a long-standing argument on the problem of East—West economic relations — whether the differences between the economic structure of the countries of Western Europe (designated 'market economy' in these discussions) and that of the socialist countries (characterised as an economy of national ownership, planning on a national scale and monopoly of trade) provide or fail to provide opportunities for intensifying economic cooperation, in a broad sense of the term. In working out their plans the socialist countries are interested in substituting quantified probabilities by quantified certainties to the greatest extent possible. That is why, according to one of the theses advanced in the argument, the socialist countries will expect from the 'outside' market only that import which they are not in a position to offer to one another, and will provide for that market only the export which is superfluous to them collectively. Otherwise, it is alleged, they would have to leave their national plan open — indeterminate — which runs counter to the nature of their economy. Hence the conclusion that it is difficult to coordinate 'market economy' with 'planned economy'.

As a corollary to that same thesis, the possibilities of expanding East—West trade are related to expectations of such structural changes in the socialist countries as would, in one form or another, alter the planned character of their economies. This logic was for long so widely accepted that, at a number of international forums, the question of the prospects for East—West economic cooperation was fused with the question of economic reforms in the socialist countries, which were expected virtually to abolish the national planning of foreign trade.

Another argument, sometimes raised as an objection to the above, is essentially very little different from the thesis it formally opposes. As the socialist countries encounter restrictions against their exports, they are compelled to husband their currency resources by a careful grading of their import requirements according to essentiality, and the centralised control of imports is necessary for the realisation of these priorities. Thus the monopoly of foreign trade turns out, by virtue of that logic, to be simply a response to restrictions by the West, and not an inherent feature of the national planning of an economy based on public ownership.

Yet another argument was put forward at the Conference of the International Economic Association in Budapest in 1974, also relating to the institutional conditions of East–West economic relations. Since the socialist countries adhere to national foreign trade plans or, at the very least, carefully coordinate the activities of their economic organisations in relations with those of other countries, it is argued that a situation of 'inequality' is created – since the partners of the economic organisations in the planned economy are the individual private firms of the Western country operating without any coordination of their activities. Hence the formulation of a requirement – no matter how strange such logic may seem – for political concessions as compensation for this 'inequality'.

The problem of the significance of macroeconomic planning in the socialist countries for East–West economic relations still seems, therefore, to call for clarification on matters of principle.

Current beliefs in the West about the nature of planning on a national scale in a socialist economy and about the management of foreign trade are frequently inaccurate, particularly when they see economic management as involving absolute centralisation and the full-scale predetermination of activities for years ahead. There is neither complete centralisation nor a fixing of immutable targets subject to change only by imperative and extraneous factors.

In actual fact the national economic plan must be regarded as an instrument of coordination, on a national (and international) scale, of the creative efforts and initiatives of the citizens and their organisations – a coordination which is sufficiently flexible to provide for adaptation to changing circumstances while utilising these changes still to attain the ultimate targets set. Admittedly, this particular function of planning cannot be considered as having yet been developed to a sufficient degree; but this is due not to the intrinsic character of planning, but rather to a host of organisational and technical difficulties which reflect *inter alia* the insufficient development of the countries' productive forces in the past. We must therefore expect that further improvement in the management of the socialist economy will entail not the cancellation, but rather the improvement of planning on a national and international scale, with a highly developed system of feedbacks and adaptation to changing conditions and opportunities.

As regards the question of direct concern here – that of the role of macroeconomic planning in the development of the economic ties of the socialist countries with the countries of the West, it is a most significant fact that the further development of planning will constitute no obstacle but, on the contrary, will promote the improvement of forms of cooperation. A national economy in possession of a sufficiently accurate, quick-acting, and reliable apparatus for coordination and for prompt reaction to any new development constitutes an open system, capable of adapting itself to any opportunity presented by the international division of labour. This makes it more dynamic in its relations with foreign partners, even if those partners are units of an unorganised market, in the classical meaning of that term.

It is thus not merely unrealistic to expect a substitution of planned trade in the socialist countries by the uncoordinated operations of individual firms, but such a change is unnecessary. The new and complex relationships now required for industrial cooperation make the old problems of plan-market relations irrelevant. Against the background of the new trends, the planned character of the economies of the socialist countries acquires a new significance, even for partner firms in the West.

Industrial cooperation involving substantial preliminary expenditure requires a large and reliable market. Planning in the socialist countries, offering coordination on a national scale (and, through the coordination existing within the entire socialist system, on an international scale as well), becomes of essential interest to the foreign partner since, precisely because of its centralised character, it offers a vast and stable market.

IV DOES CLOSE CMEA COORDINATION PRECLUDE COOPERATION WITH OTHER COUNTRIES?

The close coordination of the national plans of the socialist countries within the framework of the Council for Mutual Economic Assistance is also often suggested to be an obstacle to intensified cooperation among countries of different economic systems. Are not the links of a particular member-country of the CMEA to the remaining countries of that system an obstacle to the development of its links to countries outside that system? By way of example, does not the fact that 70 per cent of Bulgaria's trade is with the countries of the CMEA constitute a restriction on her capacities for economic cooperation with other countries? More generally, is not the fact that countries already belong to two different organisations, each of which has undertaken a high degree of internal integration, a major obstacle to the development of economic integration between the two systems to which those integrated groupings belong?

In connection with this last question it is necessary to emphasise the essential differences between the two economic groupings. This comparison is frequently neglected for fear of arousing suspicion that it aims at some propaganda effect. Nevertheless, it is most significant.

The entire institutional system of the EEC, which fences off that organisation from other countries, has one general and basic purpose — to create preference for links within the system rather than with countries outside it, even when more links with outside countries could, in the aggregate, be of greater economic benefit to a particular member state of the EEC than those within the system. To the ultimate buyer of tomatoes in the Federal Republic of Germany, Bulgarian and Dutch tomatoes are apt to cost the same — all other conditions being equal — and in that sense there exists no discrimination.

However, for the Federal Republic of Germany as an entity, the Bulgarian tomatoes on which that state charges duty, are cheaper than the Dutch tomatoes from which no duty is obtained, all other conditions being equal. Priority is given to the commodity which is more expensive to the nation as a whole rather than to the cheaper one.

The mechanism of integration within the CMEA is quite different. The essential distinction lies in the fact that there exists no division, in terms of ownership, between the importer, on the one hand, and the state budget which receives (or does not receive) duty, and thus covers the expenses incurred by any artificially created preferences. The unity of ownership ensures an economic system within each member state quite simply and directly interested in importing a particular commodity from the most advantageous source. Thus, although the CMEA is a group of national economies which really do have very close links to one another, they are not separated from the rest of the world by any institutional partition which can modify or distort the real economic advantages or disadvantages of particular international connections. The CMEA is a system of 'states-proprietors' which create their economic links on the basis of direct negotiation and agreements, and these negotiations and agreements are the instruments for mutual coordination of their plans.

It must be noted immediately that the absence of a fence creating artificial preferences and discrimination does not imply that integration within the CMEA is laid on weak foundations, and that a common fence around an aggregate of numerous owners does not provide any stronger base for integration. The existing coordination of plans (and the joint planning envisaged) is a sufficiently important integrating factor. Nevertheless, it becomes perfectly clear that if we compare the mechanisms of integration at work in the two groups of states, it is the mechanism of the CMEA that could least be considered an obstacle to the development of economic relations to the full extent of a world-wide division of labour, since each of the participating states preserves both its interest in and its possibilities of participating in any kind of economic link which it may consider beneficial.

If, after this finding, we return to the question of the relevance of national economic planning already considered, and extend this to the issue of the coordination of the individual national plans on the scale of the whole CMEA economy, we must remember what has been emphasised above – that planning, provided it is sufficiently developed and advanced, is not an obstacle to but an essential prerequisite for flexible reaction by the economic system, including taking advantage of all possibilities of advantageous international cooperation.

The comparison drawn above between the two mechanisms of integration reveals a critical attitude towards the basic mechanisms of the EEC. Naturally, the socialist countries – as partners with international economic ties – cannot be content with the fact of numerous institutional measures of discrimination against their goods on the markets of the EEC, in relation to the similar goods of the EEC member states. It is natural for the efforts of the socialist countries in the field of foreign-trade policy to be aimed at reducing the barriers to their exports in the EEC markets.

In this context, however, the accusations levelled against the socialist countries of excessive radicalism are groundless. Least of all can they be accused of lack of realism. One may recall here the words of L. I. Brezhnev in his address to the 15th Congress of Trade Unions in the Soviet Union (*Pravda*, 21 March 1972) in connection with the EEC:

> The Soviet Union is far from ignoring the real situation which has arisen in Western Europe, including the existence of such an economic grouping of the capitalist countries as the Common Market. We are carefully following the activity of the Common Market and its evolution. Of course, our relations with the participants in this grouping will depend on the extent to which they, on their part, will recognise the realities that have come into being in the socialist part of Europe, specifically the interests of the member countries of the Council for Mutual Economic Assistance. We stand for equality in economic relations and against discrimination.

In the same context, it is necessary to stress also the significance of the letter by the Council for Mutual Economic Assistance of 11 February 1976, addressed to the EEC and containing a proposal to conclude an agreement between the CMEA and its member countries, on the one side, and the EEC and its member countries, on the other, covering the basic relations between the CMEA and the EEC.

V POLITICAL MOTIVATION FOR ECONOMIC COOPERATION

In connection with the political motivation of the countries of different economic systems for the development of cooperation between them, the truth most frequently, and justifiably, emphasised is that advanced economic ties will constitute a solid basis for progress in political relations also, and thus for progress in relations in the fields of culture, of links among people and nations, etc. I shall not dwell here on this fundamental role of economic cooperation; but I must mention the reverse of the coin – the role of the political motives for economic cooperation.

It is obvious that any decision by states belonging to different economic systems to establish lasting and extensive economic ties will have to be based on a stable and favourable political atmosphere; that is, on a certain degree of political security. Otherwise, any lasting economic ties would be jeopardised.

This gives enormous significance to the comprehensive approach to the problems of security and cooperation underlying the work done by the Conference on Security and Cooperation, which is a unique forum in the history of mankind. Improvement in the political atmosphere promotes the broadening of economic cooperation (and hence of cooperation in other fields, of culture, etc.) while, in its turn, expanding cooperation in the fields of the economy, of culture, etc., helps to improve further the political atmosphere and enhance security in this field. This is how a 'favourable avalanche' process can be stimulated, and should play an extremely important role in the progressive development of mankind.

However, this is not the only aspect of the problem of political motivation to be noted. Participating in the political discussion are forces which are unfavourably disposed, as a matter of principle, towards the process of reducing tension in international relations — in both political and economic fields. To them, the broadening of economic ties, even when the economic benefit to both parties is beyond dispute, becomes undesirable since it tends to encourage a political development unacceptable to these circles.

Any hope that an effective political weapon against the socialist countries can be forged from the limitation of economic links between countries possessing different economic systems is evidently doomed to frustration. Such a policy might delay the development of the socialist countries, but it would also be to the detriment of the states applying it. In those fields of science and technology in which, for one reason or another, the socialist countries have been compelled to duplicate the research and creative technological work carried out in the West, they attained the same results in almost the same periods of time, and in many cases even earlier. One instance is the competition in space technology. If that achievement was feasible in such a field, and at an earlier stage in the development of the socialist economy, similar achievements will certainly be possible in other fields of scientific and technological endeavour, so that the aims of any short-sighted policy of blocking cooperation — prompted by political motives — will not be attained. So the question remains, why should any obstacles to the progress of mankind be erected on any side to suit the aims of a policy doomed to failure?

Attempts are sometimes made to promote a policy of restricting the ties of the socialist countries — economic ties included — by using pretexts bearing liberal labels. Such attempts, in my opinion, are due to misconception, rather than to an essential political motivation. It is perfectly obvious that growing international cooperation and division of labour, and broader economic ties and relations in the field of science, ecology, etc., are invariably to the benefit and never to the detriment of the cause of freedom and democracy.

Discussion of the Papers by Professor Lavigne and Professor Mateev

The papers were introduced by *Dr Hardt*, offering his comments under the main headings of Professor Lavigne's paper. He noted that 'intergovernmental relations' were only a part of the 'infrastructure' of East—West economic relations. Professor Mateev had drawn attention to the costly infrastructure of scientific and other research, training, etc., required for modern industrial development and to the possibility that extensive East—West cooperation in these fields — as well as in production and trade — could produce economies of scale and of specialisation benefiting both sides. But Dr Hardt suggested that the 'East—West commercial infrastructure' — of inter-state, commercial, banking, academic, contacts — was also expensive, would become more so as it expanded, and so far had shown only promise, rather than actual substantial returns. As the authors of both papers implied, not only possible CMEA—EEC relations but also existing organisations with East—West membership — e.g. the UN Economic Commission for Europe (ECE) and GATT — should be examined, to see whether the latter could be used more efficiently. Professor Shmelyov's excellent suggestion for an information centre (p. 221) might be taken up by asking the ECE or some other existing agency to take on the task. Turning to the practical possibilities of more intense East—West cooperation, he thought that the coordination of enterprise-oriented Western economies with Eastern economies planned in the national or governmental interest was not as difficult as Mr Kaser and others had suggested. In the West, large corporations were increasingly induced to pursue national interests — through credits, controls and other forms of persuasion; in the East, enterprise interests, or those of industrial ministries with growing entrepreneurial characteristics, increasingly influenced export and import plans.

He felt also that questions of benefit and equity tended to become confused in assessing the case for closer East—West economic relations. Professor Mateev's and Dr Hanson's papers both raised these questions. He would suggest that one should simply ask whether there is mutual interest in freer trade and that, in the short-run, the answer would simply depend on whether the utility of the additional imports to each partner exceeds that of its additional exports. Other considerations, such as national security, could of course enter into a long-run assessment.

Under the heading 'diversity of systems', Dr Hardt considered as too extreme both Professor Lavigne's picture of the alternative to state monopoly of foreign trade being, implicitly, market socialism, and also Professor Holzman's contrast of full commodity convertibility with complete inconvertibility. He suggested that in the CMEA countries trade policies were becoming more selective. In certain sectors traditional import strategy — compensating for lack of domestic capacity — was giving way to concern with comparative advantage or the benefits of specialisation; and this carried with it promotion of hard-currency-earning exports. Industrial cooperation was also part of the new strategy. Institutional changes had necessarily followed, with a weakening of the monopolies of foreign trade ministries, corporations and banks; access to end-users in the priority sectors had become easier, some industrial and internal-trade ministries now had their own trading rights, access to finance, etc. Similarly, in the West, corporations, banks and government organisations had adapted their traditional behaviour and institutions so as to facilitate trade with the East, by setting up, *inter alia*, bodies such as the US—Romanian Chamber of Commerce. He noted also hard-currency trading in some goods within the CMEA area and oil pricing at world market prices as other reflections of changing strategy in particular sectors.

In the context of the need for new forms of cooperation, Professor Mateev had raised the question of transfer of technology. Imports of high-technology goods alone were not enough: the need was for transfer of whole systems — illustrated by current industrial cooperation in the fields of computers and of car-production — and transfer was becoming a two-way trade. Dr Hardt said that a question asked in the West was whether we were now experiencing part of a cycle of technology transfer or whether a long-term rising trend could be expected. Transfer through industrial cooperation of benefit to all parties required reliable information on markets, credit-worthiness, etc., and some control over production costs. Professor Mateev had suggested that small countries might find it difficult to reap economies of scale for some products; Olivetti might provide a helpful example of specialisation with a world market in view. The CMEA 'Comprehensive Programme' of 1971 had also stressed the need for specialisation; and technology transfer from the West — on the Fiat model, for example — could, by the competition it offered to existing capacities, intensify the pressure for specialisation and concern with economies of scale within the CMEA area. As Professor Mateev had noted, capital/labour ratios differed less between East and West than before; this too could influence the future nature and scale of industrial cooperation and transfer of technology.

Dr Hardt concluded by agreeing with the authors of the two papers that economic interdependence of East and West was now a fact, and a necessity for both. The Helsinki 'Basket 2' indicated a promising area for promoting developments of interest to both sides. Professor Lavigne had mentioned monetary and financial relations. The USA had a special responsibility here, though the OPEC countries had precipitated the recent disastrous developments — both excessive price inflation and the recession in economic activity. These were global problems, as was the question of the adequacy of international credit flows, and he strongly advocated greater efforts to use international bodies such as the IMF, IBRD, GATT to help in their solution.

The subsequent discussion centred on

(i) transfer of technology
(ii) treaty and other relations between states and between associations with differing membership.

Professor Bogomolov stressed the possibilities of benefit to both East and West from transfer of technology. It was no longer true — if it ever had been — that the East had no comparable exchange to offer. On the microeconomic level, Western firms frequently benefited from government subventions for research and development and, in any case, they made sure that they recouped their own costs in the price of the product or in licence fees earned in Western markets; sales of licences to the East therefore produced extra, surplus,

profit. In the socialist countries, on the other hand, research and development
was state-financed and its benefits were transferred freely within and among
the socialist countries. Quantitative comparison of the benefits of East–West
cooperation was particularly complicated in this field and Western assessments
tended to understate the relative benefit to the West. *Professor Kozialek* agreed
that sectoral 'technology gaps' could be found between East and West Europe,
West Europe and North America, or other groups of countries, with the advantage to one side or the other in different sectors. This underlined the possibilities of mutually beneficial exchange; but the Eastern countries were certainly not dependent on Western technology though exchange was convenient
for them.

Professor Kozialek also took up the question of EEC–CMEA relations,
seeing – as did *Professor Zaharescu* – the major problem in this field as the
continuing refusal of mfn treatment, on both tariffs and quotas, by the EEC
to CMEA trade partners; and an extensive examination of this and related
questions was undertaken by *Professor Schiavone*. He noted the ambiguity
today of the phrase 'mfn treatment' and the confusion which this too often
introduced into East–West discussions. The Helsinki Final Act appeared to
accept that mfn treatment could be made conditional upon 'reciprocity' in
some form from the Eastern countries, though insistence on reciprocity
contradicted the plain meaning of the words. He thought that the GATT
should not apply a single rigid formula in establishing conditions of membership for socialist countries, whose individual systems and policies now showed
significant differences. He agreed with Professor Mateev that the importance
of supranationality was often exaggerated; supranational organs and institutions
did not of themselves ensure true integration. On the other hand, he doubted
whether the CMEA, despite its undoubted legal personality, could effectively
implement a common economic or commercial policy towards third countries.
Professor Lavigne's analysis of the possibility of EEC–CMEA negotiations
should be supplemented by noting that the CMEA Charter committed the
Council to 'assist the member countries in elaborating, coordinating and
carrying out joint measures for development of trade and exchange of services
between the member countries of the Council and between them and other
countries' and to 'take such other actions as may be required for the purposes
of the Council' (Article III). This implied that negotiations between the EEC
and CMEA as such were probably bound to focus on the 'common commercial policy' of the EEC.

Professor Zaharescu, after reviewing the historical forces contributing to
the present pattern of the world economy, stressed that one could indeed speak
today of 'a world economy', not merely of economic interdependence. Of
course, this 'world economy' was not equivalent to the integration of different
national economies into a single economy; but the international division of
labour had developed to a degree that made the need for cooperation between
different economies very evident. Neither cooperation within international
organisations nor economic relations between states members of different
organisations should be limited by differences in national economic systems.
Romanian policy favoured not only the most fully developed commercial
exchanges with all states, irrespective of their economic systems, but also the
development of cooperation in production as a superior form of economic

collaboration. Every state had, of course, the right to determine for itself the level and nature of its participation in international economic cooperation, in the light of its own economic objectives.

Replying to the discussion, *Professor Lavigne* stressed the evidence provided by the Helsinki Final Act of strong political motivation for East—West economic cooperation, even though the Act was not a binding treaty but a statement of principles accepted by both sides — which, in turn, explained the ambiguity of some of its clauses (e.g. on mfn). It also treated cooperation as primarily an inter-state matter even though, on the Western side, questions such as mfn treatment could in principle be settled only by the EEC; in this the Final Act implicitly recognised facts. Professor Lavigne did not share the view that the golden age of East—West trade expansion was over: there remained ample scope for further growth despite the recent and planned (in the 1976—80 plans of the CMEA countries) faster growth of intra-CMEA than of East—West trade. She accepted that the 'technology gap' was closing and also that the nature of the gap differed from sector to sector. Finally she regretted that, so far, East—West cooperation had been discussed virtually without participation by the 'South' and North—South cooperation virtually without the 'East'.

Professor Mateev replied to Dr Hardt that he saw the mutual interest in trade in technology as promising a continuing, rather than a short-term or discontinuous, development. So far as commodity trade was concerned, he wished to stress again the importance of removing obstacles to the diversification of the flow from East to West, whose concentration on materials and agricultural products did not reflect the development levels or export capacities of the CMEA countries. On the question of institutional differences, he agreed with Dr Hardt that the contrast, popular in earlier years, of the 'planned' with the 'free-market' economy, was outdated and now, happily, generally accepted as such. Large multinational corporations now planned their development and long-term relations, and for them and their Eastern trade partners it was not planning that created inflexibility or difficulty in adapting to changing needs and conditions — only, at times, bad planning.

5 East–West Trade: Selected Problems

Vladimir Wacker
CZECHOSLOVAK ECONOMIC ASSOCIATION

I have been asked to discuss some problems of the development of trade between countries with different socio-economic systems; and, by agreement with the Programme Committee of the Conference, I am going to consider (a) tariff and non-tariff obstacles, (b) policies on trade credit and financing, and (c) the composition of agricultural trade, with special emphasis on Czechoslovak trade.

Right at the beginning I wish to clarify two basic conditions for further development of East–West trade, namely, (i) the political and economic equality of both partners, and (ii) the economic effectiveness (efficiency) of this trade relation – that is, the attainment of comparative advantage. Providing that the first condition is met, the problem of economic efficiency is more or less a technical question. For one thing it is logically in the interest of all involved to maximise the benefits derived from East–West trade. It follows, therefore, that the recognition of political and economic equality must be a good point of departure not only for further development of mutual trade, but also for cooperation between East and West in general.

Acceptance of this principle implies that no trade agreement should be linked with any political conditions. It also implies the elimination of economic discrimination between the partners. While the principle of political equality is largely maintained (the only exception being the amendment to the US Trade Act 1974), that of economic equality has not yet fully been recognised. Let me add – with satisfaction – that the principle of political equality has already been incorporated into East–West relations, particularly since the Final Act of the Helsinki Conference was signed in 1975. Our efforts should now be concentrated on achieving full recognition of the principle of economic equality. It is one which now begins to play an ever-increasing role in the development of East–West trade.

I TARIFF AND NON-TARIFF OBSTACLES IN EAST–WEST TRADE

The development of trade relations between the socialist and advanced capitalist countries is still being impeded both by customs barriers and by so-called 'non-tariff obstacles', as well as by a number of other hindrances which the advanced capitalist countries inflict upon trade with the socialist countries. Such obstacles may be either expressly discriminatory – i.e. affecting only trade with the socialist countries – or of a more general nature, affecting trade with other countries also. In the customs field, it is the United States policy, above all, that belongs to the first category of discriminatory obstacles. As is well known, United States legislation – ever since the height of the Cold War in 1951 – has not permitted the United States government to grant to the socialist countries either most-favoured-nation treatment or any specific tariff reductions. Exceptions have been made in only two cases – the Polish People's Republic and, most recently, the Socialist Republic of Romania. The new US Trade Act of 1975, passed at a time of relaxation of international tensions, raised great hopes that it would put an end to this undesirable situation; but it proved a heavy disappointment since it has tied the normalisation of trade relations to unacceptable political and other conditions.

Thus, since 1951, imports from the socialist countries (with the exceptions noted) have been subjected in the USA to maximum customs duties – in most cases many times higher than those applied to imports from the 'most-favoured' nations. Naturally, this situation has been reflected in the unsatisfactory development of mutual trade relations. The discriminatory measures having been introduced, Czechoslovak exports to the USA, for example, fell by more than 80 per cent. But, in contrast, Czechoslovakia did not take full retaliatory measures and has not ceased to apply the most-favoured-nation clause in trade relations with the USA. It only rescinded certain earlier reductions of customs duties affecting some selected items of interest to the United States. Despite this, Czechoslovak imports from the USA declined substantially in the 1950s, on the one hand, because the rapid drop in exports reduced dollar earnings and thus the availability of finance to cover imports from the USA, and, on the other, because the US government, through its embargo on so-called strategic exports, itself restricted the volume of US exports.

A relatively liberal US trade policy toward the capitalist countries – manifested, in the field of customs duties, particularly through active participation in the various rounds of tariff reductions under the General Agreement on Tariffs and Trade and, above all, in the last and most important 'Kennedy round' – has in itself produced an adverse effect on trade with the socialist countries. With the lowering of normal tariff rates the differences between these and the maximum rates imposed on imports from the socialist countries have widened and thus the amount of tariff discrimination against these imports has been increasing.

No wonder, therefore, that the socialist countries have made up for the shrinking of their former trade with the USA above all by increased mutual cooperation and, secondly, that the USA's place among the Western partners in trade relations with the socialist countries has been taken by countries following a less negative line in their trade and tariff policies towards the socialist countries.

It has, nevertheless, been possible to maintain exports from the socialist countries to the USA on a modest level, and this has been facilitated both by the large differences between US tariff rates for different products, and by generally high prices on the US internal markets. As is well known, the US customs tariff is of a saw-tooth pattern – in other words, very high rates alternate with low ones or even with tariff-free items, on which the degree of discrimination is therefore small or non-existent. The high level of domestic prices in the USA in some cases makes it possible to overcome a moderate degree of tariff discrimination, though in others high tariffs and the degree of discrimination are together prohibitive. To take the Czechoslovak Socialist Republic again as an example, it has been possible recently to export to the USA some kinds of processing and textile machinery, some specialised textile goods, some traditional glass products, certain food products, artificial jewellery and natrium fertilisers. However, the volume of mutual trade relations falls far short of the economic possibilities of both countries.

Judging from the experience of the Czechoslovak Socialist Republic, in the trade relations between other advanced capitalist countries and socialist countries there has been no discrimination in the tariff field conflicting with the GATT most-favoured-nation clause, given that this clause recognises exceptions from the principle in favour of customs unions and free-trade areas. However, this is not to say that customs tariffs do not constitute obstacles to trade with countries claiming the right to such exceptions, although the rest of the capitalist countries are in a similar situation to the socialist countries in this respect.

The customs tariff of a customs union, or the tariffs of a free-trade area, each constitute a twofold obstacle to trade, in that the abolition of duties on trade among the member countries of the West European groupings (the European Economic Community and the European Free Trade Association) puts imports from all non-member countries, including the socialist countries, into a less favourable position as compared with supplies of the same goods from the member countries. However, since the tariff rates of these groupings, or their individual member countries, are in most cases relatively low, tariffs do not generally constitute unsurmountable obstacles; but they do reduce the price, and foreign-exchange earnings, that the non-member exporter can realise. However, in some exceptional cases, where individual peak tariffs have survived in these groupings – and particularly in the case of items excluded as exceptions from linear tariff reductions of the Kennedy round – the level of the tariff can be an effective obstacle to a further development of trade. The proposals on tariff harmonisation submitted in the current multilateral trade negotiations under the GATT could contribute to reducing the unfavourable impact of such tariffs. In the same way, any tariff reduction agreed upon during these negotiations will narrow the gap between tariffs imposed on goods imported to the groupings from non-member countries, including the socialist countries, and the free entry accorded to goods imported from member countries.

In this connection it is necessary to draw attention to the effects of the conclusion of agreements on association with the EEC by certain member countries of EFTA, which have relatively high levels of import tariffs – e.g.

Austria. The growing difference between the duties imposed on goods imported from the EEC countries and those on goods from the socialist countries is starting to have an adverse impact on exports from the latter countries to the 'associate'. These are not growing as fast as exports to other capitalist countries, and in some cases are showing a disturbing tendency to decline.

A similar tendency threatened to affect trade relations between Finland and some socialist countries after the conclusion of an agreement on a free-trade zone including Finland and the EEC. But Finland also concluded agreements, on mutual elimination of tariffs and other obstacles to trade, with certain socialist countries (the Bulgarian People's Republic, the Hungarian People's Republic, the Czechoslovak Socialist Republic and the German Democratic Republic) in 1974 and 1975. These countries were thereby granted the same conditions in the field of tariffs and other regulations affecting their export trade with Finland as had been granted to the member countries of the West European groupings. The favourable impact of these agreements was obvious as early as the first year after their coming into force — 1975. While Finnish exports to the capitalist countries more or less stagnated, or even fell, exports to Czechoslovakia increased by 25 per cent and to the CMEA countries as a whole by as much as 44 per cent.

Among non-tariff obstacles to trade, first place must be given to discriminatory quantitative restriction of imports, to which certain West European countries — above all the EEC member countries — are subjecting some imports from the socialist countries. To justify such import restrictions, the countries in question express their concern about the low export prices of goods from the socialist countries, which might threaten domestic production and disrupt the market for such goods. However, the share of the imports from the socialist countries in the over-all imports of the goods in question is usually so small that no threat to the domestic production and market can exist.

Let me mention a few examples of such import restrictions affecting exports from Czechoslovakia. The Federal Republic of Germany subjects to discriminatory quantitative restrictions 61 items of its trade statistics nomenclature, covering, in particular, textile products, leather footwear and metallurgical and rolled products. The Czechoslovak share in total imports of these 61 products into the Federal Republic of Germany amounts to roughly 1·5 per cent, and for textiles alone roughly 1 per cent.

In France, 42 items of imports from the Czechoslovak Socialist Republic are subjected to discriminatory quantitative restrictions, the most important being certain textile and ceramic products (facing tiles and china tableware).

In Great Britain, discriminatory quantitative restrictions are applied to 48 items of the Brussels Tariff Nomenclature. These include textile and leather products, matches, tents, rubber footwear, porcelain and earthenware, transistor radios, TV sets, valves and semi-conductors. The Czechoslovak share in total imports of these items is low and in most cases does not reach 1 per cent; exceptions are matches (10·3 per cent), hat-making and millinery products (about 5·5 per cent), and porcelain and ceramics (about 2·4 per cent). Recently, in March 1976, a new import quota was imposed for woollen clothing from the Czechoslovak Socialist Republic, German Democratic Republic and Socialist Republic of Romania.

In Italy, 92 items of the BTN are subjected to discriminatory quantitative import restrictions, particularly metallurgical products, automobiles, flat glass, footwear and textiles.

In Benelux quantitative import restrictions affect 64 items of the BTN, about one-half of them discriminating against imports from Czechoslovakia.

Denmark applies discriminatory quantitative restrictions to imports from Czechoslovakia on 48 items in the BTN, of which 15 items are affected by only partial restriction. The list includes artificial leather, leather footwear, textile products, flat and container glass, insulated conductors, furniture, chairs, tents, sleeping bags, brushes, bicycles, tiles, ceramic raw materials, confectionery. The Czechoslovak share in total imports of these items into Denmark is low (up to 1 per cent) with the exception of tents (about 44·8 per cent) and sleeping bags (about 8·3 per cent).

Ireland introduced in 1976 quantitative restriction on imports of 17 items of the BTN from Czechoslovakia.

Another grave non-tariff obstacle to trade between the capitalist and socialist countries is the import (sometimes also export) licence procedure applied by certain capitalist countries in a discriminatory way to trade with socialist countries. These licence or permit procedures are sometimes designed simply to implement quantitative restrictions, but they sometimes serve as independent administrative measures. These can be highly effective obstacles to trade, especially if applied in a discriminatory way; by imposing lengthy procedures delaying the completion of transactions, they discourage importers from choosing suppliers from a country against which the procedure is being applied. Import licence procedure is particularly lengthy in France, in Great Britain (for textiles) and in Italy (at present for 99 items).

Another kind of non-tariff obstacle applied by some capitalist countries in a discriminatory way against imports from the socialist countries is pricing procedure, producing uncertainty among customers and delaying the realisation of the proceeds by the exporter. In the Federal Republic of Germany this affects, for example, fine metal sheeting, men's clothing, dusters and wipers, felt materials for hat-making; in Benelux the procedure affects various goods, mainly textiles.

A considerable obstacle to trade is constituted by difficulties in obtaining entry visas for foreign trade representatives or labour permits for mixed companies' workers. We have noticed such difficulties, and lengthy procedures in handling requests, particularly in France, Great Britain, Italy, the Netherlands and Greece.

From the rich assortment of non-tariff obstacles to trade I have selected those most typically and frequently applied today in trade relations between states with different economic systems. Other difficulties might also be enumerated — for example, those arising from the process of examining the customs value of goods imported from the socialist countries, from anti-dumping duties, etc. However, I have limited myself to the kind of obstacles which have the most adverse influences on the development of trade.

Of course, the present crisis in the capitalist monetary system is also throwing its shadow on the development of trade relations between states with different economic systems. The capitalist states suffering from balance-of-payments difficulties introduce measures aimed to protect their balances of payments; and such measures always involve effective restriction of imports.

In recent times direct measures to restrict imports in such circumstances have mainly taken the form either of tariff surcharges or of obligatory import deposits. Formally, these are always non-discriminatory, relating to imports from all countries, and they are neither typical of nor specific to trade relations between countries of different economic systems. However, the levels of surcharges or import deposits are usually differentiated according to the kinds of goods and their significance for the economy of the importing country, and particularly important items — like sources of energy, basic raw materials or foodstuffs — may well be exempted. Thus, even if the measures are formally non-discriminatory, actual discrimination can be applied against those countries whose exports to the import-restricting country consist mostly of items subject to the higher rates of surcharge or deposit.

Recent well-known examples are, in particular, measures taken by Finland and Italy, which instituted, in protection of their balances-of-payments, import-deposit obligations. These cover imports from all countries, and thus are formally non-discriminatory. But Finland was rebuked by capitalist countries, who alleged that the deposit system in fact favoured imports from the socialist countries, which made it discriminatory. On the other hand, some socialist countries criticise Finland on the grounds that the deposit system bears particularly heavily on their exports, and that it is thus discriminatory and detrimental to them. This simply confirms the earlier conclusion that measures to protect the balance of payments, even if they may appear to discriminate against the exports of certain countries, are not essentially problems of trade relations between countries with different economic systems — which is the subject we have to consider.

II CHANGES IN POLICIES ON TRADE CREDIT AND FINANCING

Since the mid-1960s there has been some improvement in the credit facilities available to finance trade between the capitalist and socialist states, and the significance of credit policy has increased. The increased volume of credit transactions reflects the intensified trade in industrial goods. International trade has entered a new stage of development, in which competition in the field of prices is being complemented by, and often replaced by, competition in the field of credit policy. The main factors determining the competitive capabilities of the individual exporters of capital goods are the terms and conditions of credits, especially repayment deadlines and interest rates. In the course of only a few recent years conditions for granting credits have started to exert a significant and growing influence on the volume and structure of international commodity-trade flows.

Early in the 1970s the Commission of the European Communities started its attempts to work out a common credit policy toward the CMEA member countries. But there seem to be a number of reasons why this is difficult to achieve. The individual EEC countries are aware of the fact that credits have recently come to play an ever more important part in their economic cooperation with the CMEA countries, and that such cooperation can help them to acquire raw materials and fuels and to safeguard a stable market for their own industrial goods, especially engineering products. By granting credits the EEC countries can successfully resist the competition of other advanced capitalist countries (the USA, Japan, etc.) in the markets of the socialist countries; and the transition to a common credit policy is also being hampered by the raw materials, energy and monetary crises of recent years, as well as by the difficulty of establishing a sufficient legal basis for such a move.

The importance of credits in relations between the socialist and capitalist countries is growing. In most cases, an EEC country grants credits to a CMEA country for purchases of machinery and equipment, and the CMEA country usually repays by means of a counter-flow of products made in the credit-financed plants. Recently credits have become a basic prerequisite not only for a successful development of foreign trade, but also for all kinds of cooperation involving trade in licences. The importance of credit insurance is also growing.

Certain member countries of the Organisation for Economic Cooperation and Development (some EEC member countries, USA and Japan) have been striving to conclude an international credit agreement. In October 1974 they agreed that in future the interest rate on export credits should not exceed 7 per cent. The agreement was also intended to regulate repayment dates for export credits and the terms proposed were; for credits to advanced capitalist countries, five years; to socialist countries, 8·5 years; to the developing countries, ten years. The present world economic situation makes such negotiations more difficult. The granting of credits to CMEA member countries is the result of the lending countries' needs to improve conditions for the sale of their goods, to obtain sources of supply for raw materials and fuels, to attain full utilisation of capacities and to reduce unemployment. All countries try to safeguard their own interests and, in consequence, the negotiations within the OECD on an international credit agreement have as yet produced no results.

The Commission of the European Communities is trying to bring the credit policy field (including policy towards the CMEA member countries) into its sphere of competence, but also – for the time being – with no success. The Commission wanted to unify conditions for credit insurance and stipulate unified insurance premiums for all insurance institutions of the EEC member countries, to control the financing of credits granted to the socialist states through the European Investment Bank, and to subject to its own influence also the granting to CMEA countries of credits linked with industrial cooperation or trade in licences.

But trade credit policy has so far remained within the competence of the national governments of the EEC, though they have the duty to consult on projects, financing, etc. The Commission has the right to obtain information and reports on important credit agreements concluded with CMEA member countries, but cannot, for the time being, otherwise intervene in this field.

It may be expected that a credit agreement will be concluded in the OECD within twelve months; and such an agreement might then become the basis for credit relations between CMEA and EEC member countries also.

It may be noted that, so far, the socialist countries have met with discrimination in the credit field only in their relations with the USA. The US government continues to pursue a tough policy in this field, which includes, in particular, curbing the Export–Import Bank's possibilities of granting credits to the socialist countries and undertaking credit insurance. This policy has become the target of ever-growing criticism in recent years. If trade between the socialist countries and the USA is to be widened in the future, as some predict it will be, some liberalisation in the credit field — as in others — will be necessary.

III THE STRUCTURE OF TRADE IN AGRICULTURAL PRODUCTS

In international trade in foodstuffs (here defined as SITC group 0, food and live animals, and group 1, beverages and tobacco) the socialist states hold a relatively less important position than in other areas of commodity trade.

Over the period 1955–74 the share of the socialist states' exports in world food exports has stabilized, after some oscillations, at about 8·3 per cent. The share of the CMEA member countries alone has fluctuated also, but it was higher in 1974 than in 1955. The share of the socialist states in world food imports has been growing and in 1974 amounted to about 9·6 per cent, compared with 7·9 per cent in 1955, while the share of the CMEA member countries alone, after growth during 1955–65, has declined, and in 1974 was again roughly at the 1955 level.

At the same time, the shares of individual regions in the imports and exports of the socialist countries have been changing. The share of the advanced capitalist countries in the total exports of the socialist countries increased rapidly from 25·6 per cent (in those of the CMEA countries 32·1 per cent) in 1955 to about 42·0 per cent (CMEA 45·0 per cent) in 1974. The share of the developing countries in exports from the socialist countries was also increasing — from 10·2 per cent (and 2·1 per cent for CMEA) in 1955 to about 23·0 per cent (CMEA 13·0 per cent) in 1974.

The share of all imports into the socialist states (CMEA) provided by the advanced capitalist countries has also been growing — from 19·2 per cent (20·1 per cent) in 1955 to about 36·3 per cent (31·5 per cent) in 1974. The share of imports from the developing countries in total imports rose from 12·4 per cent (11·3 per cent) in 1955 to 28·9 per cent (31·3 per cent) in 1974.

In contrast, the share of the intraregional trade of the socialist countries (CMEA) in their own total exports fell from 64·2 per cent (62·3 per cent) in 1955 to about 35·0 per cent (33·0 per cent) in 1974, and in their total imports from 68·4 per cent (48·2 per cent) to about 34·8 per cent (33·7 per cent).

The development of the foreign trade in foodstuffs of the socialist countries, and of the CMEA member countries, with different regions is shown in absolute values in Table 7.

TABLE 7 FOREIGN TRADE IN FOODSTUFFS OF SOCIALIST COUNTRIES
1955, 1973, 1974 (US $ million [FOB])

Region	1955 Socialist Countries (SC)	CMEA	1973 SC	CMEA	Estimate 1974 SC	CMEA
Exports to the world	1536	1063	6310	4970	8255	6320
Exports to socialist countries	986	701	2470	2280	2889	2654
of which to CMEA	945	660	2280	2100	2322	2097
Exports to capitalist countries	550	362	3840	2690	5366	3666
of which to advanced capitalist countries	393	340	2480	2110	3467	2844
to developing countries	157	22	1360	580	1899	822
Imports from the world	1441	1375	7610	6510	8310	6230
Imports from socialist countries	986	945	2470	2280	2889	2322
of which from CMEA	701	660	2280	2100	2654	2097
Imports from capitalist countries	455	430	5140	4230	5421	3980
of which from advanced capitalist countries	276	275	3330	2600	3020	1960
from developing countries	179	155	1810	1630	2401	1948

Sources: UN, *Monthly Bulletin of Statistics*; estimates by the Foreign Trade Research Institute, Czechoslovakia.

The value of foodstuffs exports from the socialist to the capitalist countries rose from US $550 million to about $5·4 billion over the years 1955–74 – i.e., at an annual average rate of 12·7 per cent. Exports to the developing countries rose still faster – by 14·0 per cent annually; and for exports to the advanced capitalist countries the rate of increase was only 12·1 per cent. Exports of foodstuffs from the CMEA countries alone to the capitalist states reached about $3·7 billion in 1974, against $362 million in 1955, while the average annual growth rate was 13·0 per cent. Here also the annual rate of growth of food exports to the developing countries was far more striking (21·0 per cent) than to the advanced capitalist countries (11·8 per cent).

Yet still higher values, and growth rates, were reached for food exports

from the capitalist to the socialist countries, or to the CMEA member
countries. From 1955 to 1974 the value of food exports from the capitalist to
the socialist countries rose from US $455 million to more than $5·4 billion —
an average annual growth of 13·9 per cent — with a higher average annual growth
of imports to socialist countries from the developing countries (14·6 per cent)
than from the advanced capitalist countries (13·4 per cent). The value of food
imports from capitalist states to the CMEA member countries alone reached
$3·9 billion in 1974, after some decline in 1973, against $430 million in 1955
— an average annual growth of 12·3 per cent — and, here too, the average rate
of increase of food imports from the developing countries was higher (14·3 per
cent) than from the advanced capitalist states (10·9 per cent).

In this sector of East—West trade the main partners of the socialist countries
are the member countries of the EEC and EFTA and Japan, mainly as customers; the main suppliers are France, the USA, Canada, Australia, Argentina,
Brazil; and a number of other developing countries supply tropical and subtropical fruits and other produce.

TRADE IN FOODSTUFFS WITH THE EEC COUNTRIES

The suppliers to the EEC among the socialist countries are predominantly the
members of the CMEA. Food exports from the CMEA countries to the EEC —
whose members are themselves important food exporters — are significantly
hampered by protectionist import levies. Even though efforts appear to be
made, from time to time, to reform the EEC's agricultural policy, any substantial change in the principles of the common trade policy toward third
countries, including the CMEA countries, appears unlikely. The adherence to
the principles of the common agricultural policy of the original EEC of Great
Britain, Denmark and Ireland is also of importance for the export interests of
the CMEA countries. The so-called deficiency payment system of Great
Britain should by 1977 be replaced by the mechanisms of the EEC common
agricultural policy, including the customs mechanism, which means compensatory import levies. Thus, food exports from the CMEA countries to the
enlarged EEC will be seriously hampered, since some CMEA countries
(including for some products the Czechoslovak Socialist Republic) export
foodstuffs mainly to Great Britain. The import levies make practically
impossible any import from third countries (given the minimum import
price stipulated by the EEC) of any product for which there is a surplus of
domestic production. Moreover, changes in the market situation in individual
EEC member countries tend to result in the introduction of additional temporary protectionist, or even prohibitionist, measures.

Some CMEA member countries (the Bulgarian People's Republic, the
Hungarian People's Republic, the Polish People's Republic, the Socialist
Republic of Romania) maintain with the Commission of the European
Communities so-called 'technical' contacts, which govern imports of selected
agricultural products from these countries to the EEC. These CMEA countries

can thus export certain agricultural products to the EEC at guaranteed 'orientation' prices (*Mindestpreis*) and 'entry' prices (*Schwellenpreise*). They enjoy a kind of preference over other third countries, but only for supplies of a few agricultural products of interest to the EEC.

In general it can be stated that, despite the special arrangements just mentioned, the CMEA countries as a whole are subjected to more discrimination in respect of their food exports than other third countries; and the minor concessions mentioned are far from making up for the losses resulting from the implementation of the EEC common agricultural policy.

The share of food exports from the socialist countries to the EEC countries in the total of the socialist countries' food exports to advanced capitalist countries rose from 32·6 per cent in 1955 to about 62·0 per cent in 1974; and the corresponding share for the CMEA countries rose from 32·4 per cent to about 66·1 per cent.

The share of food imports from the EEC countries in total food imports by the socialist states amounted to 38·0 per cent in 1955; by 1973 it had fallen to 22·2 per cent, and in 1974 rose again to about 24·2 per cent. The importers were predominantly the CMEA countries, and the EEC share in their total food imports from the advanced capitalist states in 1955 was 38·2 per cent, falling by 1973 to 26·5 per cent, then rising to 32·1 per cent in 1974.

It follows that the EEC is by far the most important purchaser of food from CMEA countries, and its importance is continually growing despite the discriminatory measures imposed.

The EEC's discrimination against outside suppliers – and mainly against the CMEA countries – has not been lessened by the so-called gradual liberalisation of imports. This liberalisation, which has consisted mainly in the elimination of import quotas formerly in force, has been accompanied by the imposition of various compensating levies, foreign-exchange regulations, border charges and – still – import duties which, in a number of cases, are higher for imports from the socialist countries than for those from other countries. Despite the fact that the export price that can be obtained after complying with the present import regulations of the EEC often barely covers – or even does not cover – costs, food exports from the socialist countries to the EEC countries continue. This is mainly because the EEC countries are the only, or the main, market for a whole range of agricultural and food products. However, other factors also play a role, particularly the need to earn the foreign exchange to finance purchases by the socialist countries from the EEC, traditional trade relations, the relatively short-distance transport needed, etc.

When we consider the prospects for further development of food exports from the socialist countries – in practice from the CMEA countries – to the EEC, we cannot count on the elimination of discriminatory measures against food imports into the Community. Bilateral negotiations on the part of individual socialist countries may secure partial concessions, with smaller or larger advantages for certain products – which is in sharp contrast with the united, disciplined and strict observance of principles of relations with third countries formally accepted in the EEC. Certain possibilities for reducing the unfavourable consequences of the EEC's measures may also lie in cooperation agreements providing exceptional and more favourable import and export regimes for the goods produced under such agreements. Partial concessions might also be obtained by making large purchases of certain goods from the EEC conditional upon particular concessions on food exports to the Community.

TRADE IN FOODSTUFFS WITH SELECTED CAPITALIST COUNTRIES OUTSIDE THE EEC

Basic data on the development of trade in foodstuffs with capitalist countries other than those of the EEC completes a general survey of this sector of East–West trade (see Table 8).

TABLE 8   TRADE IN FOOD BETWEEN SOCIALIST COUNTRIES AND THEIR MAIN TRADING PARTNERS AMONG THE ADVANCED CAPITALIST COUNTRIES OTHER THAN THE EEC, 1960–74 (US $ million [FOB])

	1960	*1965*	*1970*	*1973*	*1974*
Exports to EFTA countries					
All socialist countries	270	274	175	320	450*
CMEA countries	255	260	170	305	412*
Imports from EFTA countries					
All socialist countries	46	92	76	145	190
CMEA countries	46	92	76	145	190
Imports from USA					
All socialist countries	–	43	79	1590	970
CMEA countries	–	43	79	1180	640
Imports from Canada					
All socialist countries	120	357	220	540	475
CMEA countries	120	260	105	340	91
Imports from Australia & New Zealand					
All socialist countries	4	226	155	135	300
CMEA countries	1	66	29	67	93
Exports to Japan					
All socialist countries	14	85	81	233	250*
CMEA countries	7	12	18	43	50*

* Estimate.
Sources: UN, *Monthly Bulletin of Statistics*; estimates by the Foreign Trade Research Institute, Czechoslovakia.

In absolute values a rising tendency was evident, for both exports and imports, in the years 1960–74, but explained by the price explosion of 1973–4. Individual years showed considerable fluctuations, obviously reflecting both trade-policies and harvest results. The commodity composition of trade has been similar to that of trade with the EEC countries.

The value of exports from the socialist countries (mainly those of the CMEA) to the *EFTA countries* was estimated in 1974 at some US $400–450 million, and imports from EFTA countries at almost $200 million.

The USA is the purchaser of a wide assortment of food products from the socialist countries but, in both volume and value, grain and fodder predominate in US exports to the socialist states. The value of imports into the socialist countries from the USA reached a maximum in 1973 at US $1·6 billion, of which the CMEA countries accounted for almost $1·2 billion. In 1974 the corresponding values were $970 million and only $640 million respectively.

On 20 October 1975 the USSR and USA concluded a five-year agreement under which the USA will supply to the USSR annually 6–8 million of tons of grain; and this ended a two-month embargo on additional sales of US grain to the USSR. The agreement was to enter into force on 1 October 1976 and stipulated that the USSR may increase annual purchases of US grain by 2 million tons provided that grain stocks in the USA do not fall below 225 million tons. The agreement further stipulates that the supplies of American wheat and maize to the USSR will be implemented under the current American–Soviet agreement on maritime transportation, which will remain in force during the whole period of the new agreement. The USSR and USA will hold regular six-monthly consultations until the agreement expires on 30 September 1981, if it is not further prolonged.

Important food suppliers – mostly of grain and oil-seed – particularly to Asian socialist countries are *Canada, Australia* and *New Zealand*. The value of Canadian food exports to the socialist countries reached its maximum in 1973 at US $540 million, of which $340 million went to the CMEA member countries. In 1974 the value of imports into the CMEA fell sharply to $91 million, and into all socialist states to $475 million. Australian food exports to the socialist states – mainly the Asian socialist states – reached their maximum value in 1974 – US $300 million, of which $93 million were exports to CMEA countries. Food exports from the socialist countries to these countries are very small.

A relatively important customer for foodstuffs from the socialist countries is *Japan.* The value of exports from the socialist countries to Japan in 1973 and 1974 amounted to some $230–250 million, of which $40–50 million came from the CMEA countries.

CONCLUSION

East–West trade in foodstuffs is concentrated on four main markets:

The EEC, or Western European, market is for the socialist countries – mainly the CMEA member countries – the largest, and decisively important, market despite the present serious trade-policy difficulties. In 1974 the share of Western Europe in food-exports from the socialist countries to all advanced capitalist countries was estimated at roughly 75 per cent; and for the CMEA member countries alone the share was as high as 81 per cent. Western European countries are food suppliers to the socialist countries, particularly important for some specialist items (Italy, Spain, Greece — citrus fruits; Greece — oriental tobacco). The share of food imports from Western Europe in the socialist countries' total imports from the industrially advanced capitalist countries was about 30 per cent in 1974, and for the CMEA countries alone the share was about 42 per cent.

The North American market in 1974 supplied almost 50 per cent of all food imports from advanced capitalist countries into the socialist countries, and 37 per cent of those into the CMEA countries. The USA and Canada are suppliers mainly of grain, fodder and oil-seed. Their share of total exports of foodstuffs from the socialist countries to advanced capitalist countries in 1974 was estimated at roughly 4–5 per cent.

The markets of *Australia, New Zealand and Japan* are most important for the Asian socialist countries. Australia's share in the socialist countries' total food imports from the advanced capitalist countries amounted roughly to 10 per cent, and for the CMEA countries alone to almost 5 per cent. Australian food imports from the socialist countries are small. Australia is an important grain supplier, to the Asian socialist countries especially. Japan, one of the principal world importers of food, in 1974 took 7·2 per cent of the total food exports of the socialist countries — mainly those in Asia — to advanced capitalist countries. Japanese food exports to the socialist countries are negligible.

The markets of *developing countries*, and particularly the markets of African and Latin-American developing countries, in 1974 took roughly 35·4 per cent of all exports by the socialist countries to the capitalist states (Table 7). For the CMEA countries alone the corresponding share was about 22·4 per cent. The share of the developing countries in imports by the socialist or CMEA countries was greater — 44·3 per cent of all imports from capitalist states in 1974 or 49·8 per cent for the CMEA alone. The developing countries are suppliers mainly of non-competing products to the socialist countries — southern fruits, coffee, cocoa beans, certain oil-seeds, etc.

This analysis has dealt with the problems of trade in foodstuffs between the socialist and capitalist countries only in broad outline and tracing general trends only. A more detailed analysis by major item of agricultural and food production would require a separate and more extensive study.

6 East–West Trade and Economic Systems

Philip Hanson
UNIVERSITY OF BIRMINGHAM

Trade between East and West is small. Commodity trade between socialist*
and OECD countries in 1974 was only 3 per cent of world commodity trade.
There are, I think, three main reasons for this. First, the two groups of
countries are separated by profound political suspicions of one another.
Second, their attempts to trade are hampered by differences of economic
system. Third, the West is richer than the East, and the rich have a distressing
preference for selling things to one another.

This paper is about some of the policy issues that come under the second
heading: 'systemic' hindrances to trade. This does not mean that I think the
political suspicions are unimportant or unfounded. Watching Western firms
rushing to supply pipeline, chemical plant and machine tools to the USSR,
and Western governments vying with one another to offer the cheapest credit
terms, the Western observer cannot help feeling a bit uneasy. What did Lenin
say? 'The capitalists will compete to sell us the rope to hang them with.'
Perhaps he was right. (Apparently he foresaw that socialist rope would break.
That is some consolation, but not very much.)

On the whole, though, I think it makes sense to separate economic from
political issues in East–West relations. So long as there is an approximate
balance of military power and the NATO and Warsaw Pact countries retain a
certain healthy scepticism about one another, they can afford to develop
mutually beneficial commercial relations. The benefits to the West may come
mainly through higher employment and profits, and to the East through
higher productivity, but the ultimate benefit is higher real incomes in both
cases.

To a liberal, of course, the mere existence of East–West trade is *prima facie*
evidence that both partners derive some benefit from it, since neither Western
firms nor Eastern state organisations are normally coerced into doing business
with one another. The questions that arise are, first, are the net benefits evenly
distributed? Second, are there constraints, due to systemic differences, which
prevent East–West trade and its benefits being greater than they are?

In the rest of this paper I shall review some policy problems under these

---

* The CMEA countries together with Albania, the Chinese People's Republic, North
Korea and North Vietnam.

two headings. On the distribution of benefits I conclude that there is nothing in the logic of economic systems that dictates that one system will generally corner most of the gains; whether there is some systemic bias in the distribution of gains is something that can only be settled empirically. On systemic constraints on East—West trade, my conclusions are less cosy. I think these constraints are severe, and will remain so unless the West adopts an Eastern economic system, or vice versa. On the other hand, there are some areas of 'systemic comparative advantage' — activities in which systemic differences actually promote trade.

I THE DISTRIBUTION OF BENEFITS

A number of arguments have been put forward to the effect that in East—West trade one side can systematically gain more than the other. I shall briefly consider some of these arguments, restricting the discussion mainly to CMEA—OECD trade.

First, it is sometimes said that East—West trade is a substantially larger share of CMEA trade than it is of OECD trade; therefore it is more important to the former than it is to the latter; therefore, the Western bargaining position is inherently stronger. In addition, it is argued that what the West mainly buys from the East — fuels, raw materials and semi-manufactures — are also available from other sources; what the East mainly buys from the West — grain, advanced machinery and know-how are not available from other sources: therefore the Western bargaining position is, on this score also, inherently stronger.

Arguments of this kind would be strong if East—West trade deals were the outcome of bilateral monopoly bargaining between two parties, 'East' and 'West'. But the general position of the two trading groups has very little to do with bargaining between individual firms and foreign trade organisations, or even with the negotiation of trade agreements between an Eastern and a Western government. There are perhaps two recent examples, however, of negotiations akin to bloc-to-bloc bargaining in which these Western advantages might have been expected to yield results favourable to the West — the economic and commercial 'Basket' of the European Security Conference, and the (very slowly) continuing CMEA negotiations with the European Community. On the other hand, even in these negotiations, the Western advantage is qualified by the highly self-sufficient character of the leading CMEA economy. Even if trade with the West now runs at close to one-third of Soviet foreign trade turnover, this still means that imports from the West are less than 2 per cent of total final expenditure in the USSR.

In any case, negotiations are not normally bloc-to-bloc. This fact has prompted another argument — that Western governments, competing to promote their own exports, are engaged in an oligopolistic price war in government-guaranteed export credit terms; their combined actions lead them as a group to provide credit subsidies to Eastern importers; the final outcome is concessions to Eastern countries which no one Western government would have chosen to make if it had been able to control the actions of its rivals.*

This argument is not, however, specific to East—West trade. It applies to the export-promoting activities of Western governments in all markets; and there seems to be little hope of doing much about it. There are dozens of more or less subtle ways in which credit terms could be softened, even if the maximum period of credit and the quoted interest rate were standardised by agreement between Western governments. The temptation to steal a march on the opposition by not charging interest on Sundays, or some such device, seems to be more than some Western governments can resist. In addition, gentlemen's agreements on credit terms are at present rapidly undermined by the ungentlemanly fluctuations in exchange rates. At the time of writing, even 6 per cent interest on loans repayable in Deutschemarks might be no competition at all for the ECGD's $7\frac{1}{2}$ per cent on loans repayable in ever-diminishing pounds.

Here we have an instance of benefits accruing to the East from the failure of Western oligopolistic competitors to get together and form a cartel. On the other hand, these things happen on the Eastern side as well. The readiness of some individual CMEA countries to deal individually with the European Commission over the treatment of their agricultural exports under the Common Agricultural Policy is a case in point.[1] Both East and West can and do play at dividing and ruling. We cannot decide *a priori* who is going to get the best of the game.

Another argument concerns conflicts of interest, not between individual countries within each trading group, but between governments and business units. It is plausible, on the face of it, to argue that CMEA foreign trade organisations, implementing a national plan, should be acting to maximise national net benefits from trade, whereas Western firms seeking profits will not necessarily be doing so. In other words, the Eastern system may be internalising externalities which Western arrangements do not capture.

This general proposition can be applied to a number of activities. For example, the plans of foreign trade organisations are devised with various

* This view has been forcefully argued by Richard Portes in 'Western Investment in Eastern Europe,' a paper delivered to a conference on European Community policy towards Eastern Europe at the University of Reading in December 1975. The importance of these subsidies can be illustrated from the Soviet case. Soviet net indebtedness to the West at the end of 1974 has been put at $4·2 billion (US Secretary of Commerce Rogers Morton, *The United States Role in East—West Trade* [Washington, 1975] p. 35). New government or government-guaranteed medium- and long-term credit extended to the USSR in the first seven months of 1975 came to $8·8 billion, of which $6·7 billion involved interest-rate subsidies by Western taxpayers (*ibid.*). Estimated Soviet drawings during 1975 have been put at $3·7 billion to $4·7 billion (CIA, *Recent Developments in Soviet Hard Currency Trade* [Washington, January 1976] p. 13). These credits are assisting a flow of Western machinery and transport equipment to the USSR which was some $2·1 billion in 1974 and some $4 billion in 1975. Converting the latter figure to 1969 investment-estimate (*smetnye*) roubles at $1·9 = 1 rouble gives a flow of machinery equivalent to about 5 per cent of Soviet planned equipment investment in 1976.

political and macroeconomic considerations in mind: the avoidance of 'undesirable' dependence on foreign sources of supply, the avoidance of balance of payments crises, and so on. Thus a Soviet foreign trade organisation will not be allowed to buy a machine in the West unless the proposal to do so is backed by statements from the relevant domestic machine-building ministry or ministries that an equivalent machine cannot be produced domestically in the required time.[2] The possibility that an imported machine may be more cost-effective for the domestic user than the domestically produced alternative is not supposed to outweigh a national policy preference for self-sufficiency.

A quite different example is shipping. In an Eastern economy it is possible for foreign trade planners to direct foreign trade organisations to make their export delivery contracts c.i.f. and their import purchase contracts f.o.b. (as far as possible) and then to allocate the freight to their own national shipping organisations. The Western exporter or importer normally has no reason to try to do the same thing in reverse. Any Western firm so patriotic as to charter high-cost national shipping instead of low-cost foreign shipping, to help the balance of payments, should apply for charitable status — which it will probably need.

It does not follow, though, that conflicts of interest between firms and governments are a systemic weakness of the West. There are three reasons for saying this. In the first place, why should we assume that government policies tend to promote national economic welfare? This is an Eastern assumption; but it is doubtful whether historical evidence supports it. It may well come from a cultural tradition of reverence for authority — a tradition to which scepticism is alien.* Thus a nation practising flag discrimination, to boost incomes in its shipping industry and protect its balance of payments, is also sacrificing some of the gains from trade and may, in the long run, be reducing its merchant marine's efficiency and ability to compete. In general, Westerners who believe that decentralised economic systems tend to be more efficient in a microeconomic sense than centralised systems, should produce strong evidence for reversing this view when they are talking about East—West trade.

Secondly, the 'framework' activities of Western governments in East—West trade are substantial, and may often help to harmonise the interests of the firm with those of the whole national community. The information provided to exporters by the US Department of Commerce Bureau of East—West Trade or the UK East European Trade Council, and the intergovernmental agreements providing for commercial representation, arbitration procedures, etc., are all fairly uncontroversial examples. Whether East—West trade promotion tends to draw Western governments into too much direct intervention in resource allocation, as opposed to 'framework' activities, is another matter.[3]

Thirdly, it would be absurd to imagine that conflicts between national and business-unit economic interests do not arise in Eastern countries. There is

---

* A cultural difference which takes other and more interesting forms. *Cf.* D. J. Richards, 'Wit and Worship — Two Impulses in Modern Russian Literature' in *Russian Literature Triquarterly*, No. 14 (forthcoming).

evidence that East European foreign trade organisations tend to constitute information barriers between domestic producers of exports and the end-user in the importing country; that domestic enterprises' incentives to produce for export often fail to match national policy requirements;[4] and that the foreign trade organisations' own incentives are not necessarily conducive to efficient trading – e.g. requirements to report low-interest credit or barter terms for machinery purchases, even when this merely means that the seller has loaded his price to offset these terms.

On balance, then, the argument that the East scores off the West in East–West trade by using its foreign trade organisations as instruments of national economic policy, does not seem all that strong. Once more, it is a point that can be decided only by an appeal to evidence. The logic of economic systems is not decisive.

A somewhat similar argument is that Eastern foreign trade organisations have an inherent bargaining advantage because they are monopolists facing competing Western buyers or, in the case of Eastern imports, monopsonists facing competing sellers. One can certainly think of instances where this has been an advantage. The Soviet 'great grain robbery' of 1972 is one obvious example – a shrewd, surreptitious and perfectly legitimate exercise which no advocate of markets and entrepreneurship can reasonably object to. But subsequent US legislation requiring grain merchants to report sales above a certain amount, and the Soviet–US grain agreement of October 1975, show that it is possible for a Western government to take corrective action.

Is there none the less a general tendency for Western firms to be outgunned by monopoly Eastern business units? It is hard to believe that this is a major problem. First of all, Eastern trade is such a small part of the world total that most Western companies negotiating with Eastern foreign trade organisations will normally have other markets or sources of supply available to them. The large part played in East–West trade by big Western multinational firms[5] reinforces this argument. Secondly, the Eastern countries do not generally coordinate their East–West trade; foreign trade organisations of different CMEA countries can therefore on occasion be competing with one another.[6] Thirdly, competition between foreign trade organisations of the same Eastern country is not unknown, even outside the more decentralised CMEA foreign trade systems such as that of Hungary. The traditional CMEA system gives each export or import agency a monopoly or monopsony of a particular range of goods, but overlaps do occur, particularly in the case of 'turnkey' projects. In the Soviet case a computer, for example, would usually be bought by Elektronorgtekhnika but it might also be included in a chemical plant 'package' bought by Tekhmashimport. Thus one occasionally hears a Western businessman claim that he has sold the same product at different prices to different organisations in a CMEA country at about the same time. Like all virility stories, these tales should be discounted by at least 50 per cent, but they suggest that the picture of Eastern monopolies facing Western competitors can be misleading.

It may be argued that as East—West trade grows, and Eastern countries become price-makers rather than price-takers in many international markets, the situation will change and the systemic monopoly advantages inherent in CMEA trade arrangements will begin to be exploited more widely. But this is surely a remote prospect; and I shall argue below that the systemic constraints on East—West trade make that trade unlikely to become a large component in the total trade of Western countries in the foreseeable future. Meanwhile, the complaints that reach Western governments about CMEA exports are not that they are priced at monopolistically high prices, but that they are priced too low — a point to which I shall also come later.

The Eastern institutional bargaining power that causes more concern at present is the importing agencies' monopsony. But even if we ignore the general counter-arguments given above, this concern seems misplaced. It is kind of Western academic economists to worry about Western companies losing money in deals with the East, but there is some evidence that businessmen are fairly good at doing business. Some mistakes and losses occur, certainly, but if Western companies are systematically selling below their normal supply price in Eastern markets, private enterprise is in worse shape than most of us normally assume.

The Vernon—Goldman argument that competing Western exporters suffer losses through under-pricing in order to 'get a foothold in the market' is not very plausible.[7] It may be true that Eastern import agencies tend, through planners' inertia or extreme risk-aversion, to have an unusually strong preference for dealing with established suppliers. (This is another important assertion about East—West trade which has not been investigated.) If so, it would follow that firms competing to break into the market would be likely to undercut one another to an unusual extent. They would hope to be able to recoup later when, as established suppliers, they would face unusually price-inelastic demand from the foreign trade organisations.

It would not follow from this, however, that there would be a serious systemic bias against Western exporters, except perhaps in the early stages of a major acceleration of East—West trade, for it should be clear in a reasonably short time whether or not the exporters' expectations about repeat orders are, in general, being fulfilled. If they are, the initial price-cutting was a successful loss-leader exercise. If they are not, expectations will be revised and firms trying to break into Eastern markets will not shade their prices any more than they would in any other market.

The charge of 'unfair competition' by Eastern exporters in Western markets is almost the opposite of the 'monopoly power' argument; and it seems to raise a more substantial issue. 'Administrative' economies, with administrative foreign-trade controls and 'goods inconvertibility', could hardly be expected to have internal prices comparable with, or open to influence by, prices in market economies. As long as their domestic price-structures differ markedly from the structure of world market prices, Eastern export pricing in Western markets is bound to seem arbitrary in relation to Western domestic costs and prices. By the same token it is bound to be very difficult to establish beyond reasonable doubt what Eastern production costs are in Western terms.

As a source of uneven distribution of benefits in East—West trade, however, this 'unfair competition' is probably not very important. Western governments have been quite quick to take protectionist action against cheap imports from socialist countries when these begin to upset domestic suppliers. Tariffs, discriminatory and global quantitative restrictions, levies under the Common Agricultural Policy, anti-dumping measures and 'voluntary export restraint' agreements affect a significant number of Eastern exports.[8] In so far as these restrict Eastern hard-currency earnings they also restrict the level of Eastern imports from the West; and, in general, this basic systemic incompatibility seems more important as a constraint on the level of East—West trade than as a source of lop-sided benefits. It will be discussed later along with other systemic constraints.

The arguments so far considered, about the distribution of benefits, have been about more or less short-run consequences of East—West trade. There are two further lines of argument about longer-run consequences. First there are the fears in both East and West that inter-bloc trade is a source of instability. Then there is the question of who gets what out of technology transfer.

So far as stability is concerned, both East and West have good reason to fear the influence of reciprocal trade. Their systemic tendencies to instability are of different kinds and not mutually offsetting. Western economies have unstable export prices, currently prone to rapid increases, and cyclical fluctuations in the volume of import demand. Eastern planners find price changes of any kind difficult and costly to deal with,* and attach a very high priority to the maintenance of stable or only slowly rising retail price indices. In recent years some of the smaller East European countries have found the import of Western inflation a serious problem. To avoid sharp rises in their own retail price indices they have had to provide large budget subsidies to retail prices and curb imports from the West. Both responses entail some cost, in terms of growth of real incomes.

The socialist countries, on the other hand, have relatively stable domestic prices and are less likely to display any absolute falls in aggregate demand. Yet their trade with the West (both in total value, and on a country-by-country basis) has tended to be less stable than intra-Western trade, with Eastern imports inclined to be less stable than Eastern exports.[9] However, this is not necessarily a disadvantage from the Western point of view; Eastern imports, for example, might fluctuate counter-cyclically with the Western world's own fluctuations.

This seems in fact to have happened to some extent. Thus CMEA imports from the West rose sharply in 1975, during the Western recession, while CMEA

---

* According to *Ekonomicheskaya gazeta* no. 46 (1971) p. 7, it took six to seven months for plan targets to be adjusted during 1971 to take into account wholesale price changes at the start of the year. Even after the adjustments many anomalies remained. The article recommends that price changes during the year be avoided.

exports fell in volume and stagnated in value. This continued rise in non-grain deliveries to CMEA countries, at a time when their payments problems were worsening, doubtless reflects to a considerable extent the time-lag between orders and deliveries of capital goods.[10] If, on balance-of-payments grounds, the CMEA countries restrict their import growth in 1976/77, they may well be doing so at a time of Western recovery. To that extent their actions may prove to be counter-cyclical; and the pattern could well be repeated, so long as major downturns in Western economic activity are not reliably forecast a year or so in advance.

The arguments so far offer grounds for expecting that the East will suffer more from the West's instability than vice versa. But if we move from macro-economic aggregates to individual product markets we find arguments tending to run the other way. The conspicuous example of Eastern grain imports has already been mentioned; but so has a possible amelioration of the problem by agreements like the 1975 US–Soviet grain imports agreement. In the case of Eastern machinery imports, however, there may be a different kind of stability problem.

Raymond Vernon has argued persuasively that it is in the nature of ad-ministrative, centrally planned economies to make technical progress via 'large-scale, lumpy, discontinuous' changes in plant and technology, rather than by the more continuous, incremental change characteristic of market economies. He goes on to argue that this may well lead to similarly large and lumpy imports of particular kinds of machinery and know-how, generating very large orders for a particular Western industry, but over only quite short periods of time.[11] He suggests that if East–West trade were to become a substantially larger element in Western trade and economic activity, such bursts of technology-importing might (without malice aforethought) cause serious problems for particular Western industries.

This is plausible and, at first glance, one might think that the historical evidence of Soviet imports from the West over the past twenty years supported the argument. Imports of chemical plant, ships and marine equipment and motor industry plant, in particular, all rose very sharply when past neglect and backwardness were suddenly attended to. On the other hand, we have not yet seen a clear peaking and falling away of any of these broad categories of capital-goods imports, at least in absolute terms. Whether the process of Eastern import of technology, for any one sector, is in the long run addictive rather than satiating, is still not clear.[12]

Technology transfer is in general a problematic part of East–West trade. A great number of plausible propositions can be advanced to suggest either that the current West–East net flow* of technology confers excessive benefits on the East or that, on the contrary, it is locking the East into a position of

---

* OECD countries' sales of machinery and transport equipment to CMEA countries have recently been of the order of four to five times the reverse flow. Naido and Simanovskii, pp. 67 and 68 (*op. cit.* in Note 6) seem to imply that for licence sales (in value) around 1970 the West–East flow was about twelve times the East–West flow.

technological dependence. Here I shall consider only some of the main points.

When an Eastern country buys designs, know-how, licences or hardware incorporating a new technology it is acquiring an asset whose present value and opportunity cost can very probably be put well above the price it pays. Both the future stream of net benefits (e.g. cost reductions from a new process) and the costs of indigenous research, design, testing, etc., that would otherwise have been necessary to develop that technology from available Western information, should be above – possibly far above – the resource cost of the exports needed to pay for it. In other words, there should be gains from trade.

The Western seller of the technology should also have found the deal profitable. Apart from selling the associated hardware, designs, engineering consultancy, training, etc., at normal or above-normal profit, he ought to have been able to extract some element of economic rent (e.g. in licence payments) for the technology itself. The technology now costs him nothing. The expenses of developing it are bygones. He will typically have required the buyer, under the terms of the licence, to keep out of the markets he wants to reserve to himself. If he undertakes to inform the licensee of further developments of the technology, he will presumably charge correspondingly more.

However, if the technology has been sold in competition with suppliers of the same technology or of close substitutes, the seller may have had most of his economic rent bargained away. This is not solely because of the monopsony power of Eastern import agencies. In other markets the seller may have the alternative open to him of supplying the product itself, rather than the know-how to make it, and he may have the further option of establishing a joint-venture or wholly owned subsidiary to manufacture inside the market. In Eastern markets, apart from the restricted joint-venture possibilities in Hungary and Romania, these alternatives may not be available. On both policy and balance-of-payments grounds, the Eastern buyer may well be interested in acquiring the technology or nothing.

Moreover, once he has licensed one producer in any one CMEA country, the licensor may well feel that he has no prospect of licensing another producer. The belief that the technology will subsequently be domestically diffused, even if the terms of the licence sale forbid it, is common among Western licensors. It may be quite mistaken, now that CMEA countries have acceded to the Paris Convention on the Protection of Industrial Property, but it is not too surprising that the belief persists. As long as access to large parts of Eastern countries is forbidden to Westerners, and there are big gaps in industrial information, suspicions of this sort will remain.

In all these circumstances the arguments that West–East technology transfer is a 'one-way street' have some appeal. Vernon and Goldman point especially to instances where Western taxpayers have contributed either to the development of the technology (through government-financed research) or to its sale (through subsidised export credit), or both.[13] Here, they suggest, is a case for intervention by the seller's government to tilt the terms of the deal in

96   *Economic Relations Between East and West*

a Westerly direction, or to prohibit the transaction altogether if the Eastern buyer will not pay a high enough price. Wolf observes that this is essentially a varient of an 'optimum tariff' policy, that the situation is not one peculiar to East—West trade and that the costs of administering such a policy would outweigh its benefits.* His criticisms are compelling; but the topic is, as he says, one that needs empirical investigation.

Meanwhile, further consideration of these arguments leads to questions about the Eastern gains from technology transfer. The newer a technology is, the more likely it is to be monopolised and the higher the costs associated with its transfer are likely to be.[14] On these grounds the Eastern buyer should delay the acquisition of a new technology until it has been diffused to several Western firms. Transfer costs should by then have been reduced and there will be scope for playing competing suppliers off against one another.[†]

An Eastern country that systematically adopted this approach, however, would be choosing an imitative strategy, with a built-in technology lag behind Western countries. This might be an acceptable policy for some industries; but for a country aiming to 'catch up and overtake' it seems unacceptable as a general strategy. The corollary is that closing technology gaps will tend to require the Eastern buyer to purchase technology when its transfer costs are still high and to pay monopoly rents to innovating Western firms. This argument, together with arguments about the virtues of learning by doing the R&D oneself, and about systemic barriers to Eastern adaptation and diffusion of imported technology, suggest that West—East technology transfer may be more of a two-way street than some people suppose. What is needed, as with all the general propositions considered here, is a close look at the actual traffic.

II SYSTEMIC CONSTRAINTS

I turn now to systemic constraints on the level of East—West trade. These are well-known and need not be discussed at length. From the usual Western point of view they include the inconvertibility of Eastern currencies; the difficulty of establishing Eastern *quid pro quo's* for Western concessions on tariffs and quantitative restrictions; the lack of market information for Western exporters and the difficulty of contacting end-users; 'unfair' price competition from Eastern exporters, for whom prices and costs are subordinate to state policy; the barriers to East—West labour migration and West—East risk-capital movements.

From the usual Eastern point of view, the constraints include the inability of Western governments to control their exporters and importers; the Western

* Wolf offers the elegant counter-proposal that where the competing sellers of a technology are all US companies the US government might veto any sale unless the Soviet buyers adopted an open bidding procedure. This would still leave many, probably most, deals unaffected because they involve international competition — as Wolf acknowledges.

† Vernon (*op. cit.* in Note 11) hypothesises that Eastern technology buying may in fact be delayed to improve the Eastern bargaining position.

reluctance to enter long-term supply agreements; the influence of protectionist lobbies on Western governments, and the Western tendency to publicise political linkages with trade.

Politics and systemic constraints on East—West trade are closely connected. Thus Eastern governments do not wish their economies to become too dependent on Western economies, and vice versa.* This is a political consideration; but what forms dependence might take and how it might come about are questions that turn in part on how economic systems work. The two systems may interact in such a way as to promote one-way dependence, and trade might then be curbed to avoid this.

For example, the CMEA countries now have a substantial outstanding debt to the West, yet they do not supply Western banks and governments with information about reserves and the balance of payments. None the less, their past payment record, their ability to control their imports and the unknown but high level of Soviet gold output and reserves have so far given most CMEA countries a high credit rating. But there is some controversy in the West about this. Are the CMEA countries using their borrowing to develop an adequate hard-currency-earning export capacity? How powerful, as the ultimate sanction against default, is the loss of all possible future credits?

The answers to these questions would be encouraging if the import of Western technology was working successfully and was liable to continue indefinitely. If it was working so badly that it was likely to be abandoned altogether, the answers would be, from a Western point of view, discouraging.[†]

Industrial cooperation provides another example. East—West coproduction arrangements, or licence or turnkey deals with product-pay-back, are at first sight a useful way to promote trade and technology transfer — under the constraint of hard-currency shortage in the East — and to buy Western management services and information. But suppose they tend in practice to lock the Eastern partner into subcontracting in labour-intensive processes or to keep development work and marketing in Western hands, perpetuating Eastern weaknesses in those fields?[15]

These reflections, together with the more obvious systemic constraints listed above, suggest that in one way or another differences of economic

---

* Friedeman Müller, 'An Attempt to Assess International Economic Dependence in East—West Relations', a paper presented to the Reading conference cited in the footnote on p. 89, provides an interesting classification of factors affecting 'economic dependence', and suggests ways of measuring it. His measure of the dependence of A on B is the reduction in country A's GNP that can be brought about by B as a deliberate act of policy. In practice Eastern and Western governments must also be concerned with their vulnerability to one another's *unintentional* behaviour. Even this is a much more limited notion than the Latin American theorists' *dependencia* — which may in fact be closer to what some policymakers in East—West relations are concerned with.

† The remaining possibility — that the import of Western technology might be so successful that it could be dropped while Eastern countries surged ahead on their own — is not very plausible. It is a notion that does violence to the pervasive technological interdependence of the modern industrial world.

systems are likely to continue severely to constrain the growth of East—West trade.

III SYSTEMIC COMPARATIVE ADVANTAGES

There are, however, at least two forms of systemic comparative advantage which help to loosen a little the constraints considered above.

One is suggested by the structural differences between Eastern and Western engineering industries and by a fairly characteristic type of East—West transaction. The central planning system tends to be associated with very large size of plant, including some mass production on a scale (e.g. KamAZ) or of a type (e.g. standard machine tools) not paralleled in the West. It also tends to be associated with a relative scarcity of small-to-medium, highly specialised engineering enterprises of a type common in the West. Very large mass-production units are particularly suitable for the utilisation of highly specialised, high-performance machines. There is therefore a particular complementarity between Western specialist machine-builders and giant Eastern (mainly Soviet) machine-users. High-performance special-purpose machine tools, for example, were not readily available in the USSR for Tolyatti and KamAZ, and have been imported in large quantities.

Another type of systemic complementarity is between Eastern research and Western development and innovation. Recently both Eastern and Western writers have drawn attention to this.[16] It appears that central planners are good at channelling large quantities of high-powered people into fundamental and applied research, but are (relatively) bad at extracting successful new products and processes from their work. It also appears that the commercially minded West skimps (relatively) on research, but is better at managing development and innovation. The scope here for mutual benefits might be considerable. The licensing of Eastern research results, as opposed to fully developed new products and processes, might conceivably become an important source of Eastern hard-currency earnings and of faster world-wide technical change.

IV CONCLUSIONS

In the first part of this paper I have suggested a sceptical view of most arguments about systemic bias in the gains from East—West trade. For every argument that one bloc will corner the gains from East—West trade there is usually another line of argument, about the same category of benefits, which suggests that the gains will on the contrary go disproportionately in the opposite direction. But there are some cases in which the arguments on one side do seem particularly strong. For one example, the Western countries may lose significantly in East—West trade from their failure to coordinate their credit policies and avoid a price war on credit terms: for another the Eastern countries, especially the smaller ones, do seem to be more at risk from Western economic instability than vice versa.

Viewed as constraints on East–West trade, rather than as sources of bias in the distribution of its benefits, the differences between Eastern and Western economic systems loom large. Western credits and industrial cooperation deals are often seen as ways of alleviating these constraints, but their effectiveness, in turn, may, be weakened by friction between the two economic systems. It is worth remembering, however, that there are some forms of systemic comparative advantage.

In this paper I have studiously avoided facts and figures and have concentrated on framing questions. The answers, unfortunately, will be much harder to find than the questions.

NOTES

1 I have discussed this topic in 'The European Community's Commercial Relations with the CMEA countries: Problems and Prospects' in Carl H. McMillan (ed.), *Changing Perspectives in East–West Commerce* (Lexington, 1974).

2 *Metodicheskie ukazaniya k razrabotke gosudarstvennykh planov razvitiya narodnogo khozyaistva SSSR* (Moscow, 1974) p. 595.

3 See Edward A. Hewett, 'Government, the Market and East–West Trade', in McMillan, *op. cit.*

4 N. Smelyakov (a Deputy Minister of Foreign Trade of the USSR) complains vigorously about the Soviet export incentives problem in 'Delovye vstrechi', *Novyi mir* (1973) no. 12. Some explanation of it, from the point of view of industrial managers, is given by G. A. Kulagin, 'Moi partnery, nachal'stvo i "pravila igry" ', *Ekonomika i organizatsiya promyshlennogo proizvodstva*, no. 2 (1975) especially pp. 84–5.

5 Jozef Wilczynski, 'Multinational Corporations and East–West Economic Cooperation', *Journal of World Trade Law* (May/June 1975).

6 On competition for Western licences among CMEA countries see Yu. Naido and S. Simanovskii, 'Uchastie stran SEVa v mirovoi torgovle litsenzii', *Voprosy ekonomiki*, no. 3 (1975) especially p. 72.

7 Raymond Vernon and Marshall I. Goldman, as cited in Thomas A. Wolf, 'Preliminary Assessment of *US Policies in the Sale of Technology to the USSR* by Raymond Vernon and Marshall I. Goldman,' (mimeo, 1974).

8 See Thomas A. Wolf, 'The Impact of Formal Western Restraints on East–West Trade: An Assessment of Existing Quantitative Research' in John P. Hardt (ed.), *Tariff, Legal and Credit Constraints on East–West Commercial Relations* (Ottawa, 1975) and *idem.*, 'Progress in Removing Barriers to East–West Trade: An Assessment', paper presented to the Workshop on East–West European Economic Interaction, Session One (Vienna, October 1975).

9 C. W. Lawson, 'An Empirical Analysis of the Structure and Stability of Communist Foreign Trade 1960–68', *Soviet Studies* (April 1974).

10 See Lawrence Brainard in *East–West Markets* (12 January 1976) p. 10.

11 Raymond Vernon, 'Apparatchiks and Entrepreneurs: US–Soviet Economic Relations', *Foreign Affairs* (January 1974) especially p. 254.

12 For details see P. Hanson, 'The Import of Western Technology' in Archie Brown and Michael Kaser (eds), *The Soviet Union Since the Fall of Khrushchev* (London, 1975).

13 See note 7.

14 For evidence about the variation in transfer costs see E. Mansfield, 'International Technology Transfer: Forms, Resource Requirements and Policies', *American Economic Review* (May 1975) pp. 372–6.

15 R. Eidem, 'East–West Economic Cooperation – Some Informational Aspects', (Stockholm, mimeo, 1975) gives a convincing rationale for industrial cooperation on

grounds of information, and also raises some doubts about its prospects. Edward A. Hewett, 'The Economics of East European Technology Imports from the West', *American Economic Review,* (May 1975) pp. 377–82, tends to strengthen the doubts with evidence from Hungarian experience of industrial cooperation.
16 Naido and Simanovskii, *op. cit.,* and John W. Kiser, in a paper in *Foreign Policy* (June 1976).

Discussion of the Papers by Professor Wacker and Dr Hanson

Introducing the two papers, *Professor Lorenz* detected few points of contact between them. Commenting first on Professor Wacker's paper which, he noted, concentrated exclusively on Western barriers to East–West trade, he was struck by the weakening of the effect of even extreme formal tariff discrimination that could result from a 'saw-tooth' tariff and relatively high internal prices (p. 75). He also noted that, recently, competition in offering credit to their Eastern trading partners had resulted in the Western countries financing a part of the CMEA countries' deficits arising from the insufficient liberalisation of Western imports and, in particular, from the often unintentional increase in discrimination produced by measures to protect balances-of-payments. He thought that Wacker too readily dismissed the 'market disruption' case for import controls (p. 76); the low price imports subject to control were, in the main, those competing with limited areas of import-sensitive domestic production (textiles, shoes, etc.), and the impact of imports from socialist and developing countries together was often far from negligible.

In connection with trade in agricultural products, Professor Lorenz suggested that a case had been made for exploring unconventional, transitional methods of easing barriers to CMEA countries' agricultural exports by, first, the usefulness of the 'technical' contacts of some CMEA countries with the EEC (pp. 82–3) and, secondly, the pragmatic attitude of GATT to the admission of individual CMEA countries. He noted that agricultural exports to the EEC were still expanding despite discrimination, though dependence on West European markets did mean downward pressure on CMEA countries' export prices; the impact on East–West terms of trade of the USSR's import dependence on North American grain was more complicated.

Dr Hanson's paper, said Professor Lorenz, discussed some of the fundamental problems of East–West trade; and he proceeded first to underline Hanson's argument for the absence of any logical basis for a presumption that the short-run distribution of the benefits of East–West trade must be biased in favour of one side or the other. He noted particularly a lesser degree of dependency for the West balanced by the effects of oligopolistic competition in credit-granting; elements at once of conflict between state and enterprise and mutual support in both East and West, and doubts about the effective power of Eastern trade 'monopolies', given the often dubious nature of apparent Western price concessions and the evidence of Eastern low-price ('dumped') exports. In considering the question in its longer-term aspects, he wondered whether the balance of disadvantage to the socialist countries on the macroeconomic level (impact of market fluctuations and inflation in the West) and to the West on the microeconomic level (Soviet buying of corn, discontinuous imports by the East), as seen by Hanson, were really comparable. He thought that Hanson's argument on the balance of benefit from transfer of technology was probably the most controversial. It was not easy to offset the argument that transfer was a one-way street — invariably benefiting the buyer more than the seller — against that which saw the buyer facing a trade-off between conceding a monopoly profit to the seller and accepting long-run technological dependence.

Professor Lorenz secondly noted that Hanson's exploration of the, still open, question whether the constraints on East–West trade resulting from differences in the two systems were significantly eased by 'systemic comparative advantages' raised an explosive question: were the Eastern European countries using Western credits to establish hard-currency-earning productive capacity, which would permit repayment of outstanding debt *and* continuing East–West trade expansion, or were they on a course likely to lead to curtailment of trade? (p. 97).

Subsequent discussion turned on

   (i) the nature and implications for trade of the technology gap(s),
  (ii) systemic obstacles to East–West trade,
 (iii) the concept of equality of treatment.

Mr Kaser agreed that trade in technology could generate monopoly rent for the exporter; it was also interesting to note that differences in technology could reflect different resource endowments, and generate commodity trade. In a Ricardian three-factor model (natural resources, capital and labour) appropriately differing technologies combined the different factor-endowments of each country so as to maximise gains from trade. But different growth strategies could also be important; at present Czechoslovak exports were more resource-intensive than Austrian, partly because of Czechoslovakia's past strategy of extensive growth.

To this systemic cause of comparative advantage, and those noted by Hanson, *Professor McMillan* added differing sectoral priorities, leading to East–West differences in sectoral rates of technological advance. He preferred to see the phenomenon as one of two-way technological 'gaps', opening possibilities of mutually beneficial exchange, rather than a one-way 'lag' – a point stressed also by *Professor Maier* and *Professor Shmelyov*, though *Professor Holzman* suggested that the question whether there was an overall 'gap' might be answered by observing that water did not flow uphill, and technology transfer was mainly West to East; but no economy could be self-sufficient. On the possibility of systemic complementarities in the R&D field itself (p. 98) *Professor McMillan* suggested that while Eastern enterprises could offer large capacities for testing new technologies, Western firms could provide access to a flexible supply system and to facilities for rapid response of R&D to market demand.

On the question of the balance of advantage in transfer of technology, *Dr Hardt* suggested that the 'new-technology market' was an extremely competitive one; far from exploiting monopoly power, the seller was more concerned to enlarge his market and to finance an R&D programme that could develop as fast as the art allowed. *Professor Wenger* also saw payments for licences, etc., by the socialist countries as helping Western firms to expand their R&D activities, thus benefiting Western economies, while trade in goods often accompanied technology transfer; moreover, the buyer of the new technology took the whole risk of its not paying off in his particular circumstances.

Considering the broader question of systemic obstacles or stimuli to East–West trade, *Professor Rothschild* suggested that foreign trade had two functions: (i) long-term structural division of labour which, as Professor Rogge had said

(p. 41), required stable long-term relations; (ii) to permit marginal stabilising adjustments in a fluctuating economy — additional supplies in a boom, additional outlets in a recession. In relation to (ii), East—West trade was particularly valuable. Both systems were subject to instabilities — economic (and electoral) cycles in capitalist countries; cumulative developments related to planning phases in socialist countries (as analysed by Josef Goldman).* But these cycles do not coincide, which gives East—West trade a stabilising influence limited, however, by the small volume of the trade. *Dr Hardt* doubted whether recent experience should be interpreted as evidence of built-in extreme cyclical instability in the West; reactions to OPEC price increases and two years of bad weather and poor harvests explained a great deal. But *Professor Kohlmey* disagreed with both speakers and with Hanson's arguments on pp. 93—4; trade cycles, inflation, changes in exchange-rates and in competitiveness all made for instability in Western trade; in the Eastern countries development priorities changed from time to time, but there were no discontinuities in demand for broad categories of imports, such as capital goods, into the CMEA area as a whole.

Dr Nitz saw a need for stable inter-firm as well as inter-state trading relations. Eastern enterprises as importers were usually dealing with large Western firms but they were at a disadvantage as exporters in having usually to deal with small firms. To ease balance-of-payments constraints on trade, large Western exporters to Eastern Europe should be willing to accept and market Eastern exports. Joint market research should be undertaken by the Western importer and Eastern exporter. He also instanced tariff and quota discrimination by the EEC as major obstacles to trade. *Dr Rogge* agreed that such obstacles existed in the West, as they did also in the East, in fact if not in form; but he suggested that the CMEA countries often failed to produce goods of a quality fully to exploit the sales opportunities they had. To this *Professor Wolf* added that many Western countries had eliminated import restrictions on just those sophisticated, high-technology goods which several of the participants from the Eastern countries had insisted ought to form a larger part of the trade flow from East to West. Empirical evidence pointed to considerable ability in some of the socialist countries to exploit such opportunities (i.e. some price-response to the lowering of barriers had been observed); but it also showed that where, in the short or medium term, CMEA exporters had succeeded in increasing their market shares, this had often been in markets for goods with relatively low income-elasticity of demand in the West, so that, over a longer period, the overall shares of the CMEA countries in markets for the more sophisticated manufactures did not increase. They thus appeared to be diversifying too much or concentrating on the 'wrong' goods — price-elastic rather than income-elastic products.

Professor Lavigne questioned the relevance of the usual microeconomic distinctions of monopoly, oligopoly, monopsony, etc., when applied to East—West trade. It was, in effect, in the hands of monopolies or oligopolistic firms

* J. Goldman, 'Fluctuations and Trend in the Rate of Economic Growth in Some Socialist Countries', *Economics of Planning* Vol. 4, No. 2 (1964) pp. 88—98; and 'Fluctuations in the Growth Rate in a Socialist Economy and the Inventory Cycle' in M. Bronfenbrenner (ed.), *Is the Business Cycle Obsolete?* (London and New York, 1969) pp. 332—49.

on both sides, the only difference being the fringe of — usually not directly involved — small and medium sub-contractors in the West who were missing in the East. *Professor Kohlmey* questioned Hanson's reference to Eastern export prices as being 'bound to seem arbitrary in relation to Western domestic costs and prices' (pp. 92—3; Hanson had not said why they should seem arbitrar or in what sense. In the West many costs (e.g. government-financed R&D) were not borne by capitalist firms and transfer-pricing by multinationals was a recognised problem. Why should prices fixed in socialist countries so as to promote their objectives of industrial or agricultural development be regarded as any more arbitrary than those fixed in another system in accordance with its nature and objectives?

Two participants referred back to the previous day's discussion of East—West relations in a North—South context. *Professor Wolf* said that the OECD discussions on the 'rules of the game' of export credit referred to by Professor Wacker (p. 79) had been superceded by negotiations in 1975/76 in which the distinctions between groups of recipient countries were no longer drawn in terms of 'Western industrial', 'socialist' and 'developing' but rather 'advanced' (in terms of *per capita* income), a middle group and 'developing', irrespective of social system. This was some small advance towards integrating the question of East—West relations into the world-wide economic development problem. *Dr Jacobsen* raised the more general question of the meaning of 'equality' of treatment. Was it enough to ask, as Wacker did, for the abolition of tariff and non-tariff barriers to trade? Free trade in a world of widely differing national levels of development tended to intensify those differences rather than eradicate them. Were the socialist countries taking this into account in determining their plans and policies? It was to be hoped so, and that they were preparing to take a far more active part in future in determining a new world economic order.

Replying to the discussion, *Professor Wacker* reiterated his belief that the dismantling of Western barriers to the expansion of East—West trade was of first priority; there must follow energetic exploration of new possibilities and new forms of long-term inter-governmental and inter-firm cooperation which could expand trade in manufactures. But the dismantling of EEC barriers to imports of agricultural products would still be essential if the maximum benefits from East—West trade were to be realised.

Dr Hanson said that he would confine his reply only to points on which there had appeared to be misunderstanding or disagreement. In reply to Dr Hardt, he thought that the link between technical change and some degree of monopoly power was fairly well established. Referring to Professor Kohlmey's observations on his references to instabilities in East—West trade, he thought there was little real disagreement between them. Professor Vernon's argument, which he had cited, was that for systemic reasons technical change was likely to be more discrete and lumpy in the East than in the West, largely because of the relatively greater importance of small, incremental adaptations of machinery and processes in the West; and he thought the case plausible though not empirically proven. This was a rather different point from that of changes in branch-wise investment patterns but, in any case, he agreed that abrupt changes in the pattern of Eastern imports of equipment and know-how were not incompatible with prospects for long-term expansion of the trade in total. He also thought that Professor Kohlmey's reference to differing price systems indicated a disagreement more apparent than real; he certainly would never describe either as 'objectively necessary' (a phrase he thought Kohlmey had used) but the two price systems were different, intrinsically related to the two economic systems of which each was a part and unlikely to be radically altered in the near future.

In reply to Professor Lavigne, Dr Hanson thought any contrast between competitive conditions in the West and monopoly in the East, in the East–West trade context, was unrealistic on both sides. There appeared to be some difference of opinion in the Conference on the empirical question whether small and medium-sized firms in the West played a significant role in East–West relations and this was a question worth empirical investigation. Finally, he confirmed by a question answered by Professor Shmelyov that the latter's reference during the discussion to a larger flow of licence sales from the USSR to the USA than in the opposite direction in recent years referred to numbers, not value; this was interesting in relation to Professor Holzman's reference to water not running uphill.

7 Effects of the European Economic Communities and the Council for Mutual Economic Assistance on East–West Economic Relations

E. S. Kirschen

UNIVERSITÉ LIBRE DE BRUXELLES

I INTRODUCTION

One of the fundamental tendencies of the politico-economic evolution in Europe during the third quarter of the twentieth century has been the integration of states within larger units, including the transfer of important economic policy instruments from a national level to a higher level (for instance, to a customs or a monetary union).

In the West the formation of Benelux, of the European Coal and Steel Community (ECSC) and of the European Economic Community (EEC) are undoubtedly examples of integration; the Organisation for Economic Co-operation and Development (OECD), the International Monetary Fund (IMF) or the North Atlantic Treaty Organisation (NATO), for examples, are not. In the East, the nature of the Council for Mutual Economic Assistance (CMEA) is somewhat less easy to define in these terms. Its role was initially restricted to a modest coordinating one, and it was only when the 'Comprehensive Programme' was adopted that the term 'integration' could describe both principle and fact. But to simplify this paper, the CMEA will be considered to have been an instrument of integration since its creation in 1949.

This tendency towards integration – a kind of organisation of the world that I consider to represent, on balance, progress – is not the only motivating concept of our times. It has developed within a context including other important preoccupations which have led to the creation of world or regional institutions – with financial and commercial aims, with military aims, with the aim of safeguarding peace.

I will devote the second part of this study to these three categories of institutions, as their existence influences and restricts the methods and the speed of integration. I have, however, excluded from the study other ideas, and related institutions, which only slightly affect European integration – for example, decolonisation, aid to underdeveloped countries and cultural relations.

I shall then examine (in Section III) the main characteristics of European integration in the West and in the East and evaluate the consequences of the Common Market for the growth of the EEC countries and, indirectly, for that of the CMEA countries. The complementary question — the influence of the CMEA on the growth of its members and of the West — could be dealt with by a socialist colleague, either during or after this Round Table. It would also be very interesting to assess the effects on growth of a closer coordination of the plans of the socialist countries.

I will finally examine (in Section IV) the interactions in Europe between the movements and institutions of integration, including an assessment of the relationship to be established between the EEC and the CMEA.

II THE PLACE OF EUROPEAN INTEGRATION IN THE WORLD

I will limit myself here to those institutions whose activities reflect the main preoccupations of our era; and for further details I refer those interested to an article I published in 1972[1] and to a chapter from a collective work published in 1975.[2]

THE WORLD FINANCIAL AND COMMERCIAL INSTITUTIONS

Their first gestation period began during the great economic crisis of 1929—35 and concluded with the tripartite agreement in 1936 between the United States of America, Great Britain and France, aiming to halt the depreciation of currencies. Though other European countries had endorsed the agreement, it had no future, because of inflation in France and, somewhat later, the beginning of hostilities. But during the war discussions restarted in ideal circumstances (for the negotiation of an agreement, of course) essentially between two Allied powers, the United States and Great Britain, who spoke the same language and who, thanks to the war, were subject to minimal pressure from their interest groups and had years ahead of them. The chain of events began in 1942 with the Atlantic Charter and ended with the birth of healthy financial twins (IMF and IBRD) in 1946 and, in 1948, that of a more fragile child who was given the strange name of General Agreement on Tariffs and Trade (GATT).

Little by little other powers were consulted, including the USSR and Free France, but the final result was essentially an Anglo-Saxon one, reflecting the balance of forces of those days: 90 per cent American and 10 per cent British. The philosophy embodied in these institutions reflected mainly the empiricism of the Western financial and commercial negotiators, tempered by a general sentiment rather in favour of free trade. The problems and the interests of the USSR (there was no other socialist country in 1942) and underdeveloped countries (this term had not yet been coined, and one still spoke of Colonies) were hardly discussed. But there has been some change during the last ten years. Four countries of Eastern Europe (but not the USSR) are at present members of GATT — a Western club that had not been created with them in mind – and one of them has also been admitted to the IMF. Their views thus receive some support within these institutions, though their influence remains weak.

Perhaps one day we will see efficient financial and commercial institutions which will be truly universal, but their elaboration will be slow, partly for ideological reasons, but mainly because of the number, the diversity and the differing demands of the countries which would want to take part in them.

THE EUROPEAN AND ATLANTIC MILITARY INSTITUTIONS

A survey of monetary and financial institutions leaves one with an impression of asymmetry between West and East. Military institutions are very different: changing from initially antagonistic relations to a degree of complementarity.

The great anti-German alliance of 1941 did not last much beyond the end of the war. The year 1948 saw the beginning of the Marshall Plan and of the Organisation for European Economic Cooperation (OEEC), open in theory to all those European countries that wanted to accelerate their economic revival through 'self-aid, mutual aid and American aid'. The socialist countries decided, however, that these institutions were to some extent directed against them, or against their ideologies and their economic systems; they refused to participate and, in the same year, created the Council for Mutual Economic Assistance (CMEA), partly as an answer to the OEEC and partly to fulfil certain commercial and economic functions that the West had delegated to the IMF (settlement and credit systems) and to the GATT.

It was the following year that the North Atlantic Treaty Organisation (NATO) was born, comprising the United States, Canada and most of the OEEC countries, because of fears created in the West by the first 'Prague coup'; and it was given new impetus in 1950 by the outbreak of the Korean war. In its turn, the existence of NATO made the Eastern countries conclude their treaty of 'friendship, cooperation and mutual assistance', better known as the Warsaw Pact (1955). Its aim was military and its creation coincided with enhanced economic and commercial activity by the CMEA (see below).

Although political tensions between Eastern Europe and the Atlantic powers have decreased during the 1960s, the share of its GNP spent by Europe for its 'defence' has decreased only slowly. Each of the two rival institutions has used the size of the other's armed forces to justify its own requests for men and equipment. One can, in this instance, generalise Galbraith's concept of technostructure to institutions theoretically antagonistic but in fact supporting each other.[3]

WORLD INSTITUTIONS FOR THE SAFEGUARDING OF PEACE

East–West relations are not limited to trade, payments and to armed forces; they also include a third aspect, namely the search for peace through diplomatic negotiations.

The idea of a 'directorate' of the five major countries goes back to the end of the Napoleonic wars (1815) when the four Allied Powers (Great Britain, Russia, Austria, Prussia) rapidly joined by France, created a system, unfair in many respects, which had nevertheless the enormous merit that it prevented wars between its members for a little over forty years. The League of Nations (1920) showed itself more egalitarian but less efficient, whereas the United Nations Organisation (1946) tried to reconcile the resurrection of a five-member directorate with a General Assembly expanding to 150 countries. Its actions have been hampered by its size, by slanging matches between many of its members and by the ideological cleavage, which became immediately apparent within the Security Council, between the only two countries of dominating power and influence. In this institution the divergencies between Eastern and Western Europe are often underlined and even magnified; but one must nevertheless give it credit for the solution of some conflicts, apparently minor, but which could have escalated. In 1976 it is difficult to conceive of a world which would forgo such a forum for discussion and, sometimes, negotiation.

III THE EUROPEAN INSTITUTIONS OF INTEGRATION

THEIR ORIGIN

The concept of European integration is both very old and very new. It was formulated in 1305 by a lawyer from Normandy, Pierre Dubois, who proposed the creation of a European state and the proposal was often reiterated during subsequent centuries, for example, by Charles V and by Napoleon. More recently, European integration was advocated by Aristide Briand and by Coudenhove-Kalergi.

Common traits have for centuries linked the Europeans: geographical proximity, Caucasian race, Indo-European language, Greek civilisation, Christian doctrine. The present geo-political structure makes the European states, with the exception of the USSR, second-class powers, though two others (France and Britain) have a right of veto in the UN Security Council. Their territories are small and the most populous states have only half the population of Japan or Brazil, or a quarter of that of the United States.

INTEGRATION IN THE WEST

Its origins can be traced back to the forced leisure of the Belgian and Dutch Governments in Exile in London during the Second World War: old animosities were buried and the creation of Benelux was made possible as early as 1948. Two years later Robert Schuman suggested a Franco–German reconciliation, based on the abolition of the obstacles to trade in the heavy-industry products considered as vital during the First World War – coal and steel.

The European Economic Community (EEC) dates from 1957, though

Great Britain and two other countries joined only at the beginning of the present decade. Despite some failures and many disappointments (the European Defence Community, for example), the integration process was very rapid when compared with the German and Italian unifications of the last century, or with those of France and Switzerland previously. There are five main reasons for this:

(a) the fact that the territory of each of the six had been invaded and totally occupied between 1940 and 1945, which proved the futility of intra-European wars;

(b) the obvious impossibility for some European countries to regain individually their former great-power status — except in the eyes of the few who still treasured illusions;

(c) the fear, especially in the Stalinist era, of Soviet domination;

(d) a little later, a few blunders by the United States in its relations with Europe, for example, during the Suez and the Vietnam wars and at the end of the 1960s, in obliging the European central banks to hold large quantities of inconvertible dollars;[4]

(e) the wish to accelerate economic growth through the creation of a large market similar in size to that of the United States.

INTEGRATION IN THE EAST

The basic motivations for integration in the East — security, solidarity and growth — probably do not differ very much from those in the West, but the immediate causes were very different.

(a) The traditional economic relations with Western Europe were shattered by the 1917 Revolution, by the war and, finally, by the complete change of economic regime that followed, sooner or later, the Soviet presence in the other countries of Eastern Europe. A desire to escape the consequences of fluctuations in world markets should also be mentioned.

(b) This isolation was aggravated by the bilateralism in commercial relations adopted in the East as well as by the restrictions imposed in Western Europe on exports to socialist countries — although the severity of this embargo has often been contested, by Z. Frank-Ossipoff among others.[5]

(c) Furthermore the East had to build from scratch a counterpart to the financial and commercial institutions which already existed in Western Europe, as part of the world-wide system.

(d) The CMEA statutes were only published a few years after its creation.

(e) Finally, integration in the West — at first attacked, if not denied, in the East — was acknowledged as a fact; and it is to some extent by a process of imitation that there developed the concept of a complex programme including in its title the term 'integration'.*

* I have not discovered any influence of Eastern integration on Western integration

THE SIMILARITIES

(a) ECONOMIC DEVELOPMENT
Nearly all the nations of Eastern and Western Europe have attained comparable development levels, based on very similar technologies; the average difference between East and West in real product *per capita* does not exceed a fifteen-year increment; i.e. approximately the gap between Europe and the United States.

(b) GENERAL AIMS
Most of the aims of general policy in European societies are also very similar, as is shown by Table 9, which summarises official texts (constitutions, laws, political declarations).

If differences in formulation are ignored (the terms used in the East are usually longer), the only important divergences occur in the concepts of 'improvement of the social order' and of 'ethical values', where no convergence can be detected: convictions remain fixed on both sides.

(c) THE OVERALL PATTERN
The pathway chosen for economic integration is, on both sides, that of developing trade and other exchanges even though the main objective is, yet again in the East as in the West, the acceleration of growth.

THE DIFFERENCES

(a) GEOGRAPHICAL
Unlike the USA, the USSR is situated in Europe. Consequently there exists a defensive reaction in the small countries of Eastern Europe facing economic integration, caused not by ideological divergences, but by the fear of seeing their national identities disappear following their intimate association with a very large and very powerful partner with a strong culture. In the West, no country — neither France intellectually nor Germany economically — can really impose itself on the others, and the dangers of a Franco—German condominium have been lessened by the presence of Britain. The United States has supported the initial stages of European integration, and even if it occasionally finds Europe not very docile, it does not seem afraid to assume the role of the sorcerer's apprentice. Of course there remain many points of friction in Western Europe, but fear of absorption is still a very minor factor, except perhaps in Scandinavia and Switzerland.

(b) INSTITUTIONAL FRAMEWORK
The fact that integration in the East is occurring within a socialist framework implies instruments unknown in the West — coordination of five-year and one-

TABLE 9 AVOWED POLICY AIMS IN THE WEST AND IN THE EAST

Shortened wording	Detailed Western wording	Detailed Eastern wording
Internal aims		
1 Material welfare	Rising standard of living	Continuous improvement in the living conditions of working people and in the satisfaction of their personal and social needs.
2 Development of personality	Opportunity to develop individual abilities to the full	Creation of conditions for opportunities and freedom for the comprehensive development of man as an emancipated human being.
3 Equity and equality	Equal treatment before the law	Equality in rights and duties regardless of differences in nationality, race, religion, language, education or social position. Equal treatment before the law or in other administrative proceedings of the state.
4 Individual freedom	Freedom of speech, expression and association	Attainment of human and civil freedom and rights. Establishment of equal democratic relations among citizens.
5 Solidarity	Reduction in tensions between different racial, ethnic, religious, linguistic, occupational and age groups	Strengthening of solidarity among working people and cooperation between people in work and in social life. Elimination of socio-economic differences between various groups (national, education, professional, etc.).
6 Law and order	Preservation of law and order	Protection and development of the socialist system of society. Protection of constitutional order and the equal socio-economic status of working people.
7 Improvement of the social order	Preservation and improvement of the free enterprise system	Building up and development of a socialist society. Humanisation of social relations. Elimination of all forms of exploitation.
8 Ethical values	Safeguarding of morals and religion	Enhancing the socialist consciousness of individuals based on the mutual cooperation of people and the implementation of the norms of the socialist way of life.
External aims		
9 Peace and security	Defence against foreign aggression, including support for collective security arrangements and other international organisations	Defence of the socialist societies from foreign aggression by mutual assistance and support, including collective security arrangements. Peaceful coexistence and avoidance of force in settling international disputes. International cooperation for safeguarding peace.
10 International solidarity	Wish to help other countries in need	Socialist internationalism. Mutual support between socialist countries to build and develop socialist society. Supporting friendly nations and helping economic and social progress in less developed countries. Support for national liberation movements and the fight against colonialism.

Shortened wording	Detailed Western wording	Detailed Eastern wording
11 Power, prestige, respectability	Power for the large nations Prestige and influence for the middle-sized ones Respectability for the small ones	Respectability in international relations. Demonstration of the achievements of the socialist system in economic, social, political and military respects.

Source: Kirschen, Blackaby, Csapo, Kamecki, Kestens[6]

year plans, ranging from a superplan common to all socialist countries (a possibility but not yet a fact) to a simple agreement that all national plans should cover the same period; a more modest coordination, covering trade, production, research and some joint ventures. And coordination in these four areas, successively, seems to have been practised during the past fifteen years.

On the other hand, the West has been able to create truly supranational institutions (though recourse to a majority vote in the EEC Council remains very rare): the best examples of this are the choice of a single negotiator in the Kennedy Round of GATT, the Common Agricultural Policy and the free movement of manpower. One must admit that the term 'supranational' still arouses emotive reactions, especially on the extreme left in Britain; and this is why its use has been avoided, supporters of European federation preferring to concentrate on practical achievement.

In the East, this stage has not yet been reached — for instance, in the three areas just mentioned; on the contrary, there is frequent insistence on the deep respect for national sovereignties in economic matters. As a consequence, no decision taken within the framework of the CMEA is directly binding on its member countries. Moreover, up to now, this institution has not established any common commercial policy, either in setting objectives (overall foreign trade, visible balance of trade) or in determining instruments (customs duties, quantitative restrictions, administrative obstacles to international trade, incentives for trade); neither has it adopted any common agricultural policy.

This situation does not prevent the secretariat of the CMEA from publicising the progress achieved or from seeking, just like the EEC Commission, to extend its power and prestige.

THE CONSEQUENCES OF THE COMMON MARKET FOR THE ECONOMIC GROWTH RATES OF ITS MEMBERS AND OF THE CMEA COUNTRIES

I now broach a concrete problem, which needs recourse to econometrics. I shall leave aside the controversy over trade-creation or trade-diversion, upon which must has been written but which I consider as now outdated. Instead I have chosen to consider the contribution of the Common Market (which is of course only part of the achievements of the EEC) to the economic growth of its members, and indirectly to that of other countries.

This problem was first discussed in 1960, in the report of a study group created by the European Coal and Steel Community,[7] which found an acceleration of the order of 0·5 per cent per annum.

Later works enable us to reach the assessments below, but we must first register a warning: in economic analysis, the adage *post hoc ergo propter hoc*, cannot easily be applied.

On the subject of the CMEA, Z. Kamecki states that 'Multilateral economic cooperation among the CMEA States is closely tied up with their bilateral cooperation. It is not possible to draw a sharp line between those problems of cooperation which are dealt with solely within the CMEA and those which are dealt with bilaterally.'[8] Similarly in the case of the EEC, according to J. Waelbroeck,[9]

> In order to assess the effect of an economic policy decision one ought to be able to compare what happens if this decision is taken with what happens if it is not. This would be easy if it were true, as imagined by Pierre Daninos, that there exist, next to our world, an infinite number of anti-worlds in each of which all the events except one are those which we have known. The astronomers would seek the anti-world identical to ours except that the Rome negotiations failed. Then it would only remain to build a telescope powerful enough to decipher statistical data at very long distances, and compare trade in that world and in ours.

Finally, E. Denison, in his study of causes of economic growth[10] attributes 50–70 per cent of the total recorded to non-measured sources and errors and omissions.

Subject to these limitations one can identify four consequences of the Common Market.

The first, and the most important, results from economies of scale: a large motor-car factory is more productive than two small ones, and the greater part of modern industry (but not necessarily agriculture) benefits from decreasing costs. On this subject, Denison estimated that for the six countries of the EEC, during the period 1955–62 (unfortunately his studies stop there) economies of scale produced growth of the order of 0·45 per cent per annum. Taking into account the entry of Great Britain (Ireland and Denmark can have practically no effect) and some exhaustion of earlier possibilities, we could round off, for the 1970s, to 0·5 per cent per annum.

A second source of acceleration of growth is specialisation, resulting from the fact that the countries of the Common Market did not all possess the same initial natural advantages. France has hydroelectric potential, Germany a powerful chemical industry, Great Britain atomic reactors and a whole network of financial (including insurance) services. Denison's figure of 0·1 per cent per annum can be raised to 0·15 per cent.

A third advantage of the Common Market arises from its weight in international negotiations. To take as an example relations with the United States: the tactics of the EEC have largely consisted in opposing the interests of Americans who want to export or import to those of other Americans who are hostile to imports. We can say that this factor — weight in international negotiations — is probably responsible for an acceleration of growth of 0·15 per cent per annum.

Fourthly, the fact that the market is larger means that industrialists cannot so easily rest on their laurels or shelter behind their agreements; livelier competition, stimulated by the anti-cartel and anti-monopoly activities of the Commission, leads to higher investment and consequently to a faster growth rate. This is probably worth 0·1 per cent per annum nowadays.

The sum of the consequences of the Common Market (including the policing of this market) would therefore be an acceleration of growth of 0·50 + 0·15 + 0·15 + 0·10 = 0·90 percentage points per annum.

The income elasticity of imports of the EEC countries from those of the CMEA is probably of the order of 1·10–1·25. Thus these imports have increased, simply on account of this faster growth in Western Europe, by about 1 per cent per annum. There is similarly an increase of imports by the CMEA countries from the EEC zone.

The preceding calculations incorporate the effects of that part of the reductions in tariffs negotiated within the framework of GATT (Dillon Round and Kennedy Round) which would not have occurred without the EEC. One must add that the products exported by the Eastern countries are becoming increasingly refined and thus improve the overall quality of production (e.g. in Poland, according to Bozyk and Gora).[11] But any further extension of these calculations would require a knowledge of the production functions of the Eastern countries.

IV INTERACTIONS BETWEEN THE EUROPEAN INTEGRATION INSTITUTIONS

THE EEC AND THE EASTERN COUNTRIES TAKEN INDIVIDUALLY

The Treaty of Rome established the principle of a Common Commercial Policy for the Community as a whole, and has entrusted to the Commission all negotiations in this field, including bilateral or multilateral trade agreements with third countries (Article 113 of the Treaty). To this end, the Commission formulates proposals for such negotiations and receives from the Council, on each occasion, a more or less precise mandate.

Initially (in 1957), the Treaty of Rome was greeted with hostility by the Soviet Union, perhaps out of fear of Germany, perhaps with the aim of hindering the political revival of Europe advocated by the United States and perhaps, finally, because she, like Great Britain, did not believe in the possibility of economic integration in Western Europe. According to an article signed with the initials LK,[12] Mikoyan stated on 23 October, 1959, 'The USSR is opposed to economic blocs that are not destined to a great future and represent the remains of the cold war.' This reflects a basic principle underlying Soviet diplomacy, which strives to prevent any union of Western countries and believes that any agreement between these countries represents *de facto* a threat to Soviet interests. All declarations made by Western statesmen concerning the need for the free world to unite in the face of communist advances are thus underlined by the press of Eastern countries and taken as proof that any kind of political, economic, commercial or customs union is part of a general plan directed against the socialist camp.

The same year, however, the review *Mirovaja Ekonomikai* published an article by Arzoumanian, according to whom 'the European integration corresponds to a new phase of capitalism and follows a double aim: on the one hand, to combat the world-wide socialist system, the democratic forces within Eastern Europe and the movements for national liberation and, on the other, to fight to reinforce the influence of an integrated Europe in the capitalist world and to redistribute markets.' Arzoumanian concluded by underlining the importance of the Common Market, 'a real fact which it is impossible not to take into account'.

In 1962, Khruschev stated his position in the review *Kommunist*. He admitted that 'the tendency of capitalist countries to unify their economies and their foreign policy is being considerably reinforced', and added: 'in spite of all the contradictions that exist within them, the leaders of the Western world have occasionally been able to create groupings of states, which engender difficulties for the young and still weak countries of Asia, Africa, and Latin-America.'

However, one had to wait until March 1972 for Mr Brezhnev to recognise the reality of Europe; this brought about favourable reactions from the Commission of the EEC, and later from the Conference of the Heads of States and Government of the Nine. The initiative then passed from the USSR to the secretariat of the CMEA (see below).

Meanwhile, representatives of the Commission had taken part — in the name of the Customs Union of the Six and later of the Nine — in the negotiations preceding the accession of Hungary, Poland and Romania to the GATT. In another field, 'technical discussions' took place between the Commission of the EEC and the socialist countries mentioned above, as well as Bulgaria, in order to allow the import of their agricultural products by the West without excessive imposts. Finally, contacts between the EEC and some Eastern countries took place in the framework of international negotiations, for example, those concerned with possible renewal of the Wheat Agreement.

On a more general level, the Final Act of the Helsinki Conference was signed by the President of the Council of the Community, as such.

THE EEC AND THE CMEA – THE PAST AND THE PRESENT

Relations between the two integration institutions began in 1973 with an unofficial approach by the Secretary of the CMEA, not to the Commission of the EEC but to the President of the Council. A month later the Council answered that contacts must be made with the Commission and, in 1974, 'The Council declares that the EEC is prepared to negotiate new trade agreements with the Eastern countries to replace the bilateral agreements of the member countries.'

In October of the same year the Commission sent the outline of a trade agreement, not to the CMEA (with which it had no official contacts), but to each of its member countries. These did not react (except for one) but it transpired that they wished to negotiate collectively via the CMEA.

In February 1975 the first official talks between representatives of the EEC Commission and of the CMEA Secretariat took place but they ended in confusion.[13] The EEC side sought to identify fields of competence common to both institutions, whereas the CMEA side wished to limit themselves to a meeting between the senior officials of both institutions, as a first step towards further negotiation.

Nothing happened for a further year; then in February 1976 the President of the Executive Committee of the CMEA handed to the President of the EEC Council the draft of an agreement between the two institutions. According to *The Economist*,[14]

> The Comecon proposals are so cleverly drafted that even to start talking about them could prove something of a trap for the EEC. Ambiguities abound. The most striking thing about the draft is that Comecon does not actually propose to recognise the EEC and its institutions. The Community as a whole would be treated as holding only those powers enjoyed also by Comecon's secretariat in Moscow, covering standardisation, statistics, forecasting and so on. The proposals also envisage the mutual granting of most-favoured-nation treatment, although it does not spell out how this would benefit the Community. A separate article puts forward plans for generalised preferences for Cuba, Mongolia and possibly also Bulgaria. On important matters like trade negotiations, the draft relegates the Community as a body to a purely technical, advisory capacity. Its general aim appears to be a return to bilateralism – the position before the EEC's common commercial policy towards Comecon came into force in 1975. This is clearly unacceptable to the Community, though nobody knows yet how far the draft merely represents a negotiating position.

Perhaps *The Economist* is right and the CMEA plan is only the prelude to a long and laborious negotiation. The Western side seems influenced by the following considerations among others: the fact that even in the absence of bilateral or multilateral trade agreements, East–West exchanges take place fairly normally;* the importance of the financial indebtedness of some Eastern countries; the wish, in the context of a world of political and military rivalries,

---

* The agreements signed between CMEA as a whole and a few outside countries (Finland, Mexico, Iraq) do not appear to be very far-reaching.

not to reinforce in any way the cohesion of the East or the influence of the USSR on her allies; the problem of giving effect to the results of the negotiations — the West cannot easily make their private sectors buy and sell, and the CMEA has very little authority over its member states.*

Finally, one must add that the pre-negotiation between the member countries of the EEC, of a trade agreement with an outside country — be it socialist, capitalist or underdeveloped — is frequently a laborious operation, because national interests must be coordinated. Furthermore, an agreement with a CMEA country sometimes poses delicate political problems in the larger countries of the EEC.

At present, the EEC is studying the proposal of the CMEA,[15] to see whether it is compatible with the Rome Treaty and with its own proposal to make individual trade agreements with each of the socialist countries; and this study also reflects a wish not to interrupt what to the uninitiated observer appears to be a dialogue of the deaf.

THE EEC AND THE CMEA – THE FUTURE

After the Helsinki Conference it is difficult to imagine the Eastern and Western integration institutions appearing to offer competing inducements to any state to join one or the other. They are too different. The differences are partly ideological (though ideology does not prevent all economic links between their respective members) and partly reflect the political and military cleavage.

In the field which interests us here, the concern for immediate or short-term political gain still dominates and relations between the integration movements are characterised above all by suspicion. But things may not always be so, and this for three reasons — listed here in order of increasing generality:

(a) Enterprises, private in the West and public in the East, must be able to *organise their purchases, their sales, their production and their research*, with a sufficient time horizon. At present, most of the trade agreements have run out, and this has not brought about any catastrophe; but there must inevitably be a slowing down of exchanges if these do not take place within a simultaneously multinational (in the case of principles and agreements on quantities) and bilateral (in the case of the detailed trade bargains) framework. Otherwise some potential complementarities between East and West will remain simply wasted opportunities.

(b) Integration — an irreversible trend towards a point of no return (in the Western vocabulary) or a historical trend (in that of the East) — presupposes *an increase in the power of the central organs*, the EEC Commission and the CMEA Secretariat. It is not in their interest to

* I mention here, only as a reminder, the specific agreements, more and more numerous, concerning loans, patents and joint ventures. These agreements between Eastern countries and Western firms are analysed by other members of the Round Table.

play second fiddle in a world diplomatic and strategic Conference led by the Foreign Offices. Each will rather be interested in justifying an extension of its own functions by reference to those granted to its homologue and rival – following the fairly successful example of those heading NATO and the Warsaw Pact, and other institutions to either side of these.

(c) Finally, to end where we began, *the world's systems of both payments and trade* must be rethought within a new framework, different from that at the end of the Second World War. The first task – reform of the payments system – is the more urgent; the second is both more difficult and more important. It is no longer possible for two or three countries to negotiate new world systems, as in 1942, but negotiations between all the members of the UN, large, medium, small and tiny, are unthinkable. The new system can only be set up by a small number of countries, the other countries confiding the task to them. One can imagine an optimum number of negotiators somewhat below ten. The Europe of the Six proved, during the Kennedy Round, that it can trust a single negotiator and Eastern Europe is certainly capable of finding a similar solution.

To the numerous reasons supporting integration in both parts of Europe, one can therefore add the need to contribute to the organisation of a polycentric world.

NOTES

1 E. S. Kirschen, 'Uberlegungen zur Wirtschaftlichen Integration in West und Ost-Europa', *Annalen der Gemeinwirtschaft*, vol. 2, (1972).
2 E. S. Kirschen, and associates, *Economic Policies Compared* (Amsterdam, 1974) vol. II, Chapter VIII.
3 J. K. Galbraith, *The New Industrial State* (New York, 1968).
4 E. S. Kirschen, *Le Seigneuriage Américain*, Société Universitaire Européene de Recherche Financiere (Tilburg, 1975).
5 Z. Frank-Ossipoff, in *Economic Policies Compared* (*op. cit.*), vol. II, Chapter X.
6 See (2), vol. I, Chapter I.
7 Communauté Européenne du Charbon et de l'Acier, Office Statistique des Communautés Européennes, 'Methodes de prévision du développement économique à long terme', *Informations Statistiques*, No. 6, (1960).
8 Z. Kamecki, in *Economic Policies Compared* (*op. cit.*) vol. II, Chapters IX and X.
9 J. Waelbroeck, 'Le Commerce de la Communauté Européenne avec les pays tiers', in Collège d'Europe, *Intégration Européenne et realité économique* (Bruges, 1964).
10 E. F. Denison, *Why Growth Rates Differ* (Washington, 1967).
11 P. Bozyk and S. Gora, in *Economic Policies Compared*, (*op. cit.*), vol. II, Chapter VII.
12 L. K. in *Revue du Socialisme Pluraliste*, No. 1 (1963).
13 *Le Monde*, (10 February 1975).
14 'Eastern Mysteries', *The Economist* (22 May 1976); 'Quand Moscou fait des avances à la CEE', *Journal de Genève* (22 March 1976).
15 'Les Neuf ont entamé l'examen du projet d'accord entre la CEE et le COMECON', *Europe* (10 and 11 May 1976); 'Accords de coopération avec les pays de l'Est: discrétion du Conseil et de la Commission', *Europe* (14 May 1976).

8 The Role of the European Communities and the Council for Mutual Economic Assistance in Promoting Economic Relations between East and West*

M. V. Senin

INTERNATIONAL INSTITUTE FOR ECONOMIC PROBLEMS OF THE WORLD SOCIALIST SYSTEM, CMEA

Economic relations between countries of East and West produce results beneficial to the countries of both the CMEA and the EEC. If we look at the history of such economic relations we may note their evolution from simple towards more complex forms; and this evolution has contributed to an increase in both their volume and their effectiveness.

I THE EVOLUTIONARY CHARACTER OF EAST–WEST ECONOMIC RELATIONS AND THEIR ECONOMIC EFFECTIVENESS

Economic interrelations between socialist states and capitalist countries based on a principle of mutual benefit produce, in general, results which indeed benefit both groups of countries.

It must be stressed that changes in the political climate and the progress now apparent in the field of military détente have brought about favourable pre-conditions for closer and wider-ranging economic relations between countries with differing social systems. In the period when we were balanced on the brink of military confrontation and at the peak of the Cold War, the scale and content of East–West economic cooperation were of no great economic significance to individual countries. In that period East–West trade in commodities developed only slowly; and rates of growth of intra-trade among the EEC countries, just as among CMEA member countries, considerably exceeded the increase in turnover between countries of the two different socio-economic systems.†

As tensions have been relaxed in recent years the progressive development

---

* The full text of Professor Senin's contribution was not available to participants in the Conference, though a summary had been circulated [Ed.].

† Thus, the average annual rates of increase in the value of mutual trade of CMEA member countries in the five years 1951–5 exceeded 13 per cent while the annual increase of trade of CMEA countries with developed capitalist countries amounted to about 8·5 per cent.

of all forms of economic cooperation has gradually gathered momentum. In particular, there may be noted the development of trade in licences and know-how, of industrial cooperation, of compensatory deals, etc. Western countries created, and in a certain sense were compelled to create, more favourable conditions for commodity trade with socialist countries, which is still the main form of mutual economic relations.* Today's problems include those of making foreign trade relations more effective and assuring their longer-term stability as well as of improving their structure and balance.

The structure of trade with their West European partners, as it has developed up to the present, is unfavourable to the socialist countries. Machinery, equipment and means of transport make up over 50 per cent of the imports of socialist countries from capitalist states, while the share of the same group of products in the exports of CMEA countries to EEC countries amounts to about 10 per cent, with over 50 per cent being comprised by raw materials and foodstuffs. It is natural that this kind of commodity structure should not satisfy CMEA member countries; and further rapid industrial development of CMEA member countries will significantly increase this dissatisfaction if the West is not prepared soon to change its policy towards the structure of trade with socialist states. Thus it is already a matter of urgency that the two groups of trade partners should elaborate, and harmonise, measures aimed at making the commodity structure of the two trade-flows more similar to each other. The Final Act of the Helsinki Conference (in particular, the section 'Commercial Exchanges') also points in this direction, in noting that the participating states are resolved 'to ensure conditions favourable' for the development of their mutual trade.[†]

On 1 August 1975, leaders of thirty-three countries of Europe, the USA and Canada signed in Helsinki the Final Act of the Conference on Security and Cooperation in Europe. This historic meeting has become a major landmark in strengthening peace throughout the world. The Final Act states that 'the growing world-wide economic interdependence calls for increasing common and effective efforts towards the solution of major world economic problems . . .' (p. 13). The consolidation of universal peace and the realisation of détente must promote cooperation in various fields of economic activity, and the states participating in the Conference on Security and Cooperation in Europe are interested in accelerating the process of giving real economic content to the political agreements, in keeping with the spirit and the letter of the Final Act.

---

* The average annual rates of growth of mutual trade of CMEA member countries in the 1971–5 quinquennium amounted to over 16 per cent, while the trade of CMEA countries with EEC member countries grew by 30 per cent per annum. The total value of foreign trade turnover between the two groups increased from $7·5 billion in 1970 to $25 billion in 1975.

† English text, *Conference on Security and Cooperation in Europe, Final Act*, Cmnd 6198 (London: HMSO, 1975) p. 14. All future references are to this version.

II THE INTERNATIONAL TRANSFER OF PRODUCTION TECHNIQUES AND TECHNOLOGY AND THE PREREQUISITES FOR THEIR MORE EFFECTIVE USE

Today the socialist countries and capitalist states are using basically the same production techniques and technologies; and the transfer of technology takes approximately the same institutional forms within each integration area. In a long-term historical context, the productive forces of socialism and capitalism have reached approximately the same level of development. However, interaction between the two systems, though increasing, remains relatively slight. The channels for exchanges of technology and technical knowledge remain restricted and the forms of exchange insufficiently developed; and artificial obstacles even to exchanges of the end-products still exist.*

But in Europe today there already exist not only the material, but also the organisational prerequisites for a more intensive all-European cooperation. The economic potential of 'Greater Europe' considerably surpasses that of any other continent. The tremendous scientific and technical potentials and productive equipment possessed by the European states of the two socio-economic systems offer the promise of greater benefits to both the CMEA and EEC countries from all-European cooperation. One-fifth of the globe's population lives in Europe, which produces 47 per cent of the world's national income and 55 per cent of the world's industrial goods; the share of the European continent in world foreign trade turnover is about the same; nearly half of the entire scientific and research personnel in the world reside and work in Europe. These facts indicate the tremendous potential represented by the still unused opportunities for intra-European cooperation.

III EAST–WEST INDUSTRIAL COOPERATION: FORMS, METHODS AND MUTUAL BENEFIT

The possibilities of useful cooperation in a number of fields — economics, science and technology, industry — have already been recognised, as have a number of possible means for their practical realisation. 'Industrial cooperation' is a most promising form of joint economic action — the term covering a complex of measures including cooperation in the field of investments, in the implementation of large-scale projects, in product specialisation, in the construction of individual installations, etc. Industrial cooperation covers both the simple supplying by each of the partners of particular components of the final product and more elaborate arrangements starting with the joint realisation of large-scale projects, cooperative deliveries of equipment for industrial

* The East–West division of labour is an area of unexploited opportunities. The Socialist and Capitalist countries together account for about 80 per cent of world exports, yet exchanges between them amount to only about 6 per cent of world trade.

complexes or construction of individual installations. It provides for a pooling of efforts, means and resources in investment, scientific, technological and other economic activities; an exchange of information, production experience and know-how; in further development of technology and improvement of the quality of final products. Industrial cooperation today takes a variety of forms.

Intergovernmental long-term agreements on economic, industrial, scientific and technological cooperation, for ten or more years, have been concluded by CMEA countries with Austria, Belgium, the Netherlands, France, Italy, the Federal Republic of Germany, the USA, Sweden, Britain and other capitalist nations. By late 1975 there were fifty such agreements in force. Under the auspices of such intergovernmental agreements a cooperation agreement was signed in April 1973 between Occidental Petroleum (USA) and the USSR for a period of twenty years. Its purpose is to assist in the construction in the USSR of an industrial complex for the production of mineral fertilisers, and the total value of mutual deliveries will be $20 thousand million. The People's Republic of Bulgaria concluded a ten-year agreement with the Italian Montedison company governing exchanges of know-how and licences, production and exchange of computers, chemical and petrochemical products, etc; and plants will be built in Bulgaria for the production of ethylene oxide (80,000 tons annual capacity), propylene (100,000 tons) and benzene (240,000 tons).

The economic organisations of CMEA countries also give technical assistance in setting up industrial projects in capitalist countries. For instance, Soviet organisations are taking part in the construction of an iron and steel complex in Southern France (Faux-sur-Mer) and others have contracted to supply Soviet equipment worth Fr. 60 million to expand and modernise the Elf-Erap oil refineries in France. Romanian organisations are helping with the construction of a tractor assembly plant in Saskatchewan, Canada.

Thirdly, there is the planning and realisation of joint projects in third countries. Thus, the Polish foreign trade company Polimpex-Cekop concluded a contract to supply plant, equipment and instruments to the value of Austrian schillings 250 million for the joint Polish–Austrian construction of a chemical plant in the People's Republic of Congo.

An important part in industrial cooperation is played by licensing agreements and the division of the production programme for components for some final manufacture. For instance, the Czechoslovak enterprise Kdinské strojirny cooperates with the British firm D. E. Calaghan & Son Ltd in joint production and sales in third countries of automatic equipment for the textile industry. The Hungarian enterprise Metrimex and the French firm Thompson-Houston have concluded an agreement on joint production of TV systems in Budapest, the value of mutual annual deliveries amounting to $500 thousand.

Industrial cooperation can also take other forms, such as the establishment of joint industrial enterprises and associations, mutual participation in the construction of projects, scientific and technical cooperation, etc.

In 1973 Romania entered into agreements for the establishment of four 'mixed enterprises'. For instance, the Ministry of Machine-tool Building and Electrical Engineering and the US company Control Data organised one; the share of the US firm in the value of fixed and circulating assets is 45 per cent and the enterprise will produce peripheral equipment for computers.

The number of industrial cooperation agreements concluded by CMEA countries with firms in capitalist states increased from 350 in 1970 to 1000 in 1975. About three-fifths of the agreements are in the field of machine building, one-fifth in the chemical industry and the rest in such branches as metallurgy and the light and food industries.

The character of cooperative arrangements has been changing, in the sense that they are being concluded for longer periods of time and covering a wider range of cooperative activity. The extension of industrial cooperation promises to produce significant results for both sides; and the CMEA countries – and the Soviet Union in particular – intend to seek continuously for new ways of developing mutually beneficial cooperation with states of different social regimes. A new form, to which great attention is being devoted at present, is the compensatory, or product-pay-back agreement.

An example of this kind of agreement is provided by the pipes—credits—gas deal – involving intergovernmental agreements and contracts – of the USSR with Austria, the Federal Republic of Germany, Italy and France. As of today there has been constructed and put into operation a trans-European gas pipeline 5000 kms long with an annual capacity of 30 billion cubic meters of gas. In anticipation of deliveries of Soviet natural gas, the importing countries granted the Soviet Union credits to purchase large-diameter pipes, gas-pumping plants and other equipment. Contracts concluded between Soyuzgazexport and the Petroleum administration (Austria), the state oil and gas association ENI (Italy), the joint-stock company Ruhrgas (FRG) and the state company Gaz de France (France) provide for deliveries of gas to them for a period of twenty years. Deliveries of pipes and equipment are financed by the largest banks in the gas-importing countries.

Exports of Soviet gas to Austria were started in January 1973, to the FRG in October 1973, to Italy in May 1974, and deliveries to France were to begin in 1976. Through the same pipeline, gas from the USSR is being delivered to the GDR and the Czechoslovak Socialist Republic; and by the beginning of 1976 over 25 billion cubic meters of natural gas, in total, had been delivered. This compensatory agreement is mutually advantageous. The Soviet Union has obtained an additional possibility of putting its natural resources and raw materials to economic use, and of developing areas east of the Urals which require large amounts of capital investments and special equipment. Western countries are importing the much-needed fuels and raw materials for their chemical industries, which are in short supply, particularly in the conditions of the energy crisis.

There is strong interest, on both sides, in compensatory agreements as one of the forms of mutually beneficial cooperation offering the best prospects for future development. However, these prospects do depend on a change in the focus of such deals towards industrial branches producing manufactured goods. They will then serve as a means of increasing the share of manufactured products in the exports of CMEA countries to capitalist states.

During the present economic recession in the West, when serious signs appeared of a slump in trade among Western countries, an ever-greater number of companies and firms have been displaying interest in establishing business relations with the countries of Eastern Europe.

All Western countries have made their own calculations as to the economic advisability of economic relations with foreign partners. Foreign orders expand employment possibilities, which is of great importance in present conditions of massive unemployment (early in 1976 there were over 17 million unemployed in the developed capitalist countries). For instance, in the USA they have calculated that the export of goods to the value of $15,000 ensures employment of one person for a whole year. In the Federal Republic of Germany the firm AEG has calculated that in order for one more worker to be employed for one year it is necessary to spend about DM 20,000. If one takes this figure as a basis, exports of the FRG to CMEA countries in 1975 of about DM 20 billion (10 per cent of the country's total exports) represent 100,000 additional workers in employment. Herr Schmidt, the Federal Chancellor, when making a Government statement at a meeting in the Bundestag, noted the great importance of the growth of exports to East-European countries 'in the period of a general economic slump, from the viewpoint of ensuring employment and supporting the country's economy'.

Indeed, to capitalist states, economic relations with CMEA countries have become of great social importance. One should remember that East–West cooperation is a question of hundreds of thousands of employed workers, since the trade-flow runs to several dozens of billions of dollars. Naturally, the products obtained in the West are used in the national economies of CMEA member countries, and promote their economic growth.

Exchanges of know-how have become an important field of cooperation between socialist and capitalist states. Usually, in this form of cooperation, exchanges of scientific and technical documentation are accompanied by reciprocal training of specialists, transfer of the most modern technology to the partner, exchanges of personnel and upgrading of their skills, transfer of patent rights, sales of samples, transfer of commercial information and participation of specialists from the partner country in the production process. The increasing volume of exchanges of know-how between countries of East and West attests to their profound mutual interest in such exchanges. For example the State Committee for Science and Technology of the USSR Council of Ministers has concluded an agreement with the West German firm Siemens on scientific and technical exchanges in the field of computer equipment, instrument-building, communication technology, electric household appliances, etc.; and the agreement is being successfully carried out.

In most cases an enterprise which has bought a licence pays for it with deliveries of the goods, or some components of the goods, produced under the licence, sharing also in the profits gained from on-sales of its products. For instance, Romania and the French firm Renault concluded an agreement under which the Romanian side delivers to France gearboxes in exchange for the licence and part of the equipment for manufacturing cars. In exchange for the licence for cement-plant equipment provided by the firm Schmidt (Denmark), Poland delivers to the firm furnaces and mills manufactured under the licence.

Trade in licences increases with every year. The Soviet foreign trade association Litsenzintorg alone has sold hundreds of licences to Western partners in recent years. A licence for an evaporation cooling system for blast furnaces was bought by firms from Britain, The FRG, Italy, France and other countries. The West German firm Klekner Humboldt Deutz bought a licence for the 'kivcet-process' — a method of extracting metals from polymetallic concentrates.

The socialist states can offer technical assistance in electro-metallurgy, welding, metal-working, organising the production of some kinds of chemical products, medical equipment, shipbuilding, atomic-instrument building, aviation, extraction of many kinds of minerals and in other fields and branches.

The expansion of the great variety of economic relationships between socialist and capitalist states is facilitated by a network of banking facilities for financing various activities, including foreign trade operations. Successfully operating Soviet banks are the Commercial Bank for North Europe in Paris, the Moscow Narodny Bank in London and the Woskhod Handelsbank AG in Zurich. In 1973 the Polish Trade Bank and the Gessische Landesbank Giro-zentrale signed an agreement establishing a joint bank which assists measures of cooperation. Operating in Frankfurt-am-Main is the Mitteleuropeische Handelsbank.

The number of banks and firms with representation established in CMEA countries is on the increase and their number now runs into several dozens. Today the normal and stable development of economic relations — and of production and commercial activities in particular — cannot be maintained without large supporting credit facilities.

In the words of the US Co-chairman of the Board of Directors of the American—Soviet Trade Council and the President of Pepsico Corporation, D. Kendall, a credit of $2 billion granted to a trade partner augments US exports by $6 billion and thus provides jobs for 400,000 Americans for one year. An increase of the credit to $6 billion would augment US exports by $9 billion, and so on. In February 1975, in the course of top-level negotiations, the Soviet Union and Great Britain reached an agreement granting credits of approximately £1 billion to the Soviet Union; in the first seven months of 1976 Britain exported more goods to the Soviet Union than in the entire year 1975. British imports have also grown considerably. The amount of credit available, the rate of interest and other conditions are at present a powerful lever in the competition to obtain advantageous contracts; and of this, business-men are well aware.

Thus, examples of the new form of East–West cooperation – industrial co-production – are numerous. But, naturally, their impact on the whole economy is still small. Nevertheless, it is important that experience is being accumulated and is bringing to light problems which can, and should, then be solved.

IV CMEA–EEC: RATIONAL COOPERATION OR DESTRUCTIVE COMPETITION

Cooperation between the CMEA and EEC can be an important field, and even a pre-requisite, for the further strengthening of economic interrelations in Europe. Economic conditions within Europe are in many respects determined by the relations between the Council for Mutual Economic Assistance and the European Economic Community, as well as between the individual countries of the CMEA and EEC. Relations between the CMEA and EEC, as such, have recently improved; and mutual recognition of the economic realities of present-day Europe will be of great importance for the future. The recent new initiatives of the CMEA are fully in keeping with the interests of the peoples of Europe, and with the Helsinki Final Act.

With the aim of expanding mutually beneficial economic cooperation within the European continent and eliminating obstacles to trade between the European socialist and capitalist states, the Chairman of the CMEA Executive Committee, Deputy Chairman of the GDR Council of Ministers G. Weiss, at the request of the Council and the governments of all CMEA member countries, made a proposal on 16 February 1976 for an agreement between the CMEA and the CMEA member countries, on the one side, and the EEC and the EEC member countries, on the other, on basic relations between the CMEA and the EEC. Herr Weiss handed over to the Chairman of the Council of Ministers of the European Communities, the Prime Minister and Minister of Foreign Affairs of Luxembourg, M. Gaston Thorn, a message from the Council for Mutual Economic Assistance addressed to the European Economic Community, together with a Draft Agreement on Basic Relations envisaging the establishment of favourable conditions for cooperation between the two organisations and their member countries. The socialist states are very ready to cooperate.

The CMEA initiative is aimed at creating the conditions necessary for the further development of mutually beneficial cooperation and trade between the CMEA and EEC countries. The main features of the proposed Draft Agreement are:

(i) The provisions relating to mutual trade and commerce reflect the need to apply most-favoured-nation treatment in relations between the CMEA member countries and the EEC member countries – i.e. to conduct relations between the CMEA members and the EEC members on a non-discriminatory basis and to abolish limitations on the import or export of any goods if such limitations are not applied to all third countries. It goes without saying that mutual trade in any goods should not limit or damage the internal market for these goods. The CMEA and EEC are called upon to promote trade between the member countries of the two associations on a stable, long-term and equitable basis, which involves the granting by countries to each other of most-favoured-nation treatment; i.e. each nation undertakes to extend to its partner all the benefits and advantages in the field of trade which it grants or will grant to third countries.

(ii)   The Draft Agreement requests the CMEA and the EEC to study monetary and financial questions and to adopt decisions which would promote the stable growth of commodity trade. This would involve, for instance, the mutual granting of credits by the organisations' member countries on the best possible terms.

(iii) The CMEA and the EEC should contribute to the development of trade in agricultural goods between the CMEA member countries and the EEC member countries on a stable, long-term and equitable basis.

(iv)   The Draft Agreement envisages that general questions of trade and economic relations between the CMEA and the EEC be settled in bilateral and multilateral agreements while individual, specific issues could be resolved through direct contacts, arrangements and agreements between the CMEA member countries and EEC authorities, as well as between the two organisations.

(v)   The Draft Agreement provides also for developing cooperation between the CMEA and the EEC in such fields as standardisation, environmental protection, statistics, and economic forecasting in areas of production and consumption of interest to both sides.

(vi)   With respect to the forms which relations between the two organisations can take, the Draft provides for joint studies and research on problems, regular exchange of information on the main activities of the CMEA and the EEC and systematic contacts between representatives and officials of the CMEA and the EEC, including the organisation of conferences, seminars and symposia.

The Draft Agreement takes into account earlier proposals made by both sides on possible relations between the CMEA and the EEC; and it is envisaged that the provisions of the proposed Agreement should not affect the rights and obligations of members of either association under bilateral and multilateral treaties and agreements in force, or their rights to conclude such treaties and agreements in future. To facilitate the implementation of the proposed Agreement, the Draft provides for a mixed commission of representatives of the contracting parties. However, its functions will not affect the functions of the mixed commissions operating within the framework of bilateral or multilateral agreements between CMEA member countries and EEC member countries.

The conclusion of this Agreement would promote a stable increase in trade between the CMEA and the EEC member countries, the diversification of

this trade and full use of the possibilities presented by the economic development of these countries. It would help to eliminate obstacles today impeding
the development of cooperation in various fields. It would also contribute to
further relaxation of international tensions, a matter of deep concern to both
sides.

The CMEA member countries are prepared to extend and improve
economic cooperation with the EEC countries; and they can offer wide-ranging
opportunities. The growth of output of some most important industrial
products in the CMEA member countries and the EEC member countries is
indicated in Table 10.

TABLE 10 OUTPUT OF SOME INDUSTRIAL PRODUCTS IN THE CMEA AND EEC
COUNTRIES, 1970 AND 1975

		CMEA		EEC	
		1970	1970	1975	1975
Electricity generation	bn kwh	988	1386	850	1020
Oil	mn tons	365·3	510	13·3	10·5
Steel	mn tons	155·6	193	138	126
Mineral fertilisers					
(100 per cent nutrient)	mn tons	20·5	33·5	14·9	16·9
Cement	mn tons	137·5	182·4	131·8	128
Fabrics of all kinds	bn m^2	13·0	14·9	6·4	6
Sugar	mn tons	14·0	15*	8·4	8·8

* Excluding Cuba.

According to the economic development plans of the CMEA member
countries, the volume of their industrial output will reach about 2·1 times the
1970 level by 1980. Thus the socialist community has become the most
dynamic economic force in the world; and in many respects its economic
development has now either come very close to, or surpassed, that of the EEC
region. Industrial specialisation and diversification are proceeding rapidly in
both regions, and the need for external outlets for their products is growing.
This is an objective and inevitable law which makes the development of
cooperation a necessity. There is no alternative save destructive confrontation.

V PROSPECTS FOR EXTENDING EAST–WEST ECONOMIC COOPERATION TO THIRD COUNTRIES

Continuing the discussion of the prospects for extended 'East–West' economic
cooperation, it is important to stress that this must embody the principles of
mutual interest, mutual benefit and equality. The development of long-term
concrete programmes of economic cooperation, involving mutual obligations
to contribute on an extensive and mutually beneficial basis, would be in the
interests of both sides. The most promising forms of economic relation
between East and West include those already discussed – industrial coopera-

tion, exchanges of know-how, compensatory deals, cooperative marketing arrangements, etc.; and the new need that has now arisen is to expand the field of compensatory agreements to include processing industries, thus giving a new impetus to industrial cooperation. In our view the most promising fields for such cooperation include development of power resources and the sharing of electricity supplies, research into new sources of energy, the mining and processing of minerals, development of the communications network and the creation of an all-European transport system, cooperation in outer space and in the world's oceans, etc.

It is likely that third countries will be increasingly involved in European economic cooperation; and there are examples of this already. Thus in November 1975 in Teheran, talks which began in May 1974 were completed and documents were signed envisaging deliveries of natural gas from Iran to West European countries through the territory of the USSR. Iran's natural gas will be supplied to the Federal Republic of Germany, Austria and France through the territories of the Soviet Union and Czechoslovakia. Two multilateral agreements were signed and a joint statement made by the governments of the participating countries. One agreement (in fact a contract) was signed by the national Iranian Gas Company with the West German company Ruhrgas, the French national company Gaz de France and the Austrian oil directorate. Under this contract Iran will, from January 1981 until the year 2003, supply annually 13,400 million cubic metres of natural gas to the region of Astara on the Soviet–Iranian border. The Federal Republic of Germany will take half of this, France approximately one-third and Austria 17 per cent. The minimum price for the gas supplied to Astara will be fixed on the basis of the current price of fuel oil, and if the price for fuel oil goes up the price for gas will also increase.

The second agreement – on the transit of gas through the territories of the USSR and the Czechoslovak Socialist Republic – was concluded between the directors of the above-mentioned companies and the Soviet foreign trade company Soyuzgasexport. It spells out the conditions and terms for the transit of gas between Astara (the Soviet–Iranian border) and Weidhaus (a town on the border between the Federal Republic of Germany and Czechoslovakia). The distance between Astara and Weidhaus is about 4000 kilometres, of which 3000 kilometres are on the territory of the USSR. The payment for the transit of gas is to be made by the customers in freely convertible currency, and they will also make available to the gas transport authorities free gas – approximately 1500 million cubic metres a year for the USSR and 400 million cubic metres for Czechoslovakia – for the operation of compressor facilities. Czechoslovakia has in fact preferred to receive payment for the transit of gas through its territory in gas – approximately 1100 million cubic metres a year – rather than in currency. Thus, the total volume of gas deliveries from Iran when the project is in full operation will reach about 14,500 million cubic metres a year.

The USSR Foreign Trade Bank has negotiated with the corresponding banks of the Federal Republic of Germany, France and Austria a credit to the Soviet side of 650 million roubles in freely convertible currency, which will be repaid from the payments received for the transit of gas.

A major construction effort is to be undertaken in Iran, where a new gas pipeline about 1500 kilometres long will have to be laid from gas deposits in southern Iran to Astara. At the starting point its capacity will be 25,000 million cubic metres of gas a year. Huge capital investments will also be required to build the gas pipeline system from southern Iran to the eastern border of the Federal Republic of Germany (5500 kilometres). The volume of gas deliveries is also vast — in the twenty-three years of the operation of the contract the deliveries of gas from Iran will exceed 300,000 million cubic metres, and at today's prices for gas this represents 18,000 million dollars worth of supplies.

Contacts between scientists of socialist states and capitalist countries are useful and necessary. Our Round-table Conference is a testimony to this. I feel that we should proceed from mutual provision of information and discussion of general questions of cooperation, which are of course of great significance, to the discussions of more concrete problems of cooperation and, particularly, of all-European economic relations. Our forums can deal with a whole range of problems discussed in the Helsinki Final Act, in congresses, symposia, seminars and other forms of contacts, the participants in which would take into account the degree of interest of their countries and their readiness for closer relations. Scientists can undoubtedly make an effective contribution to the cause of developing cooperation. It would seem advisable to choose for our future meetings major specific problems such as protection of the environment, transport links, forms of cooperation in the fields of science and technology or in the spheres of production and trade, etc. We might then find it necessary to elaborate and discuss recommendations of a scientific nature on a particular range of related issues.

In any case greater activity by scientists in this field can, must and will, in my view, promote trust and confidence among our countries, as well as a search for constructive and mutually acceptable solutions of the problems raised by the scientific and technological revolution and the growing intensity of economic interrelations within the world. This would meet the aspirations of the peoples of the countries of Europe and of all other continents of our planet.

Discussion of the Papers by Professor Kirschen and Professor Senin

Professor Senin having asked to elaborate on the brief summary of his paper that he had circulated, *Professor Kohlmey* limited his introductory remarks to Professor Kirschen's paper. He acknowledged the value of Kirschen's historical method but disagreed with some of his interpretations and conclusions. Kirschen had overstressed the formal institutional aspects and the geographical aspects of the Eastern and Western integration processes and objectives, while neglecting real political, social, economic (essentially system-determined) contrasts. An example was Point 7 of his 'avowed policy aims' (p. 112); in fact, capitalism today meant increasing monopoly power not increasingly free enterprise, and thus the stated Western objective appeared unreal and impossible to attain. Similarly, Point 10 blurred the difference between the objectives of socialist and capitalist states by ignoring the unresolved problem of the contrasts between the riches of the imperialist states and the impoverishment of the less-developed countries.

Professor Kohlmey agreed that the fact that the USA was not a member of the EEC while the USSR was a member of the CMEA affected the integrationary forces and the forms of integration within the two groupings; it was a pity that the paper had not given more attention to the development of the integration experiences over time, since this would have revealed more of the longterm processes at work and of the nature of the transformations being brought about in the national economies. He regarded Professor Kirschen's conclusions on EEC–CMEA relations as realistic but too little concerned with positive suggestions for ways of achieving far-reaching all-European cooperation.

After Professor Senin's indication of the content of his own paper, *Professor Kirschen* intervened on two points: (i) Speaking as one committed to rapid Western European integration, he regretted the time spent by the EEC and CMEA in shadowboxing, rather than trying to develop working relations; the practical negotiation of a new world economic order would inevitably require negotiation between representatives of groups of countries, rather than the (now 130) individual nation states. (ii) The results of integration, he thought, were better measured in terms of growth rates rather than of trade development, which was not an end in itself. He had estimated that some 0·75–1·00 per cent of the recorded annual percentage rate of economic growth of the EEC area could be attributed to the effects of the Common Market; were there any comparable calculations for the CMEA area?

Subsequent discussion turned on

(i)   differences between the natures of the EEC and the CMEA;
(ii) relations between the two groupings and developing countries;
(iii) the forces making for economic integration or 'internationalisation' of European economies.

Dr Jacobsen drew attention to the formal rejection of 'supranational' powers for the CMEA emphasised in Chapter 1, Section 1, Point 2 of the 'Comprehensive Programme' and implied by the many references – in its statements of

principles, agreements and the Draft Agreement sent to the EEC – to
'interested' countries. On the other hand, the world-wide movement towards
'internationalisation' of production and other processes could be seen also
within the CMEA, in the form of joint projects and the establishment of
international economic associations. Did these developments represent a
tendency towards greater 'supranationality'? He was inclined to think so, and
to think that intensifying integration within the CMEA – and thus the
diminishing the importance of the 'interested countries' formula – was a force
motivating the apparent desire for CMEA–EEC relations rather than, or in
addition to, bilateral relations between individual CMEA countries and the
EEC or its individual members.

Professor Schiavone also drew attention to 'mutual assistance' as a key
ingredient of 'socialist internationalism' as interpreted in the CMEA, and to
the fact that even an 'interested' member state was obliged at first only to
'consider' a recommendation from a CMEA organ; only if it then informed
the secretariat of its acceptance would the recommendation acquire, in its
case, binding force. But he also doubted the genuine 'supranationality' of the
EEC, since the last word rested with the Council, composed of instructed
delegates of the member states. Both in the EEC and the CMEA political
resolve of the member states was, and would be, much more important than
institutional arrangements for the implementation of any programme of real
integration. However, a further difference between the two bodies could be
added to those listed by Professor Kirschen – the EEC was open only to
European states, the CMEA to a 'region' (socialist countries anywhere in the
world) limited by political and ideological, rather than geographical, criteria.

Professor Bogomolov saw no reason why closer East–West cooperation
should be inhbited by formal differences between the CMEA and EEC or by
differences in the economic systems of their member states, while *Professor
Zaharescu* doubted whether economic or political fusion were in prospect in
either community. *Professor Lavigne* appreciated Professor Senin's exposition
of the draft CMEA–EEC treaty and asked for elucidation of the issues
considered suitable for EEC–CMEA, EEC–CMEA member, CMEA–EEC
member and inter-state agreements, respectively.

In the context of EEC and CMEA relations with the rest of the world,
Professor Yamamoto agreed with Professor Kirschen that inter-group discussions would be increasingly necessary; he thought that a South-East Asian
group such as ASEAN, within a new looser 'Organisation for Asian Economic
Cooperation' as a peripheral circle, could increase Asia's influence with the
major powers and with other groupings. *Professor Savov* disagreed with
Professor Kirschen's comments on the initiative taken by the CMEA in seeking
an agreement on cooperation with the EEC. Such an agreement would be a
useful first step towards economic cooperation between the two different
'integration communities' in Europe based on the realisation of mutual benefits
from an intensified international division of labour. But CMEA–EEC cooperation should not, of course, be limited to trade: immense possibilities existed
in industrial, technical, scientific and other fields. Closer intra-European relations should be seen as an essential step towards the establishment of a new
economic order of worldwide cooperation and the further strengthening of
the economic basis for peaceful coexistence. Political conditions for this were

now very favourable, as the recent discussions in the United Nations had shown. He did agree strongly with Professor Kirschen that the approach must be via negotiation between existing integration groupings, and perhaps other groups of countries also. *Professor Shmelyov* also urged consideration of a cooperative EEC–CMEA approach to the design of a new world economic order.

Dr Diakin contested Professor Kirschen's assessment of the effects of EEC integration; it could not be claimed to have encouraged economic growth while the integration process left more than 5 million workers unemployed within the EEC area. Inflation and recession had forced even the large monopolies of the EEC to look outwards for markets and investment opportunities. East–West cooperation could contribute to a solution of these problems through the undertaking of large-scale joint projects or the establishment of mixed enterprises, in the CMEA area and/or the developing world. Some legal problems in this connection had already been overcome in the CMEA countries. Dr Diakin then instanced several examples of successful East–West industrial cooperation. *Dr Rogge* also anticipated an increasing capital outflow from Western Europe but said that the socialist countries tended to appear at the bottom of lists of 'safe' countries for direct investment; more assurances of welcome for foreign capital – as a partner in projects inside or outside the CMEA area – were needed, covering such questions as patent protection, remittance of profits, immunity from nationalisation, etc.

Replying to the discussion, *Professor Kirschen* said that he saw about half the Eastern European countries and Britain and France as defenders of 'states' rights' within their respective groupings, and the rest of the CMEA countries, the Federal Republic of Germany and Benelux as 'integrators'; there were thus political forces pulling in opposite directions within each group. So far as the economic benefits of the EEC were concerned, he suggested to Dr Diakin that it was certainly not obvious that without the EEC the recent West European recession would have been less acute or barriers to trade lower; the situation might well have been worse in both respects. He suggested that comments on his table had missed one significant implication – the fact that, while he would not claim 'convergence', both today's conditions and future objectives in the EEC and CMEA countries were closer to each other than either group was to the developing world.

Professor Senin considered that the internationalisation of the economic life of different countries was now an objective law of development, not the manifestation of the will of one or another politician, state or group of states. The CMEA was not a supranational authority able to force its members to integrate their economies; its operative principle was national sovereignty and mutual interest, not 'supranational directives', and it was on this basis that the socialist countries cooperated within the CMEA. The 'Comprehensive Programme' also offered the possibility of advantageous cooperation to any country, even if it was part of another social system and did not approve of the system of the CMEA countries; and CMEA relations with Finland were an example of such cooperation.

9 Monetary, Credit and Financial Issues in Economic Cooperation between East and West

Zdzisław Fedorowicz
WARSAW SCHOOL OF ECONOMICS

I INTRODUCTION

The share in world industrial production of those socialist countries which are members of the Council of Mutual Economic Assistance exceeds 30 per cent, but their share in international trade is considerably smaller. In 1974 these countries' share of total world imports was only 8·6 per cent, and of world exports 8·4 per cent.[1] This proves that the CMEA countries do not yet profit sufficiently from the opportunities for international division of labour. In the 1970s the development of trade among the socialist countries has accelerated, as has their trade with other countries. Between 1970 and 1973 East–West trade increased by 107 per cent, while total international trade increased by only 80 per cent;[2] and this indicates some progress in economic cooperation between East and West. But it can satisfy nobody who believes that the development of economic cooperation between East and West is advantageous for both sides.* To attain more significant levels of cooperation, it will be necessary to change substantially the structure of the trade between Eastern and Western countries.

During 1966–8 the share of raw materials in the total exports of socialist countries to Western countries was 56 per cent. It has been estimated, that by 1980 exports of manufactured commodities from Eastern to Western countries should reach a value of about US $12 billion and represent some 63–75 per cent of the total value of this export-flow. At the same time the value of raw materials exported from Eastern to Western European countries should reach $4–7 billions, or 25–37 per cent of the total, estimated at $16–19 billions.[3] This would represent a fundamental change in the structure of exports from East to West, requiring great efforts in the fields of industrial production and industrial cooperation, in marketing of goods and in improving the transfer of technology and know-how. Such a development of, and structural change in, economic cooperation between East and West will also require the solution of some monetary, credit and other financial problems.

---

* But the policy of developing economic relations with socialist countries still has its opponents in the West (see T. D. Zotschew: 'Der Handel zwischen den Systemen', *Deutsche Studien*, vol. 38, (Kiel, 1972) pp. 143–4.

This paper will concentrate on a number of issues which seem particularly interesting, either from a theoretical or from a practical point of view.

II CONVERTIBILITY OF EAST EUROPEAN CURRENCIES

All socialist countries in Eastern Europe today use, in their settlements with Western countries, freely convertible Western currencies. From the point of view of the Western countries this should not be an obstacle to developing trade and economic cooperation with Eastern partners. Western firms and banks are accustomed to dealing in these currencies; they are well informed on prices of commodities and services denominated in them, on exchange rates and on tendencies on financial and capital markets. But the question remains, whether the inconvertibility of socialist countries' currencies does not hamper the development of economic cooperation between East and West, because Eastern countries, not being able to pay for their imports from the West with their own currencies, have to limit such imports to the amount of convertible currencies earned from exports to the West and borrowed from Western banks. Moreover, socialist countries have to hold reserves in convertible currencies to provide a sufficient liquidity in relation to their transactions with Western partners; and this also diminishes their ability to import. Thus, at first sight, making socialist currencies convertible — even for foreign firms, banks and persons only — could be advantageous for Eastern countries, because in such a case Western firms and banks would hold some reserves in their currencies, so improving the balances-of-payments of socialist countries.

On the other hand, the convertibility of socialist currencies would entail consequences which are sometimes neglected in theoretical argument. The convertibility of a currency — even external convertibility, limited to foreign firms and persons — means that everybody has the right to convert foreign currency into the home currency of a socialist country and, in consequence, the right to buy any commodity from that country at its internal price in the national currency. But the domestic price structures in the socialist planned economies differ greatly from the price structures in the so-called market economies. In general, socialist countries establish price levels, and the relative prices of different commodities and services, according to their own social and economic conditions and the planned goals of social and economic development. Pricing systems in these countries are connected with incomes policy, with consumption policy, with investment policy, etc. Thus, prices of foodstuffs in socialist countries are comparatively low, and prices of motor-cars and some other consumer-durables are comparatively high, when compared with prices in Western countries. There are also considerable differences between the relative prices of many raw materials and semi-finished products in socialist and capitalist countries, reflecting both differences in costs of production and policies of substitution of some materials by others which form part of the socialist countries' long-term development programmes.

Socialist countries cannot, therefore, allow their internal prices to be also the prices at which they sell abroad — for instance, selling coal at half the world-market price, or attempting to sell other commodities at prices higher than those in other countires. On the other hand, if the socialist countries adjusted the structures of their internal prices to the world-market price structure they would be obliged to subordinate their economies to the drastic cyclical changes which occur in capitalist countries — for example, to inflationary pressure imported from abroad. They would soon be obliged to sacrifice planning and their long-term social and economic aims. It is obvious that such an option does not exist for socialist countries.

The possibility of convertibility can, in my opinion, be discussed only in relation to the common currency of the socialist countries, used in their mutual settlements of foreign trade and other international transactions — the transferable rouble. Prices in transferable roubles are derived from world market prices, using the average prices of the last five years in order to eliminate the influence of cyclical and speculative factors. If necessary, some other adjustments of these prices can be made, especially in individual trade contracts negotiated by the directly interested countries and their enterprises. However, the general proportionality of foreign trade prices in transferable roubles to prices in convertible currencies should be maintained, in order to avoid competition between the market of socialist countries and the world market. This general similarity of relative foreign trade prices in transferable roubles to relative prices in convertible currencies — together with the possibility of adjustments in individual contracts — eliminates the main argument for keeping the transferable rouble inconvertible. But this is not the case of the national currencies of socialist countries which, in my opinion, should remain inconvertible.

It should be added that the evolution of the transferable rouble towards convertibility has already started. The deposits of socialist countries in transferable roubles with the International Bank for Economic Cooperation (IBEC) in Moscow are already partially convertible and, according to the rules of the Bank, other countries participating in this system of settlements would be able to convert their transferable rouble deposits into Western currencies even more easily. The problem of extending the scope of settlements made in transferable roubles is however still being discussed by the countries belonging to the IBEC.

III EXCHANGE RATES BETWEEN CONVERTIBLE CURRENCIES

Floating of the exchange rates of convertible currencies seems now to be accepted by all major industrialised countries in the Western world, in default of any other feasible system. Though it was declared in the Rambouillet Agreement that 'erratic' fluctuations of exchange rates should be reduced, in practice drastic fluctuations still occur. The British pound, Italian lira and French franc supply examples of such fluctuations.

But floating exchange-rates do not favour the development of international trade – and especially not of long-term contracts for industrial cooperation – because of the uncertainty of relations between future costs and benefits accruing in different currencies. Therefore the stabilisation of exchange rates would be very desirable, especially for the East European countries, since they do not dispose of the sophisticated banking systems of the West, which may be able to offset exchange-rate fluctuations by compensatory operations of various kinds.

Of course, the stabilisation of exchange rates remains a mere desire, if the causes of the resort to floating are not eliminated. These causes are different rates of inflation in different countries, internal economic disequilibria in individual countries, disequilibria between regions or groups of countries (especially between industrialised countries, oil producing countries and developing countries), incompatible monetary and financial policies applied by the individual countries fighting against inflation and depression, lack of adequate mechanisms for the adjustment of balance-of-payments deficits and surpluses, excessive monetary liquidity and speculative movements of 'hot money' from country to country.

Rates of price inflation in some countries remain at moderate levels of under 10 per cent a year; others have rates of 10–20 per cent; in some cases rates exceed 20 per cent a year, even if we leave aside cases of hyperinflation. The fight against inflation is extremely difficult, taking into account the impact of anti-inflationary measures on internal economic activity. Thus we observe in many countries the new phenomenon of 'stagflation', resulting from the contradiction between anti-inflation and anti-recession policies. Assuming that the fight against recession will have priority, we must expect rather long-term inflationary trends of prices in Western countries.

For Eastern European countries the declining purchasing power of Western currencies is less important than changes in the structure of price relationships on the world market and the economic recession in the industrialised Western countries. The rise in the general level of prices denominated in Western currencies can be matched by appropriate adjustment of the exchange rates and 'currency coefficients' used by socialist countries in their national economies. In this way 'imported inflation' can be limited, if not completely eliminated. It is sometimes even argued that the depreciation of Western currencies is advantageous for Eastern countries, in diminishing the real burden of their debts. This is hardly correct; expected rates of inflation usually influence the calculation of rates of interest on loans, and – what is more important – inflation is in fact accompanied by changes in price structures, which affect the terms of trade between socialist countries and the outer world. These terms of trade are now, in general, worsening for Eastern Europe, though individual countries suffer in differing degrees.

The impact of depression in the industrialised Western countries on economic cooperation between East and West is particularly harmful. Socialist countries meet with growing difficulties in exporting their commodities to the West, especially when discriminatory measures are applied to diminish imports from Eastern countries as, for instance, in the case of imports of agricultural products by EEC countries.

Although floating exchange rates reflect more fundamental processes within the market economies, it nevertheless seems necessary to look for some instruments or procedures which would prevent erratic fluctuations and their unfavourable consequences for economic cooperation between East and West.

IV CREDIT RELATIONS BETWEEN EAST AND WEST

The development of economic cooperation between Eastern and Western countries depends to a great extent on the availability of credit facilities in the West for socialist countries. In order to increase their exports of manufactured products, and of goods produced under industrial cooperation agreements, to Western countries, the socialist countries have to import advanced technical equipment, technology, know-how, licences, etc. These imports require some credit assistance; but so also does any increase of traditional Eastern exports of raw materials to the West, because of the capital-intensive nature of the development of extractive industries. Eastern countries' demand for credits is growing very quickly.

This demand is reflected in the increasing deficits of Eastern countries in their trade with the West. In 1972 these deficits amounted to US $2·4 billion; in 1974 they were already $8 billion, and in the first half of 1975 $7·6 billion (compared with $3 billion in the first half of 1974).*

Eastern countries are interested first of all in long-term loans for investment purposes, mainly for the purchase of technical equipment and licences from Western industrialised countries. The policies of the latter countries on loans to Eastern partners vary with the economic situation of the creditor and other factors. The Western countries most interested in promoting their exports are especially active in this field. Thus, Italy started very early to support exports to Eastern countries with credit facilities – with a loan of $100 million to the USSR in 1961 followed by participation in the financing of construction of motor-car factories in the USSR and Poland. Other important credit contracts between Italy and Eastern countries – among them a loan of $2 billion to the USSR – are currently in course of negotiation. France opened a line of credit of Fr. 3·5 billion to the USSR in 1964, and in 1974 another of Fr. 1·5 billion, linked with the modernisation of the Moscow motor-car factory, with the construction of the Kama truck factory and with other industrial projects. French credits to Poland between 1972 and 1974 amounted to Fr. 4·5 billion, and a further Fr. 7·5 billion line of credit was opened in 1975; and these credits were linked with deliveries of French technical equipment to fertiliser

---

* Including China, North Korea and Vietnam (Adam Zwass, 'Kredite im Ost-West Handel', *Quartalshefte der Girozentrale und Bank der österreichischen Sparkassen AG,* vol. 4 (1975) p. 56).

and petrochemical factories under construction in Poland. France is also developing credit-supported cooperation with Romania, the German Democratic Republic and other socialist countries; the GDR, for example, received credits of Fr. 550 million in 1970 and $50 million in 1975. Great Britain, also, is actively supporting exports to Eastern countries with credit facilities. The many contracts for industrial cooperation between British and Eastern firms include an important contract between the Ferguson Company and a Polish tractor factory, based on a loan of about $300 million (about £150 million).*

Italy, France, Great Britain and some other Western European countries grant credits on exports of technical equipment to Eastern European countries on special terms of reimbursement and interest. As a rule interest rates are below market levels and subsidised by the respective governments.

In other Western European countries, less deeply concerned to increase their exports, credits to Eastern European countries are granted on normal market conditions. The government of the Federal Republic of Germany, for example, does not normally subsidise exports, the only exceptions being credits granted to Yugoslavia, and recently to Poland, at very low interest rates and for very long terms and subsidised by the state budget. But these are considered as a form of recompense for war damage and are not typical. However, in some other cases the rates of interest on loans granted by West German banks are extremely low. This is true of two loans, each of DM 1·2 billion, granted to the USSR for the purchase of steel pipes for the construction of a gas pipeline; and the loans will be repaid by deliveries of gas from the USSR to the FRG. The Federal Republic of Germany is, in fact, very active in credit relations with socialist countries; in 1975 alone, the Federal Republic granted loans of $100 million to Hungary and of $250 million to Bulgaria. Between the Federal Republic of Germany and the German Democratic Republic credit relations are of a special character, with a swing-credit operating; the amount outstanding at the end of 1974 exceeded DM 2 billion.

The approach of Western European countries to credits to socialist countries is distinguished by their willingness to accept reimbursement in deliveries of predetermined lists of products. This type of contract is considered very advantageous by the socialist countries who, as was pointed out earlier, meet with difficulties on Western markets. It is also advantageous for Western countries, in assuring them of long-term deliveries of important products — raw materials, energy, components for goods produced under industrial cooperation agreements — and, last but not least, such a contract guarantees the repayment of the loan.

Unlike West European banks, United States banks prefer not to predetermine in this way the source of funds for the repayment of loans, though they examine very carefully the creditworthiness of the borrowing country and its institutions. Credit relations between the USA and socialist countries from

---

* All figures in this and the two following paragraphs are from the source in the footnote on p. 139.

the beginning of the 1950s until 1968 were virtually limited to credits granted by the Commodity Credit Corporation for the purchase of surpluses of agricultural products. Lending by American banks was limited by the Johnson Act, prohibiting the extension of credits to socialist countries for longer terms than six months.[4] This, in practice, made it impossible for the socialist countries to import machinery and technical equipment from the USA, since other exporters of equipment usually finance their contracts with three- to five-year bank credits.

In 1968 the US Export–Import Bank included East European countries in its Medium Term Guarantee Programme, but this authorisation was withdrawn after three months and only in the 1970s did the Eximbank again undertake to grant loans on American exports to East European countries. Usually the Eximbank participates to the extent of 60–80 per cent of the loan, the remainder being lent by commercial banks. The Eximbank is permitted to charge rates of interest below the market rates, but does not always do so.

A special factor affecting American commercial bank credit to East European countries is the legal lending limit, prohibiting the granting to one debtor of loans exceeding 10 per cent of a bank's capital. This limit can be very easily reached, even by the great banks, because of the extremely concentrated nature of the banking systems of the socialist countries. Each socialist country is, as a rule, represented on Western credit markets by only one foreign-trade bank, which undertakes foreign borrowing for all the industrial and commercial companies of the country. Thus loans for two or three large projects – all to one borrower – can very quickly reach the legal lending limit and make new contracts impossible. Attempts by industrial corporations in the socialist countries to apply directly for loans from American banks, without the mediation of the national foreign-trade bank, have not succeeded because the legal lending limit – according to the interpretation of the American Chamber of Commerce – applies in the case of a socialist country to the total indebtedness of all banks and firms having legal site in that country. In other words, according to this interpretation, the legal lending limit is applied to the whole country as a single borrower. This interpretation is neither justified – since industrial and commercial corporations in Eastern countries, though state-owned, dispose of separate assets and are financially independent – nor does it correspond with what is needed to promote economic cooperation between East and West.

East European countries, in search of credit facilities, borrow also on the Eurocurrency and Eurodollar markets; and, especially in recent years, this method of financing imports has become relatively important. In 1975 the USSR borrowed $650 million in the Eurodollar market and Poland $290 million.

The socialist countries of Eastern Europe, with the exception of Yugoslavia and Romania, are not members of the International Monetary Fund and therefore have no access to the credit facilities offered by the World Bank. Romania has, however, borrowed about $290 million from the Bank for terms between twenty and twenty-five years.

This short outline of credit relations between Eastern and Western countries permits one to conclude that there are still many problems to be explored in this field, and solved to the advantage of both sides.

V COOPERATION IN THE FORM OF JOINT VENTURES WITH MIXED CAPITAL

Up to now joint ventures, in the form of companies with mixed capital provided partly by Eastern and partly by Western countries, exist only in Romania, Hungary and Yugoslavia. Having no experience of my own in this field, I shall describe briefly the characteristics of joint ventures on the basis of Romanian Decrees Nos 424 and 425 of 1972 (published in the *Official Bulletin of the Socialist Republic of Romania*, No. 121 of 4 November 1972) which concern the formation, organisation and operations of mixed companies and the taxation of their profits.

Mixed companies with foreign capital may be established in Romania in stated fields, mainly in industry. They are legal entities in Romanian law and operate in accordance with the laws of that country. The share of Romanian partners in the initial capital must be at least 51 per cent. The Romanian government guarantees to the foreign partners the possibility of transferring abroad both currently earned profits and also the value of shares transferred to Romania and of the foreign partners' share of the proceeds of the realisation of the assets of the firm after its closing down. In forming the initial capital, shares may be subscribed in the form of money or of goods necessary for real investment by, and for developing the activities of, the company, etc. The value of the investment by both parties in forming a mixed company is determined in the currency specified in the agreement on the formation of the company and in the company's rules and regulations. Expenditures of mixed companies are made in the currency specified in the agreement; they can buy raw materials and other means of production, either on the domestic market or abroad. The sale of the products of mixed companies is accounted in the same currency. Mixed companies have separate accounts with Romanian banks in foreign exchange and in Romanian currency; they may transfer money from one account to the other according to the exchange rate determined for non-commercial operations. The Romanian personnel are remunerated in Romanian currency (or partly in foreign exchange). Foreign personnel may transfer a predetermined part of their remuneration abroad.

Profits of mixed companies are taxed at 30 per cent. The tax is calculated on the amount of undistributed profit, after deducting write-offs from the reserve fund of up to 5 per cent of the profit; but on profit reinvested for a period of at least five years, the tax is reduced by 20 per cent.

Cooperation in the form of joint ventures seems well worth putting into practice. Direct investments are not subject to such restrictions as the legal lending limit for bank credits already mentioned, and the Western partners of socialist countries in such undertakings are more interested in running the factories and in selling their products than in the case of simple loans to finance industrial projects. This form of economic cooperation between East and West thus deserves more attention in the future.

NOTES

1 *Mały Rocznik Statystyki Miedzynarodowej, 1975* (Warsaw, 1975) p. 9.
2 Professor Angelos Angelopulos, Governor of the National Bank of Greece, *Quelques propositions sur la relance de l'activité économique internationale et sur la reforme du système monétaire mondial* (Vouliagmeni, Greece, 1975) p. 2.
3 UN Economic Commission for Europe, *Economic Bulletin for Europe*, vol. 22 (1971) p. 46.
4 Oswald Judar, 'A Businessman's View on East–West Trade', in S. Wasowski (ed.), *East–West Trade and the Technology Gap* (New York, 1970) p. 159.

10 CMEA's Hard Currency Deficits and Rouble Convertibility*

Franklyn D. Holzman

TUFTS UNIVERSITY

Over the past fifteen years, the CMEA countries[†] have consistently run hard currency deficits in their trade with the West. I will first consider very briefly the extent and causes of these deficits. In Sections II and III, various Eastern convertible-currency proposals, which are related to financing these deficits, will be discussed. The policy issues will be summarised in the final Section. Because of the limitations of space, some of the issues discussed below will be considerably oversimplified.

I EXTENT AND CAUSES OF CMEA'S HARD-CURRENCY DEFICIT

According to Western estimates, CMEA's hard-currency indebtedness was in the neighbourhood of $32 billion at the end of 1975.[1] This is considerably above the $22·3 billion estimated for the end of 1974; and the 1974 figure represents an approximate $5 billion increase over 1973.[2] About half of the present debt is attributed to the USSR and Poland. These debts represent something like a 20 per cent debt service/export ratio for the USSR and ratios probably of a similar order of magnitude for the rest of Eastern Europe, with the Bulgarian ratio on the high side and those for Czechoslovakia and the GDR on the low side. These are fairly high figures by most Western standards and there is some feeling in both East and West that the CMEA may be beginning to approach a credit ceiling. As early as 1971, an experienced Hungarian economist remarked that 'To maintain East—West trade even at the present level, the unbalanced payments situation must be recognised'. He also observed: 'a deficit balance of the Eastern European nations seems to be a constant phenomenon of these relations'.[3]

Why is it that the CMEA's deficit balance with the West is a 'constant phenomenon?' It is my view, presented at length elsewhere,[4] that these deficits can be attributed largely to (a) the practice of central planning with direct controls and, related to this, (b) excessive tautness in the plans — what

* This paper has benefited from discussions with Charles Kindleberger, Rachel McCulloch, Robert Tarr and Gordon Weil. I also gratefully acknowledge support from the Bureau of East—West Trade of the US Department of Commerce, Contract 6—362—42, in writing this paper.

† We will be concerned with the Eastern European (including the USSR) members of CMEA.

some have called 'overfull employment' – and (c) distorted domestic prices.*
Briefly the arguments are as follows:

(1) Almost three-quarters of the exports of advanced industrial nations
are manufactured products (SITC categories 5–8). This is also true of
intra-CMEA trade. In trade with the West, however, CMEA's exports
of manufactured products are no more than one-third whereas imports
are more than four-fifths of the total. This – as it might be called –
comparative disadvantage in manufactured products is due, according
to Imre Vajda, to lack of innovation and to deficiencies in 'performance,
reliability . . . appearance, packing, delivery and credit terms, assembling
facilities, after-sale services, advertising . . . selling itself . . .'.[5] These
deficiencies, in turn, are due to the relative lack of competition in both
domestic and intra-CMEA trade as a result of distribution according to
plan, excessive tautness and consequent pervasive sellers' markets, and
other well-known deficiencies of the existing systems of success
indicators.

(2) Excessive tautness in plans, like inflationary pressures in the West, puts
pressure on the balance of payments as excess demand seeks satisfaction
both through higher imports and through diverting exportables to
domestic use.

(3) Central planning by direct controls results in so-called 'commodity
inconvertibility'. Foreign buyers cannot make unplanned purchases
because of the disruptive effect this would have on the exporting
country's plan. This significantly reduces the competitive ability of
CMEA exporters. It also contributes to the inconvertibility of CMEA
currencies.

(4) Again to avoid plan disruption, CMEA countries are prevented from
rapidly adjusting imports downward to levels which can be supported
by exports. Hence the Western recession in 1975, and decline in
Western imports, may have resulted in greater deficits for CMEA
nations than would have been the case for some comparable capitalist
nations.

(5) The distorted domestic prices in CMEA countries† necessitate using
adjusted world prices in intra-CMEA trade and using world prices
unrelated to CMEA domestic prices in East–West trade. This, along

---

* The analysis presented immediately below is less relevant to Hungary than to other
CMEA countries because of Hungary's relatively radical economic reforms.

† In the words of three Polish economists: 'Because of the autonomous system of
domestic prices in each country, an automatic and purely internal character of the
monetary system and arbitrary official rates of exchange which do not reflect relative
values of currencies, it is impossible to compare prices and costs of production of
particular commodities in different countries . . .' (cited by Z. Fallenbuchl – (from a
Polish source), 'East European Integration: Comecon,' in Joint Economic Committee,
Congress of the United States, *Reorientation and Commercial Relations of the
Economies of Eastern Europe* [Washington 1974]).

with commodity inconvertibility, makes the domestic currencies of the CMEA, and also the transferable rouble (TR), all inconvertible. It also deprives their exchange rates of any real price function. Devaluation, for example, cannot affect East—West trade and can only affect a small percentage of transactions in intra-CMEA trade. Inability to use devaluation as a tool for achieving an equilibrium in the balance of payments is a serious shortcoming and is certainly responsible, in part, for hard-currency problems.

(6) Commodity inconvertibility results in rigidly bilateral trade within CMEA (see below). The use of world currencies and world prices frees East—West trade from this straitjacket.

Having traced briefly the extent and causes of the hard-currency balance-of-payments problems of the Eastern nations, I will now examine two important proposals which have been made regarding convertibility. One is for the CMEA to develop an externally convertible rouble (ECR) which would be used exclusively in East—West trade. The ECR would be a purely financial instrument which could not be used to buy goods within the CMEA but only for exchange into Western currencies. Of course, to the extent that any Western trader holding ECRs was able to use them to purchase goods in other Western countries, there would be no hindrances from the CMEA side. The second proposal, one which has been around for at least a decade, is to make the transferable rouble (TR) a convertible currency. Both of these proposals have implications for the hard-currency problems of the CMEA. Making the TR a convertible currency is a much more difficult and profound change than the establishment of an ECR and in effect would make an ECR unnecessary. It would also have important implications for intra-CMEA trade. Therefore let us consider first the possibilities and implications of establishing an ECR.

II THE EXTERNALLY CONVERTIBLE ROUBLE

To my knowledge, the ECR as such was proposed first by Peter Wiles.[6] More recently (October 1975) at a conference of Eastern and Western international monetary experts held near Athens, the proposal was made by a number of Eastern European bankers. A related proposal — using the TR in East—West trade without solving the commodity convertibility problem — has been advanced by Soviet economists on at least two occasions recently[7] and was also suggested in Section 7, Articles 5 and 12 of the 'Comprehensive Programme' of 1971 (see below).

The idea of an ECR is attractive: if successful, it could provide another financial link between East and West, one upon which more profound monetary relationships might be developed. From the standpoint of the Eastern nations, the proposal must have positive political value since it would give them for the first time representation among world currencies. Still another possible advantage of financial convertibility mentioned by Wiles[8] is that it would enable CMEA countries which joined the IMF to comply technically, if not substantively, with Article VIII which requires members to strive for currency convertibility. Financial convertibility might satisfy this condition, though in a way not envisaged by the Bretton Woods fathers since they never anticipated the existence of financial convertibility without commodity convertibility. On the other hand it might not – unless the CMEA could join the IMF as a group – since the ECR is not identified with individual nations.

A main purpose of the ECR, however, must be that it would provide the CMEA with some economic advantages. What economic advantages might be expected? Gains accruing to a nation which issues currency that is used in international transactions are usually called seignorage. Normally seignorage results when a nation pays a lower rate of interest on outstanding holdings of its currency than it is able to earn, either at home or abroad, on the investments* made possible by the fact that foreigners are willing to hold its currency. Related to this is the fact that foreigners, by their willingness to hold others' currencies, in effect extend credit and allow debtor nations to live beyond their means, at least temporarily. In the 1950s and early 1960s, the United States was able to live beyond its means because foreigners were willing to hold dollars, and to hold them at low or zero rates of interest. Seignorage on this score was partly offset, of course, by various constraints and costs which the United States was forced to bear as a result.[9] The question to be raised here is whether the CMEA can expect to get more and cheaper credit if an ECR is created. Other possible gains to the CMEA must also be considered, however. As we have seen, the CMEA nations suffer from other disadvantages in international trade. Therefore it would be worth enquiring whether the use of the ECR would ameliorate these problems – inability to devalue the currency, commodity inconvertibility, and excessive bilateralism in trade.

It is simple enough to create ECRs. The member nations of CMEA must make deposits in their International Bank for Economic Cooperation (IBEC) or some other financial institution against which they can draw ECRs with which to pay hard-currency debts to Western nations. Some portion of these deposits must be in convertible currencies and/or gold so that the bank can convert upon request outstanding ECRs held by foreigners. This means that the CMEA members as a group must hold larger hard-currency reserves than before, because now they are needed not only to satisfy transactions demands but also to guarantee ECR convertibility. If Westerners are willing to hold more ECRs than the additional value of hard-currency reserves necessarily impounded, an increase in CMEA ability to buy Western products results. The extent of the increase in available credit will depend in part on the percentage of hard-currency reserves to foreign-held ECRs that it is deemed necessary to hold.

* Actually, earnings on investments also have to cover the costs of bank services and a normal profit before seignorage results.

What are the determinants of, and what is likely to be, the demand by foreigners for ECRs? Will there be an intrinsic demand for the ECR as there is for gold and dollars or will the CMEA have to pay foreigners a high rate of return to prevent them from converting? Whether or not positive seignorage results from issuing ECRs will largely depend on the answer to this question.

There are at least four reasons why foreign currencies are demanded and held:

(1) for intervention purposes — to buy or sell against one's own currency, usually in order to maintain a fixed exchange rate;
(2) as a vehicle currency — that is, as a third currency in which two nations' traders denominate and conduct their trade;
(3) for transactions purposes — when a nation's traders use their own currency in trade;
(4) as a store of value.

The demand for currencies used for intervention and as vehicle currencies is, of course, much greater than the demand for currencies for other purposes and only the major currencies fall into these first categories. An intervention currency is bound to be one which is widely used and relatively stable in value; it is, in effect, a standard of value against which other currencies are measured and this puts it in a class by itself. There are also strong economic reasons for transacting trade in a few major vehicle currencies rather than in the more than 100 national currencies. First, vehicle currencies are usually those which over the long-run have been relatively stable in value; and their wide use is partly attributable to low exchange-rate risk. Secondly, use of vehicle currencies enables a nation both to conserve reserves and to reduce transaction costs. To understand this, we must note that a nation's transactions-demand for currencies depends to a considerable extent on the country composition of its trade and the currencies in which trade is denominated.[10] If there is any uncertainty at all regarding the amount and direction of trade, then obviously the amount of foreign exchange reserves which a nation needs to hold is reduced if trade is transacted in vehicle currencies acceptable to all nations rather than in dozens of national currencies. Use of one or a few vehicle currencies also reduces the amount of money-changing which takes place and thereby reduces transactions costs. However, despite these advantages of using vehicle currencies, any two nations which trade a lot with each other will undoubtedly find it convenient and inexpensive to conduct some part of their trade in their national currencies.

Now, with these factors in mind, compare the qualifications of the proposed ECR with those of the dollar and other world currencies. The dollar currently serves as the main world intervention and vehicle currency. In 1973, with world exports totalling a little more than $500 billion, the United States exported over $70 billion worth of goods, considerably more than any other country. Further, the USA had more investments in other countries, and more countries had investments in the USA, than is true of any other nation.

Other factors also contribute to the universality of the dollar. Existence within the borders of the USA of the largest financial market in the world guarantees a relative stability in the face of possible internationally generated financial shocks. Confidence is also generated by the size and variety of US output – a foreigner with dollars can always find things to buy at reasonable prices within the United States. Finally, the dollar has demonstrated as high a degree of stability of value as any currency over the past thirty years.

The British pound and French franc also play fairly important roles as vehicle currencies, and to some extent also as intervention currencies. For one thing, the British and French are among the world's largest five trading and investing (abroad) nations; for another, they have had close political and economic relationships for a century with many smaller nations which use their currencies as reserves and as units of account. The West German Mark is also used quite heavily in world trade and as a reserve asset. This is explained by the facts that West Germany's trade is second only to that of the United States and that the Mark has been possibly the strongest currency in the world over the past decade, with very large foreign exchange reserves to back it.

What about the trade of the CMEA nations? Their truly multilateral hard-currency trade with the West in 1973 was less than $15 billion and may not have exceeded $10 billion – approximately the level of Sweden's trade and less than half that of Italy or the Netherlands, for example. Further, their investments in the West are negligible and local financial markets non-existent. It seems highly unlikely, in light of these facts, that there would in the foreseeable future be a demand for ECRs either for purposes of intervention or as a vehicle currency. This would imply a sharp limit to the value of ECRs which foreigners (private or official) might demand or be willing to hold, all other things being equal, which would, in turn, reduce the probability of substantial seignorage resulting from the issuance of ECRs. It is indeed sobering to consider that even the British receive little or no seignorage from the very wide use of pounds sterling in world trade.[11] It is even more sobering to consider that on balance even the United States may not have derived a net gain from the almost universal use of the dollar by the rest of the world in the postwar period.[12]

Under these circumstances, what is the likelihood of the ECR replacing Western vehicle currencies in East–West transactions? Arguments against this occurring on a wide scale are stated in the previous paragraph; what we have perceived as the advantages of vehicle currencies are disadvantages of the ECR. Use of the ECR would increase both the transaction costs and amount of reserves Western trading partners would have to hold. While these costs would not loom large, because East–West trade is such a small part of Western trade, they might loom relatively large in terms of the value of the trade (East–West) in connection with which they would be incurred. Another obstacle to the use of the ECR as a transactions currency, at least initially, would be the artificiality of drawing up contracts in ECRs, particularly when prices in ECRs would really be world prices mechanically translated into roubles. Further, Western traders are used to their own currencies and to the vehicle currencies in which they usually transact business. These factors present psychological obstacles that might significantly impede the introduction of ECRs or, alternatively, raise the costs of introducing them; admittedly, these impediments might be overcome in time.

Two further impediments to the use of the ECR as a transactions currency are the facts that it would be a currency without a country and that like all Eastern currencies, including the transferable Rouble, it would have very low if not zero commodity convertibility. That there would be low or zero commodity convertibility is attested by the very name of the proposed currency — it is only 'externally convertible'; commodity inconvertibility would appear to be compounded by the fact that the ECR has no real referent in a specific country.* It is a fairly obvious historical fact that the currencies which have been used the most in the world, with the exception of gold which has a unique mythology, have been currencies of the major trading countries which provide, in fact, a maximum of commodity convertibility. It is all well and good to guarantee 'financial convertibility'; but it must also be recognised that a currency with financial convertibility not backed up by commodity convertibility will have a lower value to prospective holders than one with commodity convertibility. When Western currencies have been financially inconvertible, as after the Second World War, the values of these currencies always fell. But there was always a limit to the loss of value as a result of the fact that one could always convert the currencies into a wide range of commodities, admittedly a second-best solution. The value of an ECR must be almost exclusively based on financial convertibility, since its commodity convertibility would be much more limited if not zero.

The upshot of this discussion is that there is nothing inherently attractive about ECRs to encourage Western traders, banks, or treasuries to hold them. This suggests that if the ECRs are to be launched successfully, they will have to be endowed with special features which will create a demand for them, essentially as a store of value. By special features I mean both the terms of convertibility and the interest to be paid on ECR deposits.

Wiles proposed that in a period of world inflation, like the present one, ECR deposits be indexed to the US dollar price level.[13] There certainly would be a demand for any asset which proved to be relatively inflation-proof — so long as inflation persists. In periods of rapid inflation, the implicit interest rate on such balances could be very high; but should prices once more become stable, demand for new ECRs on this account would undoubtedly collapse. Wiles thinks that it would be a real coup for CMEA to introduce ECRs on this basis. He seems to forget that it could be costly to redeem such a currency if prices had been rising rapidly.†

---

* Some reluctance has been observed even with respect to the SDR, and also the European Unit of Account (EUA) and the European Currency Unit (ECU) (*Cf. The Economist*, 14 February 1976, p. 13).

† Actually, Wiles's proposal is quite arbitrary. A more flexible approach would be to

The ECRs could also be guaranteed against devaluation. Presumably the CMEA could guarantee holders of ECRs the exchange rates which prevailed on a particular date around the time of issuance. On the assumption that inflation continues, that most exchange rates are pegged, and that adjustments between other currencies are made more by devaluations than by revaluations,* the ECR would gradually become worth more and more in terms of all other currencies. This would make it a fairly attractive asset with an implicit interest rate equal to the average rate of devaluation of world currencies – perhaps approximating the rate of world inflation.

The ECR might also be tied to the SDR and thereby to an average of major exchange rates. Like a share of stock in a mutual fund, an ECR so denominated would eliminate some of the exchange-rate risk attached to holding foreign currencies, retaining its value better than those currencies which depreciate the most, but not as well as those which depreciate less than the average or even appreciate. The implicit rate of return on ECRs held under these terms would not be high.

Other possible convertibility terms can be conjectured of course, but this is not necessary for our purposes. To the extent that the terms of convertibility yield an implicitly high rate of return to those holding ECR deposits, explicit interest payments may not be necessary. On the other hand, under less favourable convertibility terms – like tieing the ECR to the SDR – it may be necessary to pay interest on deposits if creditors are to be cajoled into holding ECRs.

The question to be asked is: given the need to overcome depositor reluctance, what possibility is there that positive seignorage would be realised on the use of ECRs? Normally, seignorage would be measured by comparing the interest costs on deposits with the returns from investments which are made by banks with their free resources. In this case, the interest costs are those, both implicit and explicit, on ECRs held by Westerners; and the returns on investment are properly viewed as the rate of return on, or profitability of, imports financed by the ECRs. In comparing interest costs on liabilities with returns on assets (i.e. imports), it is necessary to take account of the fact that some assets must be held as reserves in liquid form to insure convertibility.† The returns on these reserves are likely to be relatively low and on gold and cash, of course, zero. The possibility of profitably using ECRs to finance imports will vary inversely with the percentage of liquid reserves to total assets which it seems prudent to hold and with the gap between the rate of return

---

view the ECR deposit as equivalent to a kind of short-term interest-bearing security and to let the interest rate on it be set (determined) with reference to competitive money market instruments.

* In a world of universal float, adjustments would probably be made roughly equally by devaluation and revaluation and, presumably, the ECR would also float.

† The return on imports is not much affected by inflation since their values rise with other prices. On the other hand, to the extent that Western currencies are held as reserves, CMEA runs a devaluation risk.

on imports and rate of interest paid on deposits. If it is profitable to issue
ECRs, then CMEA's ability to import Western products is expanded beyond
the value of its hard-currency reserves by an amount which depends on the
ratio of reserves to ECRs that must be maintained. How large must this reserve
ratio be?

Let me answer this question by considering a crude diagrammatic representation of the static relationship between the interest rate on currency deposits

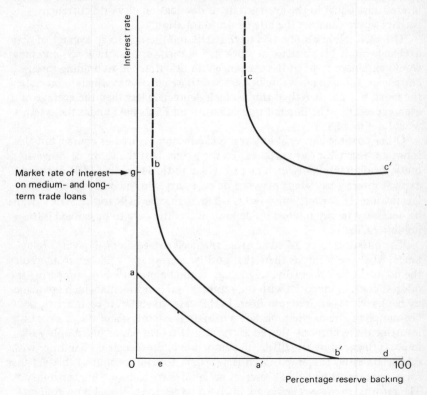

Fig. 1. Relationship between the percentage of reserve backing and the
interest rate on currency deposits held by foreigners.

(or near-moneys) held by foreigners and the ratio of hard-currency reserves to
the value of these foreign-held deposits. As implied above, the relationship
will be inverse — the lower the percentage of reserve backing, the higher the
interest rate required to induce foreigners to hold the currency.

In Figure 1 the three lines reflect this trade-off; and the relative distances
of the lines from the axes reflect the various factors mentioned above. Line
$aa'd$ may be taken to represent an intervention currency (say, the dollar) which
is held interest-free or at a very low rate until the reserve/deposit ratio falls to

a', after which a small interest payment is required. Line $bb'd$ could be taken to represent a slightly weaker currency — say, a vehicle currency like the pound sterling. It should be noted that a very low reserve/deposit ratio (say, oe) probably reflects a serious balance-of-payments problem, in which case any but one of the most traditional vehicle currencies would probably cease to serve as such, and the whole curve would shift to the north-east. Finally, line cc' is taken to represent a hypothetical ECR. It is my belief, for reasons set out below (and above), that even with large reserves to back the ECRs, interest on ECR deposits held by foreigners would have to approximate the market rate on foreign trade loans (og) if deposits are to be maintained; and that if reserve ratios were to be lowered, the required interest rate would rapidly become prohibitive.

Let me now return to the main line of argument.*

To complete the framework it is also essential to consider alternative ways of financing deficits. Is there any reason to believe, for example, that the interest rate which CMEA nations would have to pay on ECRs would be any lower than that which would be necessary to raise funds in the Eurodollar or other private financial markets or to get additional official credit from, say, the French Government?† In a perfect financial market, there should be no difference between interest rates; and if there is no difference, it might be possible for the CMEA to make its resources go further by borrowing directly than by issuing ECRs. This is because, unlike raising credits, the issuance of ECRs would require the CMEA to hold additional hard-currency reserves to ensure ECR convertibility, thereby immobilising resources which could otherwise have been spent in the West. How likely is it that there will be little difference in interest rates between credits and ECRs? Probably much more likely than in the West. This is because in the East the borrower and issuer of currency are one and the same economic unit — a government or group of governments — whereas in the West borrowers may be governments and their institutions, private businesses, private banks or some combination of these. This leads us to conclude that the CMEA nations can probably do as well or better by borrowing in world credit markets than by issuing ECRs.

To sum up so far: there would appear to be little or no reason for ECRs to be demanded as vehicle currencies or for transactions purposes. Given a high enough rate of interest (explicit or implicit) on ECR deposits, they would be held by foreigners as a store of value. Under these circumstances, of course, there would be no positive, but probably negative, seignorage on ECRs. The fact, noted above, that the pound sterling earns little or no seignorage would

---

* This is not the place to discuss in detail the factors determining the shapes and positions of the curves in Figure 1, including the possibilities of shifts in position over time.

† We abstract here from the important fact that ECRs would be backed and used by CMEA as a group whereas securing credits is on an individual-country basis. Clearly, under an ECR system, the financially weaker CMEA nations would benefit relatively to the financially stronger, who actually might lose.

lead one to predict negative seignorage for ECRs. This fits with the current theory[14] that seignorage results only when the currency-issuing nation is possessed of monopolistic powers in world money markets, which would not be the case for the issuer of ECRs any more than it is for most other nations.

Even if a case could be made, in general, for ECRs, this would be a poor time to introduce them. The debt-service/export ratios of all the CMEA nations are at present high. As noted, over the past year (1975), very large deficits were sustained because of the Western recession and the disastrous Soviet grain crop. Large deficits were predicted for 1976. Imagine how holders of ECRs would have felt in 1975 when the news of the disastrous Soviet grain crop was announced or when, as the impact of the recession reduced CMEA exports, reports of rapidly rising deficits were made public. Surely, demands for conversion would have created serious problems, if not a convertibility crisis!

Before leaving the ECR, it is worth questioning briefly whether its use would help to resolve other major difficulties which have beset CMEA foreign trade — bilateralism, commodity inconvertibility, and inability to use devaluation as an instrument for achieving trade balance. While bilateralism is a serious problem in intra-CMEA trade, it is absent from East—West trade. East—West trade is conducted largely in Western vehicle currencies. Since there is at present general convertibility in the West, CMEA nations can spend their export earnings wherever they wish. The trade data show that earnings are spent relatively multilaterally, not bilaterally. Since the ECR is proposed for East—West trade, it can contribute nothing to solving the problems of intra-CMEA bilateralism.

Unlike bilateralism, commodity inconvertibility and inability to devalue are problems which do affect East—West trade. However, both of these problems are intimately connected with central planning by direct controls as it is practised in Eastern Europe today; their amelioration requires, in my opinion, nothing more and nothing less than a significant decentralisation of planning and pricing, as discussed below.

III CONVERTIBILITY OF THE TRANSFERABLE ROUBLE (TR)

Before 1963, trade between CMEA countries was conducted bilaterally and each pair of countries attempted to achieve a balance as close to perfect as possible. Occasional deviations occurred as a result of specially planned trilateral arrangements, planned credits, and failures of plans to be fulfilled. Because of the heterogeneity of distorted price structures which existed among the Eastern countries, negotiations were based on adjusted world prices and usually held stable for at least five years. Domestic prices and currencies of the CMEA countries played no role whatsoever in this process. While each country reported its trade in its own currency, this represented simply a mechanical translation from adjusted world prices at some exchange rate (often an unrealistic one) and the domestic-currency values reported implied prices in fact quite unrelated to the actual domestic price structure. No currency needed to be exchanged since trade was balanced. In fact, trade was balanced because of the desire of each country to avoid holding the currencies of other CMEA countries — a consequence of commodity inconvertibility and distorted prices.*

In 1963, the International Bank for Economic Cooperation (IBEC) was formed. A major purpose of IBEC was to free intra-CMEA trade from the shackles of rigid bilateralism. Toward this end a transferable rouble was created. All intra-CMEA trade was to be transacted in TRs and members were encouraged to trade with each other multilaterally, settling their imbalances in TRs. But rigid bilateralism remained despite the use of TRs. In particular, the CMEA countries which 'tended' to be in overall surplus insisted on balancing their trade with those which tended to be in overall deficit. With commodity inconvertibility, it mattered not whether countries held zlotys, roubles and other national currencies *or* TRs — none of them could be spent freely.

So the search for a multilateral settlement system has continued. Section 7 of the well-known CMEA *Comprehensive Programme* of 1971 was devoted to 'Improvement of Currency-Financial Relations'. Measures were to be developed and implemented by 1973 which would expand the use of the TR for multilateral settlements (Article 9). The TR is to be used, like other currencies, for settlements with third countries (Articles 5 and 12). Mutual convertibility of the TR and other CMEA currencies is envisaged (Article 15). Conditions for this mutual convertibility are to be worked out by 1973 (Article 18). IBEC is to be used to secure convertibility of the TR (Article 26).

The year 1973 has come and gone and so far as I am aware, nothing has been accomplished to *significantly* reduce bilateralism or achieve convertibility. Some insight into the causes of this lack of progress is gained by considering in traditional theoretical terms, what attributes of money the TR has. V. F. Garbuzov, Soviet Minister of Finance, states a view which can be found in several Soviet writings about the TR. He argues that experience demonstrates that 'the transferable rouble performs all of the basic functions of an international socialist currency: measure of value, means of payment, means of accumulation'.[15] It seems doubtful to me that this view can be as widespread among Eastern economists as the printed word suggests. I say this because, in my opinion, the TR embodies less 'moneyness' than almost any other currency presently in use and I totally disagree with the Garbuzov view cited above.

Is the TR a measure of value? Only in the most trivial sense of the term. This can easily be seen by asking first how prices in TRs are set? Prices in

* It is probably more correct to say that the country suffered from commodity inconvertibility than that commodity inconvertibility was a characteristic of the currency — for even holders of gold and dollars could not freely purchase products, particularly intermediate products, in CMEA countries, because of the havoc this would wreak on the central plans.

intra-CMEA trade are 'fixed on the basis of world prices freed of the harmful influence exerted by the interplay of speculative forces on the capitalist market which ensures its stability and excludes all influence on it by the crisis-like phenomena inherent in the capitalist currency system'.[16] In other works the relative values of products are based on capitalist relative values as expressed in world markets at some point in time, then adjusted (as noted above) and maintained fixed, usually for a period of five years. At this point, these capitalist prices are transformed into TRs at an arbitrary rate of exchange, based on the fact that a TR is declared to be worth 0·987412 grams of gold. The point is that the TR has nothing to do with the relationships among prices; these 'measures of value' flow basically out of the capitalist market. For purposes of CMEA trade, it wouldn't matter whether they remained in dollars, or were translated into TRs, Dutch guilders, Mongolian tugriks or, for that matter, into (American) Indian wampum.

Another problem arises regarding the validity of the TR as a measure of value when one considers that both the TR and the Soviet rouble are declared to be worth 0·987412 grams of gold yet (1) since the TR was established, world prices (hence prices in TRs) and Soviet internal prices have changed at different rates* and (2) relative prices in the USSR have often been quite different from those used in CMEA expressed in TRs.[17] In fact, a Soviet economist, Iu. Ivanov, published in 1968 an article demonstrating how to translate exports and imports in foreign trade prices into domestic prices.[18] Can the rouble (zloty, lev, etc.) and the TR both be valid measures of value when they attribute different relative and absolute values to the same pairs of commodities?

Is the TR a 'means of payment' or, as Western textbooks say, a medium of exchange? Again, only in a trivial sense of the meaning of the term. The power of a currency as a medium of exchange is related to the degree of option that one has in spending it. An American citizen with a dollar can spend it in literally thousands of different ways. The same is true of a Soviet citizen with roubles or a Polish citizen with zlotys. The possessor of a TR is in no such fortunate position. As a result of commodity inconvertibility, he can only spend it on a particular product in accordance with advance plans. Each TR is like a ration card — it is designated in advance to buy a particular product. No one to my knowledge has ever called a ration card 'money'. Money is, after all, generalised purchasing power.

There are at least two ways to interpret bilateral exchanges of goods valued in TRs between two CMEA countries. On the one hand, one might say that each country has thousands of ration cards denominated in TRs, each for the purchase of a separate product. On the other hand, since a planned balance of total trade is usually the immediate goal of each pair of trading partners, it

---

* At this point, it should be noted that, at least until the recent rapid increase in world prices, the 'adjusted world prices' used by CMEA were substantially higher than real world prices.

could be argued that the TR does not even serve the function of a ration card. To the extent that trade is balanced, as planned, one might view the trade process as an instance of a gigantic barter. The fact that the products are denominated in TRs relates to the measure of value, or unit of account, function discussed above rather than to the medium of exchange. Only the imbalances, in this interpretation, could qualify for status as medium of exchange and this would represent a tiny fraction of total intra-CMEA trade. Further, it would be subject to the commodity inconvertibility qualification already mentioned.

Is the TR a 'means of accumulation' (store of value). It is a means of accumulation but, certainly, not a desirable means of accumulation. If it were a desirable means of accumulation, the various CMEA countries would not strive so hard to balance their payments with each other so as to avoid accumulating TRs. Not only is the very low rate of interest paid to holders of TRs undoubtedly far below the social rate of return on investment in all of the CMEA countries, but the existence of commodity inconvertibility and distorted domestic price structures creates great uncertainty regarding the true value which might be realised on each particular TR that one might hold.* A 'store of value' at the time of its realisation becomes a 'medium of exchange'.

The Eastern literature does not ascribe to the TR a role as a 'standard of deferred payment', typically one of the characteristics of money listed by Western economists. In fact, it would seem to me that the TR, particularly in times of inflation like the present, is a better standard of deferred payment than most capitalist currencies.

We have argued so far that the TR serves very poorly the major functions of money. Not having strong characteristics as 'money', it is easy to understand why the introduction of the TR was of no assistance in reducing intra-CMEA bilateralism. So long as the CMEA does not have a truly convertible currency, CMEA nations will continue to have to trade on a largely bilateral basis.

Would convertibility of the TR be difficult to achieve? Some observers are optimistic. At a Conference in Venice in 1975, Yuri Ivanov, President of the Soviet Foreign Trade Bank, is reported to have said that the CMEA is considering introducing convertibility of the TR, particularly in relation to Western industrial countries, and that this could 'easily' be done.[19] I would be much less optimistic. The TR is inconvertible for the same reasons that national CMEA currencies are inconvertible – commodity inconvertibility and price structures which are distorted in the sense described earlier and which, therefore, are unrelated to world prices. What would it take to eliminate commodity inconvertibility and arbitrary prices? In my opinion, this can only be achieved by radical economic reforms which substitute decentralised planning for the

---

* By extension of the above logic, it can be argued that any multilateralism introduced into CMEA trade by IBEC credits in TRs should not be attributed to the inherent qualities of the TRs.

central planning with direct controls which dominates the CMEA at present (Hungary being a partial exception). The establishment of free internal markets and free prices in which both domestic and foreign buyers and sellers can operate, subject only to indirect state controls, would lead eventually to an organic connection between internal and external markets and price structures, as is the case among Western countries. This would create necessary conditions for the convertibility of CMEA currencies. It would not be sufficient, however: it would also be essential that each country get itself into approximate balance-of-payments equilibrium, thereby establishing the conditions for 'currency' as well as 'commodity' convertibility.

The elimination of commodity inconvertibility and arbitrary pricing and the achievement of payments equilibrium would permit each country to make its currency convertible and would eliminate the need for bilateral balancing of trade. Each currency would then serve in the international market as a measure of value, medium of exchange, and store of value. What about the TR? There would, in fact, be no need for a TR if national currencies became convertible. (There would also be no need for an ECR, of course.) What probably would happen is that trade would be conducted in one of the vehicle currencies, say dollars, or if the USSR continued to be the major trading partner of most other CMEA countries (which it might not be under the assumed conditions set out below), then the Soviet rouble might assume the role of vehicle currency for the Eastern group of nations.

So far, I have discussed the impact of radical reforms primarily on bilateralism in intra-CMEA trade, not the subject of this Conference. However, such reforms would also have a profound impact on East—West trade relations. Most important, such reforms might serve to reduce the Eastern balance-of-payments pressures in trade with the West, although there might be a medium-term transition period before beneficial effects were experienced in which the reverse was true. An end to allocation according to plan and excessive tautness in planning, along with greater Western competition in the domestic markets of the CMEA countries, should gradually raise the quality and saleability in the West of CMEA manufactured products. Competition should also improve incentives to innovate and to diffuse innovation. The combination of these factors should eventually reduce CMEA demand for Western manufactured products and technology and increase the amount they can profitably sell to the West. Ability to sell to the West would also be strongly enhanced by commodity convertibility. There seems little doubt that if Western importers were able to compete freely for currently produced Eastern products and were not faced with the delays and uncertainties connected with having to get desired products into the 'planned export' category, more exports to the West would result. Still another advantage of radical internal reforms and convertibility would be that CMEA nations which were encountering hard-currency balance-of-payments problems would have available to them the possibility of devaluing their currencies in order to get into equilibrium. It is my belief, discussed elsewhere,[20] that inability to devalue is an important factor behind the CMEA's persistent deficits with the West.

To sum up: I see no possibility of making the TR convertible in either intra-CMEA or East–West trade so long as present methods of central planning with direct controls dominate CMEA practice. Radical economic reforms would make possible a convertible TR but would also render it unnecessary, since the reforms required for TR convertibility would also lead to convertibility of the national currencies of the Eastern nations. Such reforms would also make the ECR unnecessary. Finally, radical reforms would remove some of the problems that have led to CMEA's persistent hard-currency deficit with the West and by this token reduce the demand for credit.

IV WHAT POLICY FOR CMEA?

Faced with persistent hard-currency deficits in East–West trade and with persistent bilateralism in intra-CMEA trade, CMEA policy-makers and economists have been casting about for solutions, some of which relate to creating convertible supranational currencies. I have argued that these efforts are misguided, and that the way to mitigate or eliminate these foreign trade problems is by introducing radical economic reforms in which planning is decentralised. The question is: should CMEA introduce radical economic reforms in order to eliminate its foreign trade problems, not to mention other (internal) problems attributable to central planning with direct controls?

This question cannot be answered in strictly economic terms but is more properly a question of political economy and of politics. While radical reforms might result in improvements in foreign trade performance, for the reasons noted above, they might well conflict with other CMEA goals. For example, CMEA constitutes the most tightly knit trading group in the world. Intra-CMEA trade is at present probably in the neighbourhood of 55–60 per cent of the total trade of the CMEA countries, or about three times the degree of concentration of trade among them in the pre-war period. The introduction of decentralised planning and freer trade would certainly lead to a much sharper reduction in intra-CMEA trade than would otherwise be likely to occur. The leaders of the Eastern nations may consider this an undesirable result.*

The Eastern leaders may also have a political or ideological preference for planning with direct controls rather than for allowing their economies to experience some of the so-called anarchy of the market. They are, of course, entitled to such a preference. In the West, the preference is for the anarchy of the market. In the pre-war period, market anarchy in the West led to the Great Depression and, in the past ten to fifteen years, it has led to stagflation. Great Depressions of the magnitude of that experienced in the 1930s are probably a thing of the past; but stagflation, with the socio-economic disrup-

---

* The smaller CMEA nations, with their higher trade participation ratios, are likely to be influenced relatively more by economic than by political factors in their preferences regarding foreign trade policies.

tion it involves, is an unsolved problem. Stagflation could be wiped out by the introduction of planning and controls. However, the preference of most Western economists and political leaders is to stick with the market and to try to find a market solution to stagflation – although the prospects at the moment are not bright.

Convertibility and freer trade would do violence to other accepted goals of the socialist nations. Dedication to full employment, job stability and stable prices, particularly of consumers' goods, is much more absolute in the East than it is in the West. Radical economic reforms, convertibility and so forth, would open the economies of the CMEA nations to much of the relative instability that characterises Western capitalist countries. Would any Eastern country allow itself to import the Western inflation of the past ten years? As Professor Csikós-Nagy says, 'The importation of inflation is incompatible with the economic policy of the socialist countries.'[21] Or would Eastern authorities allow foreign exporters freely to outcompete some domestic industries, all of which are nationalised? (In the West, after all, governments do not always allow foreign exporters to outcompete even their private industries!) It seems unlikely, in my opinion, without a total transformation of values and goals. As Janos Fekete, Deputy President of the National Bank of Hungary has put it, 'Convertibility in the Western sense would introduce such spontaneous elements into our planned economies which we cannot undertake.'[22]

There is no need to expand this list of examples further. Both the planned and market economies have their problems and both prefer to try to solve them in ways which are consistent with political and ideological predilections. Radical changes under either system will be delayed while there is still a chance that conservative solutions will work and while economic performance, if not entirely satisfactory, is still adequate.

In light of the above, I feel that radical reforms to solve foreign trade problems are not likely to be undertaken by the CMEA in the near future. As indicated earlier, I feel that an attempt to establish an ECR for East–West trade would be misguided. The CMEA nations have received large amounts of Western credits and are unlikely to enlarge their imports significantly and at reasonable cost through ECRs. Further, the use of Western currencies ensures multilateral East–West trade and so there is nothing to be gained on this score. Even more misguided are those who talk of making the TR a convertible currency. Given the inconvertibility of TRs, and unwillingness to adopt radical economic reforms, there is in my opinion no first-best solution to the problem of intra-CMEA bilateralism. The goals for convertibility set in Section 7 of the *Comprehensive Programme* of 1971 will not be implemented, given central planning with direct controls.

On the other hand, some multilateralism may be achieved through the planning for integration on a multilateral basis which is envisaged in other sections of the *Comprehensive Programme*. This is, of course, a much less effective way of achieving multilateralism even if it can be so achieved.* Any multilateralism so achieved should not be attributed to the TR, as some

Eastern economists have done. As K. Nazarkin, President of IBEC has admitted, multilateral balancing which is planned in advance is not 'real transferability'.[23] When Iu. Konstantinov, head of the Currency-Financial Division of the Secretariat of CMEA says 'The planned organisation of commodity flows is essentially the factor that assures the effectiveness of the "work" of the transferable rouble, its actual convertibility into commodities, and real utilisation of assets in the collective currency,' he is partly echoing Nazarkin's insights; but he is also confusing the issue in suggesting that the TR is doing any work at all: it is not.

A few other possibilities of ameliorating intra-bloc bilateralism do exist and were proposed by this writer in 1964.[25] One is to establish a market for national CMEA currencies in which interest rates on outstanding balances would be allowed to reflect flexibly the relative desirability of each currency. Growing deficits would be accompanied by rising rates of interest sufficient to attract holders. Such market prices on outstanding currency balances would facilitate multilateral currency and trade exchanges and would also give the deficit-prone nations an incentive to balance their accounts. Another possibility would be to introduce commodity convertibility in consumers' goods. This would be much less disruptive of planning than commodity convertibility in producers' goods and other intermediate products.* I am not sure how feasible either of these proposals is. My third proposal was for the CMEA nations to accumulate hard-currency balances and to use these to multilaterialise their payments. More recently it has been proposed that the process be started by requiring small percentages of any imbalance to be paid in hard currency and that this percentage gradually be increased until all imbalances are settled in hard currency. In 1964 I felt that this was an impractical proposal and that is still my opinion. The reason is the very great shortage of, and therefore premium on, hard-currency balances in CMEA. With all CMEA nations short of hard currency, no nation will willingly accept a creditor position in trade when only, say, 10–30 per cent of the balance is payable in hard currency. On the other hand, as the percentage of deficit payable in hard currency rises, the debtors will gradually become more and more reluctant to incur deficits with CMEA partners. So, until CMEA is in some kind of hard-currency equilibrium with the West it would not seem possible to use hard currencies to multilateralise intra-CMEA trade since at least one partner will always insist on a bilateral balance. Such multilateralisation as might take place would, in any case, not affect the basic inconvertibility of the TR. It would not, therefore, affect CMEA's position in East–West trade.

---

* Mme Lavigne says that coordination has been largely bilateral thus far (Marie Lavigne, *The Socialist Economies of the Soviet Union and Europe* [White Plains, New York, 1947]).

* Mme Lavigne says that this proposal seems to be currently under consideration (*op. cit.* pp. 315–16).

[*Professor Holzman has asked, since the conclusion of the Conference, for the following note to be added to his paper* (Ed.).]

Since this paper was completed, it has been reported that the IBEC Council decided in October 1976 to allow traders and banks of non-communist nations to accept and hold TRs in payment for exports and to use them in settlement of accounts (Moscow Narodny Bank, *Press Bulletin,* 8 December 1976, pp. 14–18; *Financial Times,* 17 December 1976). Apparently importers cannot use TRs directly for purchases in CMEA countries and banks holding TRs must have the prior agreement of the governments involved. This may be inferred from the statement in the *Press Bulletin* (p. 14) that 'The requirement of agreement between competent organs of the interested countries on purchase/sale of goods or services under settlement in transferable roubles remains in force.' The interest rate on TR accounts opened with the IBEC remains, as before, at 1 per cent per annum. Careful reading of the *Press Bulletin* suggests that once having accepted TRs, instead of convertible currencies, the Western exporter or bank cannot exchange the TRs into convertible currencies (unlike the envisaged ECRs) but can only use them in settling accounts within its own country or purchasing imports from CMEA countries; and this despite the fact that Western banks receiving credits in TRs from the IBEC are allowed to repay in either TRs or convertible currencies!

The new regulation thus appears to be an attempt, on the lines of the ECR proposal, to secure cheap credit. For the reasons noted above in connection with the ECR, it seems doomed to failure. It seems very unlikely that a Western exporter would agree to accept in payment for goods more than a token amount of TRs. Not only is the 1 per cent interest rate non-competitive, but the TR deposit appears to be inconvertible into Western currencies. Further, the IBEC requirement that the use of these deposits to pay for imports from a CMEA country requires an intergovernmental agreement underlines their commodity inconvertibility.

NOTES

1 L. Brainard, 'CMEA: Rising Deficits', *East–West Markets* (12 January 1976), p. 10.
2 L. Brainard, 'Financing Eastern Europe's Trade Gap, the Euromarket Connection', *Euromoney* (January 1976) p. 16; International Monetary Fund, *International Financial News* (Washington, D.C., 15 March 1976) p. 91.
3 B. Csikós-Nagy, 'Foreign Trade and Monetary Policy in Eastern European Countries' in *Foreign Trade and Monetary Policy* (CESES Milan, 1974) p. 207.
4 Franklyn D. Holzman, *Foreign Trade under Central Planning* (Cambridge, USA, 1974) pp. 225–9; 'Theories of the Persistent Hard Currency Deficits of Centrally Planned Economies' (manuscript, 1976).
5 Imre Vajda, 'External Equilibrium and Economic Reform', in I. Vajda and M. Simai, *Foreign Trade in a Planned Economy* (Cambridge, 1971).
6 Peter Wiles, 'On Purely Financial Convertibility', in Y. Laulan (ed.), *Banking, Money and Credit in Eastern Europe* (NATO Colloquium: Brussels, 1973).
7 K. Miroshnichenko, 'International Collective Currencies', *International Affairs*

(March 1973); K. Nazarkin 'IBEC and the Monetary System of the Socialist Community', *International Affairs* (March 1974).

8 As in Note 6, p. 124.
9 R. Z. Aliber, 'The Costs and Benefits of the US Role as a Reserve Country', *Quarterly Journal of Economics* (August 1964).
10 A. Swoboda, *The Euro-Dollar Market: An Interpretation,* Essays in International Finance, No. 64 (Princeton, 1968).
11 B. J. Cohen, 'The Seignorage Gains of an International Currency', *Quarterly Journal of Economics* (August 1971).
12 As in Note 9.
13 As in Note 6, p. 123.
14 H. Grubel, The Distribution of Seignorage from International Liquidity Creation', in R. Mundell and A. K. Swoboda (eds), *Monetary Problems of the International Economy* (Chicago, 1968); Ronald I. McKinnon, *Private and Official International Money: The Case for the Dollar,* Essays in International Finance No. 74 (Princeton, 1969).
15 V. F. Garbuzov, 'The Development of Currency and Financial Relations of Comecon Member Nations', in *Soviet and Eastern European Foreign Trade* (Summer 1973), translated from *Ekonomicheskaia gazeta,* No. 7 (1973) pp. 76–7.
16 *Comprehensive Programme for the Further Extension and Improvement of Co-operation and the Development of Socialist Economic Integration by the CMEA Member Countries,* Section 7, Article 3 (CMEA Secretariat, Moscow, 1971).
17 Holzman (1974) as in Note 4, Chapters 10, 13, 14.
18 Iu. Ivanov, 'Matrichnoe opisanie sistemy natsional'nykh schetov i balansa narodnogo khoziaistva', *Vestnik Statistiki* No. 5 (1968) pp. 51–60.
19 *East–West Trade News* (15 May 1975) p. 4.
20 Holzman (1974) as in Note 4, pp. 687–8; 1976.
21 As in Note 3, p. 206.
22 Janos Fekete, *Some Reflections on International Monetary Problems and East–West Economic Relations* (Budapest, 1975).
23 Nazarkin, as in Note 7, p. 47.
24 Iu. Konstantinov, 'Increasing the Role of the Transferable Rouble', *Problems of Economics,* translated from *Economicheskaia gazeta* (1975): 8.
25 Reprinted in Holzman (1974), as in Note 4, Chapter 6.

Discussion of the Papers by Professor Fedorowicz and Professor Holzman

Dr Rieger suggested that discussion of the two papers – both dealing with problems crucial for the further development of East–West economic relations – might usefully concentrate on two main subjects:

(i) the various convertibility proposals and whether they could mitigate the CMEA countries' deficits with the West, save reserves or improve balances of payment;

(ii) the extent of the socialist countries' hard-currency deficits and the medium-term outlook in the context of possible world-wide balance-of-payments developments.

He was ready to rule out both the 'externally convertible rouble' (ECR) and convertibility of individual CMEA currencies, as outside the realm of practical politics. He saw perhaps slightly more chance of the transformation of the transferable rouble (TR) into a convertible currency, though noting that the national economic reforms that Holzman considered necessary for such a step to be possible – and also as making the TR unnecessary – included abandonment of domestic price systems which Fedorowicz considered vital. Fedorowicz saw these price systems as essential measures of national economic policy and insulation against Western trade-cycle influences, justifying inconvertibility of national currencies and, presumably, the economic cost of – as most Western observers saw it – an 'irrational' domestic price system. In this context, Dr Rieger recalled Professor Kohlmey's useful reminder that arbitrary elements were to be found in the pricing systems of the Western economies also (p. 104), and added that in no country could a precise identity of domestic and foreign trade prices be found.

After summarising Professor Holzman's arguments on the ECR, Dr Rieger said he was convinced that such an instrument would contribute little to the solution of East–West trade problems, especially commodity inconvertibility and the inability of CMEA countries to devalue.

Dr Rieger noted that Professor Fedorowicz saw the fact that foreign trade prices denominated in TRs already derived from world market prices as eliminating the main argument for keeping the TR inconvertible; his statement that 'the deposits of socialist countries with the IBEC are already partially convertible' (p. 137) was probably news to many members of the Conference, who would welcome further elucidation. It could be argued that the introduction of convertibility of a collective currency of a group of countries differing considerably in their degree of economic development would encounter more difficulties than would convertibility of a single national currency; it would surely presuppose a fairly high degree of economic policy integration and, probably, pooling of reserves. He hoped Professor Fedorowicz would comment on this.

Considering the present state of East–West trade and balances of payments, Dr Rieger noted that to Holzman the CMEA countries' perennial hard-currency payments problem and the unfavourable commodity structure of trade were the inevitable consequences of 'over-full' employment, 'distorted' domestic prices unrelated to costs and lack of competition – with its impact on quality of manufactured goods – in both domestic and intra-CMEA trade.

Fedorowicz expected a major improvement in trade structure, but his quoted projections of CMEA exports (p. 135) were now obsolete.* Dr Rieger regretted the absence of official data on balances of payments and hard-currency indebtedness of CMEA countries. His bank's experts estimated outstanding Western credits at $25–27 billion, but he did not share Holzman's view that the CMEA countries 'may be beginning to approach a credit ceiling' (p. 144). One could not assess their creditworthiness in terms simply of the ratio of debt service to annual total, or hard-currency, exports. The CMEA countries' total outstanding debt looked quite modest against Italy's $17 billion; their outstanding borrowings in the Eurocurrency and Asian-dollar markets were about 10 per cent of the total, or only slightly greater than their share in world trade. It might reasonably be argued that to look only at total, all–CMEA, debt understated the problem of the largest individual debtors; but it had been suggested that one reason for the accepted creditworthiness of individual Eastern European countries was a tacit assumption that the USSR would at need act as lender of last resort to them. Was this an illusion?

Dr Rieger circulated the OECD 'scenario' – rather than forecast – of possible balance-of-payments developments, assuming in 1980 (i) an increasing import-absorptive capacity of the OPEC countries, and (ii) substantial official outward transfers from the OECD area and some from the OPEC countries (see Table 11).

TABLE 11 ESTIMATES OF CURRENT ACCOUNT BALANCES

Current balance excluding official transfers	1973	1974	1975	1980(a)
		($ billions)		
OECD	11	$-22\frac{1}{2}$	$5\frac{1}{2}$	20
OPEC	$3\frac{1}{2}$	66	39	$27\frac{1}{2}$
Non-oil developing countries(b)	-9	$-23\frac{1}{2}$	$-33\frac{1}{4}$	$-32\frac{1}{2}$
Other(c)	-4	$-10\frac{1}{2}$	-15	$-17\frac{1}{2}$
Discrepancy	$1\frac{1}{2}$	$9\frac{1}{2}$	$-3\frac{3}{4}$	$-2\frac{1}{2}$
Current balance including official transfers				
OECD	$2\frac{1}{2}$	$-33\frac{1}{4}$	$-6\frac{1}{2}$	$7\frac{1}{2}$
OPEC	$3\frac{1}{2}$	64	$36\frac{1}{2}$	25
Non-oil developing countries(b)	$-2\frac{1}{2}$	-15	-23	-20
Other(c)	-4	-10	$-14\frac{1}{2}$	$-17\frac{1}{2}$
Discrepancy	$-1\frac{1}{2}$	$5\frac{3}{4}$	$-7\frac{1}{2}$	-5

(a) 1975 prices but 1980 terms of trade.
(b) Excluding OECD countries and similar non-OECD Mediterranean countries.
(c) Sino-Soviet area, S. Africa, Israel, Cyprus, Malta and Yugoslavia.

* For evidence of this see UN, ECE, *Economic Survey of Europe in 1975.*

Implicit in this was a formidable payments disequilibrium to be adjusted by the national and international financial markets and by international monetary cooperation. Western financial markets, and particularly the Eurocurrency market (a Soviet invention!), had shown extraordinary flexibility and growth in recent years, the latter financing a large part of the post-1973 deficits of Eastern as well as Western European countries and many developing countries also. This support to import-capacities had made the Western recession less severe than it might otherwise have been. Nevertheless, the prospective future problems required a new effort either to expand international liquidity through the Bretton Woods institutions or to forge new international financial instruments; many people saw this as an opportunity for East—West cooperation to help to establish a truly world-wide monetary system.

Subsequent discussion centred on

  (i) the hard-currency payments problems, indebtedness and credit-worthiness of the CMEA countries;
 (ii) possibilities of convertibility of CMEA currencies or of the transferable rouble;
(iii) more general problems of balance-of-payments adjustment.

Seeking to assess the causes of the increased indebtedness of the CMEA countries to the West, *Professor Wenger* listed differential rates of inflation in East and West, shrinking Western markets due to recession, and the absence of any benefit to the socialist countries from recycling of petro-dollars; but the ratio of annual debt-service to export earnings (only some 20—30 per cent for Eastern countries against much higher ratios for some Western countries) did not support the idea that a credit ceiling had been reached, and profitable direct investment opportunities also could still be offered to Western firms. *Professor Fedorowicz* stressed that much of the CMEA countries' external borrowing had been matched by investment in export capacities; but although capacity to repay and 'creditworthiness' had thus been increased, that capacity could be rendered partly ineffective by Western recession or new trade barriers. *Dr Guzek* and *Dr Rogge* both emphasised the importance of using foreign credit, directly or indirectly, to develop *specialised* hard-currency-earning capacities. *Professor Kunz* agreed with Professor Fedorowicz and added that, while the CMEA countries were still generally considered 'creditworthy' in the West, they had to balance the value of Western credits as a means of economic growth against their cost; this meant, *inter alia*, considering debt-service commitments in relation to the likely rate of inflation in the capitalist world.

Mr Kaser pointed out, in reply to Dr Rieger, that one CMEA country — Hungary — did publish data on its hard-currency balance-of-payments, reserves and liabilities in its 'Placing Memoranda' for hard-currency loans, thereby enhancing its credit rating in the Eurocurrency market. *Professor Holzman*, like others, doubted the usefulness of debt-service/export ratios as indicators of creditworthiness; a country such as Hungary where according to Professor Csikoś-Nagy (p. 192) virtually all productive investment was export-producing or import-saving could justify a higher ratio than a capitalist country where this was not so. *Dr Hardt* doubted whether the hard-currency deficit problem required major changes in policies or institutions in the CMEA countries. Their creditworthiness, in the eyes of Western governments and financial institutions was enhanced by the state's ability (a) to mobilise not only gold and convertible currency reserves but also stocks of 'hard goods' (particularly oil and metals), and (b) through industrial cooperation to ensure the generation of future hard-currency earnings. It was, of course, for the deficit countries to decide whether it was worth their while to accept the cost of financing continuing deficits — including the mortgaging of future export earnings — rather than immediately to cut back imports, but if the imports were crucial to future economic performance it might well be worthwhile.

But *Professor Wolf* doubted whether the CMEA countries were really better able to control their hard-currency deficits than were market economies. If a country initially had a deficit, world inflation — even if not imported (*cf.* Csikoś-Nagy, p. 199) — would increase it if import and export values changed in equal proportions without any deterioration of the terms of trade; with worsening terms of trade it would grow still more. Of course imports could be cut to some extent; but export increases could be difficult to achieve in slack foreign markets and these countries could not effectively devalue vis-à-vis the West. In the OECD countries, however, balance-of-payments adjustments had become easier with the acceptance of flexible exchange rates. The textbook view of the greater possibilities of control in a planned economy was not supported by recent experience; some deficits might have been 'planned', but not on the scale realised.

Professor Lorenz saw the hard-currency deficits of the CMEA areas as to some extent a structural phenomenon, reflecting differences in levels of economic development in East and West. But the Eastern European situation also in some respects paralleled that of Western Europe in relation to the dollar area in the early 1950s. Generally overvalued European currencies had helped to prolong the 'dollar problem', and thereafter an undervalued DM had produced new disequilibria. In East–West trade the exchange-rate problem was not perhaps important for the traditional exchange of Eastern primary products for Western manufacturers; it could be by-passed by co-operation agreements (*cf.* McMillan's paper) and by barter arrangements, though these could pose marketing problems for the Western partner. But any Eastern country which simply adjusted its foreign-currency selling price for a manufactured product, so as to achieve the effect of a devaluation without taking that formal step, was liable to face accusations of dumping.

On the question of convertibility of CMEA currencies, or of balances arising in intra-CMEA trade, *Professor Fedorowicz* explained that five countries (the USSR, Poland, Hungary, Czechoslovakia, the GDR) had agreed to settle in convertible currencies 10 per cent of any balances with the IBEC exceeding their negotiated credit margins. In addition, bilateral contracts sometimes provided for hard-currency payment by the importer for hard-currency inputs into goods supplied by a CMEA partner (e.g. Polish ships supplied with engines produced under a Swiss licence had to be paid for partly in hard currency). So far as trade with the outside world was concerned, Finland and Yugoslavia had both expressed interest in joining the transferable rouble settlement system, though some technical problems had still to be resolved. He expected the use of TR settlement to expand and some degree of TR convertibility into hard currencies to develop. But differences between national and external price structures precluded the opening of the national market through convertibility of the national currency so long as domestic price-fixing remained an essential tool of national economic and social policy. However, he disagreed with Holzman's analysis of commodity inconvertibility. This implied a far greater inflexibility of trade plans than was in fact the case. The CMEA countries were glad to negotiate – among themselves and with Western partners – long-term contracts which were then incorporated into trade and production plans; but trade plans were otherwise often fixed only in value terms for fairly large categories of goods, leaving enterprises to seek sales outlets for specific goods as it appeared worth their while. *Professor Wenger* thought that full currency convertibility and fluctuating exchange rates could well hamper trade; but he saw possibilities of partial convertibility of the TR for e.g. developing countries.

Professor Shastitko, however, argued that because trade on the CMEA market was regulated by national plans, monetary and financial arrangements had to be seen as secondary instruments, whose use was also determined by the plans. The question of convertibility of the transferable rouble had therefore to be considered in the context of the role the currency should play in a CMEA market set in a general context of planned cooperation. The planned balancing of deliveries and settlements among the member countries virtually ruled out automatic, free convertibility of the TR and, indeed, made such free convertibility superfluous. But it might be advisable to provide for partial convertibility of unplanned balances arising in bilateral trade. As prerequisites, it would be necessary to create reserves of convertible currencies, and commodity reserves and production capacities, adequate to ensure convertibility of the collective currency, as well as to devise an appropriate mechanism for regulating 'convertible currency' relations among the CMEA countries. However, since the bulk of intra-CMEA trade was based on firm trade-agreement quotas, TR convertibility could have little significance. Full convertibility of the TR and the national currencies of the member countries, on the other hand, would imply the complete restructuring, on a 'market' basis, of the existing system of planned economic relations and cooperation among these countries. The CMEA countries had rejected this approach as not according with the principles of socialist economic activity.

Professor Kunz agreed generally with Professor Shastitko's views on the undesirability and irrelevance of convertibility of the TR. But he also agreed with Professor Fedorowicz that the degree of commodity inconvertibility of CMEA currencies had been exaggerated.

Mr Kaser suggested that East–West differences in price systems and the degree of convertibility of currencies did not necessarily reflect different principles of resource allocation (including attitudes to foreign trade); but the principles were reflected in the plans in the East – and later translated into transactions accounted in transferable roubles – and in price structures in the West. He asked for explanations of the exchange rates applied in IBEC for compensation of TR balances or conversion into hard-currency (a CMEA Finance Committee decision in 1973* stated the TR as equal to 1·2 USSR

* See H. Matejka, 'Convertibility in East Europe', *Annals of International Studies*, vol. 5 (1974) p. 176.

valuta roubles, yet comparison of Soviet and CMEA foreign trade statistics
and IBEC settlements showed that a 1 : 1 rate still applied); and what exchange
rates were applied in transactions with Yugoslavia and other non—CMEA
socialist countries? He was also interested to know whether Professor Holzman
would see the same difficulty in indexing ECRs to a basket of CMEA export
commodities as he would in indexation to a world-traded basket.

Considering the likely development of balances of payments, a number of
participants questioned Dr Rieger's projections (p. 165), *Professor Wolf* asking
what exchange rates were assumed and *Mr Kaser* asking for the crucial assumption about the ratio of oil prices to general world prices in 1980. *Professor
Bogomolov* expressed uneasiness at the growth of the USA's short-term
indebtedness in the form of Eurodollars over the last decade or so, which he
saw as representing a transfer of real resources to that relatively rich country.

On the question of balance-of-payments adjustment mechanisms in a world-
wide setting, *Professor Rothschild* reminded the conference that the problems
of trade policy discussed earlier and those of financial arrangements and credit
policy currently under discussion were aspects of a complex interrelated
system — the rules of the game of international trade and credit, balance-of-
payments adjustment and development assistance. Reform of one part of the
system could not be successful without consideration of the possible need for
complementary reforms of other parts. The simple Bretton Woods and GATT
rules worked out during the Second World War had proved an effective first
step towards preventing a relapse into the chaos of the 1930s; but they were
no longer adequate to cope with today's problems of international economic
relationships. He agreed with Dr Jacobsen that trade between countries at
different stages of development could not be adequately regulated by a simple
mfn rule (p. 104); he would add that any new international financial institutions would have to be supplemented by appropriately differentiated trade
policy programmes, covering not only long-term rules and production and
exchange agreements, but also arrangements for flexible adjustment of trade
flows to make possible *different* means of adaptation of *different* economies
to new situations. To ensure that future balance-of-payments crises were overcome without danger of cumulative restriction of international trade, simul-
taneous reforms in trade, currency and credit policies and rules were needed,
based on careful analysis of today's conditions in East, West and South and
recognition of the economic aims, history, institutions and systems of each
group.

Replying to the discussion, *Professor Holzman* emphasised that he had not
suggested that the CMEA countries should give up central planning or otherwise modify their national economic systems in order to achieve currency
convertibility. These countries had stated that convertibility of some kind was
their aim; he had simply tried to explain why, if their stated goals of national
economic and social policy were taken as given, it was not reasonable to
consider convertibility — or even automatic transferability and multilateralism
within the CMEA area — as consistent with those goals. He did not regard it
as unreasonable for them in fact to attach higher priorities to full employment,
price stability, control of income distribution or economic growth. Professor
Fedorovicz appeared to agree that convertibility of national currencies was
inconsistent with the present Eastern economic systems; they disagreed on the

possibility of making the transferable rouble convertible. In his, (Holzman's) view, proportionality of prices in TRs and world-market prices was a necessary but quite insufficient condition for convertibility; so long as there was persistently greater repressed demand for Western goods than for Eastern goods nobody would willingly exchange hard currency for TRs. Incidentally he did not regard this built-in propensity to hard-currency deficit as a sign of the 'inefficiency' of the CMEA countries' economic systems; they were, for example, efficient generators of economic growth; but in the context of the convertibility argument this was not the point.

In connection with the two forms of 'partial convertibility' mentioned by Professor Fedorowicz and others, Professor Holzman pointed out, first, that the total of CMEA countries' annual bilateral deficits in intra-CMEA trans-actions amounted to only some 3 per cent of total intra-CMEA exports or imports and that some of this represented planned imbalances against negotiated swing credits; 10 per cent of the remainder must be a minute value. In any case, whether a real step towards convertibility had been made would soon be indicated by the increase, or otherwise, of bilateral deficits and surpluses in intra-trade. Secondly, he thought that hard-currency payment by the CMEA importer for the hard-currency-input content of goods exported by another CMEA country was more of a retreat from than an advance towards convertibility. For Poland to buy goods for dollars but refuse to sell them, after processing, for TRs was comparable with the hard goods for hard goods and soft goods for soft goods balancing in intra-CMEA trade agreements.

He could not agree that Kaser's argument supported the idea of the TR as either a medium of exchange or a store of value; 'money' in a money trans-action that simply ratified a plan did not have these characteristics. He also saw little benefit for the CMEA countries in an ECR indexed to a basket of CMEA export products; if prices rose 50 per cent in the world market and some holder of roubles then demanded their conversion the CMEA would still lose in real terms.

Professor Fedorowicz took up the question of the reserves needed for convertibility. If the TR were convertible, individual CMEA countries could hold smaller reserves of other convertible currencies, though the TR would certainly require both a central reserve of currency and the backing of assured capacities for exportable goods. On the question of floating exchange rates, acceptability in the West did not mean that there were no disadvantages for the rest of the world; the risks for the socialist countries in planning their Western trade had increased. This led to considerations of whether the socialist countries could integrate their system more closely into some world-wide trade and payments system. But it was hard to see what it could be. 'Join the IMF' was not the answer, since the Bretton Woods agreements no longer operated and no one could tell how they would be reactivated or amended.

11 The International Organisation of Inter-Firm Cooperation*

Carl H. McMillan
CARLETON UNIVERSITY, OTTAWA

I INTRODUCTION

It has been widely observed that relations among domestic firms within capitalist industrial societies have frequently and significantly departed from the traditional realm of market transactions to assume the form of joint business arrangements, of a wide variety and covering a broad range of economic activities.[1] This development has increasingly come to be designated 'inter-firm cooperation'. Inter-firm cooperation has extended to the international sphere also, gaining particular momentum in the post-war period, and resulting there too in an intricate web of inter-firm relationships.[2] While several useful typologies have been constructed,[3] the nature of inter-firm cooperation remains ill-defined and its determinants imperfectly understood.

This essay seeks to explore the concept of cooperative international relations among firms. In the first sections, the nature of inter-firm cooperation will be examined, and its principal variants distinguished. The choice of organisational alternatives will then be introduced. The determinants of choice in the East—West setting will be explored in a fourth section. A concluding section will propose avenues for further research.

II THE CHARACTERISTICS OF INTER-FIRM COOPERATION

Two basic categories of relations at the level of the enterprise are stressed by the theoretical literature on international economics. One comprises those relations which are conducted by autonomous firms through the market — primarily in the form of trade in goods and services, but also in the form of purely financial transactions. The second covers the interaction of subordinate

* The author gratefully acknowledges the generous encouragement and advice he has received from Gilles Paquet as well as the helpful comments of Jean Laux and Lynn Mytelka on an earlier draft. In addition to the sources listed in the bibliography, the propositions advanced here are based on a survey of East—West inter-firm cooperation conducted by the author in 1975, which was supported by grants from the Carnegie Endowment for International Peace and the Canada Council. The Wiener Institut für Internationale Wirtschaftsvergleiche facilitated the author's research in innumerable ways during his visit to the Institute. 'East' in this paper refers to the Soviet Union and Eastern Europe; 'West' to Western Europe, North America and Japan.

units of a single, multinational firm, the result of a national firm's international expansion through direct foreign investment. For our purposes the conceptual framework needs to be broadened to accommodate a third category of relations of an intermediate character.

The 'pure' market and the 'pure' multinational firm may be imagined as lying at opposite extremes of a figurative spectrum of possible relationships linking economic units internationally (Table 12). Within these extremes may be found a range of hybrid forms which combine elements of both the 'market' and the 'firm'. In these arrangements, firms associate themselves in various cooperative ventures which allow them to conduct relations outside the marketplace, but without the loss of their essential operational autonomy.

TABLE 12 THE ORGANISATION OF INTERNATIONAL ACTIVITIES AT THE ENTERPRISE LEVEL

Function:	←——————— Coordination ———————→		
Generic form:	Market	Cooperative association	Multinational firm
Mechanism for coordination:	Price system	Provisions of inter-firm agreement	Centralised managerial directives

Basic to the distinction of the three categories is the difference between supranational mechanisms for coordinating the activities of the different national actors. The market performs the fundamental functions of coordinating and enforcing decisions on the international allocation of resources through the well-known mechanism of the price system. Within the centralised multinational firm, resources at its disposal are allocated according to an enterprise plan, administered and enforced by managerial authority. *The negotiated terms of a cooperation agreement substitute for the coordination and enforcement mechanism of the market-price system, on the one hand, and the managerial prerogatives of the multinational firm, on the other.*

Through a cooperation agreement the parties commit themselves to a continuing pattern of behaviour with regard to designated activities. While market relations involve the parties in isolated transactions, cooperation typically associates them in a set of complementary activities. Moreover, the coordination performed by the agreement characteristically extends directly to activities (production, research and development) which are only indirectly determined by the operation of the market in the case of trade relations.

The provisions of a cooperation agreement (established and amended through negotiation and consultation) impinge on the coordinating functions of the market-price system, setting terms which may deviate from those of the market place.[4] The conditions on which goods and services are exchanged between the parties to a cooperation agreement may take the form of 'transfer prices', analogous to those internal to a firm. The extent to which such terms may be employed is restricted, however, by the accounting independence of the parties, and therefore varies with the degree of integration established by the arrangement (see Section III below).

The discipline imposed by the market is attenuated by the nature of inter-firm cooperation, which consciously restricts competition; and special control procedures and penalty provisions are therefore usually established. The more fundamental guarantee of enforcement of the terms of the contract, however, is the direct interdependence between the parties which the cooperative arrangement creates.

The three mechanisms differ in degree of centralisation and visibility. The decentralised coordination of the market is anonymous; while the centralised administration of the firm takes the form of overt managerial regulations and directives. The cooperative association is again intermediate. Important relations between the parties may be left to determination by market forces, while others are consciously regulated by inter-firm agreement. The latter, however, may take the form of an oral, rather than a written, understanding and, as we shall see, need not be administered by a jointly established body. An analogy may be found in the domestic cooperative, where members associate in a loose 'federation', establishing a mechanism through which some, but not all, of their activities are centrally regulated.[5]

It must be emphasised that the distinctions drawn here between the international market, the international inter-firm cooperative and the multinational firm are not based on differences in ownership in the conventional sense. Either the mechanism of the market, or that of a cooperation agreement can coordinate relations among parties who may be linked through formal ownership claims. One trading partner may own shares in the other, as may one cooperating partner.

I have been using the term 'multinational firm' to designate an extreme form of extra-market coordination through a comprehensive central plan binding on the members and administered by managerial directive. But coordination of the activities of branches of a multinational firm need not approximate this extreme. Firms granted operational autonomy by a single, multinational parent may both trade and cooperate.

A more complex concept of ownership as constituting separable property must therefore be applied to the analysis.[6] As Pejovic points out, 'property rights refer not to relations between men and things, but to relations among men that arise from the existence of things and pertain to their use'.[7] In terms of this approach, the three mechanism represent fundamentally different property-rights systems, with further property-rights configurations constituting sub-categories.

Customarily, when goods and services are transferred through the market, a complete set of property rights to them is exchanged between the parties (as specified in the contract governing the transaction). In the case of the centralised, multinational firm, formal title, together with use, income and disposal rights to the resources invested are transferred to the firm (as specified in its charter).[8]

Falling between the extremes in this sense as well, the cooperative case essentially involves more complex property-rights allocations. The typical pattern here is for each party to make some resources available for cooperative activities while retaining independent title to them. Use and disposal rights to pooled assets may, however, be significantly attenuated by the obligations of the agreement (provision for quality control by the partner, for example, attenuates autonomous-use rights). Each party receives income directly from its portion of the assets pooled, but in accordance with a fee schedule established by the agreement. In other respects, relations among cooperating resource owners follow the trade pattern. That is, full rights to goods and services are transferred between the parties as the goods and services themselves are exchanged in implementation of the agreement. (Variations on this basic pattern are discussed in Section IV.)

The spectrum which I have divided into three classes (the market, the cooperative association and the multinational firm) is a continuum of organisational possibilities. The intermediate character of cooperation may make it difficult in specific instances to distinguish between the market, on one side, and the firm, on the other. Nevertheless, from the discussion certain criteria for cooperation emerge:

(a) It associates operationally autonomous actors, obligating them to pool certain of their capabilities in a common endeavour.

(b) Complex property rights relationships result, involving the separation of use and disposal rights from formal ownership claims and the attenuation of income rights. The arrangements thus permit the indirect exploitation of proprietary rights through the partner.

(c) Joint activities are coordinated and policed by the terms of an inter-firm agreement (the result of continuing negotiation and consultation) rather than by the market-price system or by a central managerial authority. No special institutional machinery for coordination is necessarily established.

(d) The association covers a set of complementary activities, in contrast with the isolated transactions of the market place, and extends directly to line production activities as well as to research and development, financing and marketing.

(e) The association involves continuing commitments and obligations by the parties for a specified or indefinite time period.

III PRINCIPAL VARIANTS

We have been using international inter-firm cooperation as a generic term to designate the wide middle section of the spectrum depicted in Table 12. Cooperation is a heterogeneous class, covering a variety of arrangements, and its nature may be better understood if it is further broken down into broad sub-categories (within which, as will be apparent, further sub-classifications are possible but will not be developed here).

Table 13 extends Table 12 accordingly. As we move from left to right through the cooperative sector of the spectrum, an increasing number of relations which had been conducted between the parties through the market are encompassed within the cooperation agreement. Cooperation increasingly assumes the character of intra-firm relations, as non-market coordination

TABLE 13   FORMS OF INTER-FIRM COOPERATION

Market ←	Inter-firm Cooperation	→ Firm
Commercial harmonisation	Production collaboration	Institutional integration
Examples	*Examples*	*Examples*
Sourcing	Horizontal or	Contractual joint ventures
Market-sharing	vertical production	Equity joint ventures
Licensing	specialisation	Decentralised multinational
Franchising	Coproduction	firm or conglomerate
	Joint R&D	

increases in scope, becomes more institutionalised and more centralised. Simpler forms of cooperation tend to telescope within more complex arrangements. Thus agreements for production collaboration often include commercial harmonisation, and institutional integration typically incorporates harmonisation and collaboration. The characteristics of the three sub-categories may nevertheless be conveniently treated separately, in terms of the scope of cooperation, the property-rights allocations involved and the mechanism of coordination. A hypothetical example will be used in illustration of each.

COMMERCIAL HARMONISATION

Harmonisation involves the parties in the least intensive forms of cooperation, although the activities coordinated may be large in scale. In these arrangements, the parties harmonise commercial policies with respect to the acquisition and provision of goods and services. Commitments are of limited scope and duration, and there is minimal attenuation of independent property rights.

Special 'sourcing' arrangements (sometimes involving exchanges of products and materials by the partners) fall into this sub-category. It is not merely the regularity of sourcing but its specialised character that gives the arrangements a cooperative character. Thus accustomed supplier—purchaser relationships which are placed on a continuing basis evolve into simple cooperation of this sort.

Joint development and construction projects (for either partner or a third party) where the partners coordinate their participation, are another example. Cooperation is carried a step further when the project is to extend the capacity of one of the partners, who then commits a portion of the resulting output to the other partner or partners. In such instances, joint development is combined with longer-term harmonisation of supply and purchasing.

Another common form of harmonisation is licensing and franchising, where the licensor or franchisor continues under the arrangement to exercise some proprietary rights to a patent or trade mark. Suppose that firm A licenses firm B to use its patented technology to produce a product, and the agreement includes, for a ten-year period, conditions with respect to quality, brand name, royalties, marketing rights and the rights to any ensuing new technical developments. Terms which would otherwise be set in the market-place are thus established by direct inter-firm negotiation and administered by *ad hoc* consultation. While A, the granter of the license, thereby transfers significant proprietary rights to B, the agreement enables A to continue to exercise some rights indirectly over their use, their disposal and the income from them. It is in the joint exercise of these rights that the licensing agreement falls into the category of inter-firm cooperation as distinct from the simple sale of a patent through the market. Licensing agreements of this nature evolve easily into the next sub-category of cooperation.

PRODUCTION COLLABORATION

Here the parties directly coordinate line production operations (and possibly related research and development) through the terms of inter-firm production-specialisation agreements. Collaboration may extend vertically, through successive stages of processing, or horizontally, over the combined product range. More complex collaboration may involve both vertical and horizontal coordination. Collaboration is frequently supplemented by the transfer of specialised capital equipment and know-how between the partners.

Vertical coordination may be one-way or two-way. The simplest type of the former is sub-contracting, where one partner makes an existing productive capability available to the other. In the latter case, each partner contracts with the other to supply specified inputs (component parts in the typical manufacturing case), which each then incorporates into the final product. Such arrangements are often termed 'co-production'.

Since collaboration involves the coordination of complex production processes, it generates the need for greater partner involvement in operations. Whereas in the case of harmonisation the partners often deem that quality requirements can be controlled at a distance, the more direct exercise of joint-use rights is characteristic of collaboration. On-site partner personnel, for example, ensure direct and continuing sharing of operational authority. The distribution of income from the coordinated use of productive assets is determined by the agreed terms of exchanges of goods and services between the partners.

Suppose (developing our harmonisation example) that firm A licenses firm B to produce a patented type of equipment and also furnishes, in addition to some of the necessary capital equipment and initial technical assistance, certain (usually more technically sophisticated) components. Firm B combines these with the remaining components which it produces itself or procures independently, to assemble the final product. Firm A subsequently phases out its own production of the components which B produces, relying on B for future sourcing. Both then produce the final product on the basis of this collaboration, marketing it on agreed terms in agreed areas. As the relationship progresses, meaningful collaboration extends to related research and development programmes.

This example is typical of the agreements in this sub-category.[9] The buyer—seller dichotomy of market transactions, which still remains visible in harmonisation agreements, now tends to disappear. Cooperation extends to core production and development operations on both sides, its scope thus expanding qualitatively as well as quantitatively. Nevertheless, no permanent joint bodies are established under the arrangement. The terms of the agreement are implemented through contacts between the special officers and divisions of the partner firms charged with this responsibility, and through on-site representatives. The establishment of special machinery for coordination moves us into the next sub-category.

INSTITUTIONAL INTEGRATION

Institutional integration differs from collaboration more in form than in substance. The cooperative activities encompassed may be identical, but their coordination is institutionalised.[10] In the case of either a contractual or an equity joint venture, the partners create a special institutional framework for their arrangement; or cooperation may occur within the framework of a decentralised multinational firm or conglomerate, where only certain auxiliary functions — accounting, or research and development — are centrally administered.

To illustrate the case of a contractual joint venture, suppose that the collaborating firms in the preceding example decide that the demand for their joint product on a third market may be most conveniently served from B, and that this requires expansion of B's plant capacity. They contractually agree to share the capital costs of the expansion, to collaborate in production on the basis of the new capacity, jointly to market the output and to share in the profits. No new company need be established but joint management of production and related activities is institutionalised in a mixed committee or board.[11]

The organisation of property rights in this case is similar to collaboration, in that separate title to assets is maintained. While both parties invest in the joint venture, only B enjoys formal title to the assets thus created. Limitations on disposal rights may nevertheless ensure that A recovers his initial investment when the venture is dissolved, or by stages over the lifetime of the venture. Characteristically each shares in joint income from the venture in proportion to his capital contributions, in contrast to the fee schedule for goods and services provided by the partners which determines the distribution of income in collaboration and harmonisation agreements. The partners exercise use-rights jointly over the pooled assets, through their participation on the mixed management board (usually on an equal basis regardless of relative capital contributions) and through appointment of key operational personnel to the venture. Joint management tends thus to be carried further than in the case of collaboration.[12]

IV THE CHOICE OF FORMS

What forces give rise to these different arrangements? What considerations motivate firms to depart from the autonomous pursuit of objectives through the market and to associate in a variety of possible cooperative arrangements, or to merge into a vertically organised, multinational firm where decision-making is concentrated in a single managerial authority? How different are such considerations in various national and international contexts?

It would be much beyond the scope of this paper to treat these complex questions thoroughly. Nevertheless, some of the more fundamental motive forces involved in the choice of organisational form may be indicated. The choice of extra-market forms of coordination must rest on the perception that goals can be more effectively pursued by collective than by individual action. Such perception is generally seen as linked to limitations on the market mechanism, either inherent or imposed.

EXTERNAL FORCES

The organisational choice is inevitably conditioned by forces external to the firms involved. The environment within which the arrangements occur may set important constraints on enterprise decisions. In particular, legal norms may limit, or establish conditions which influence, the choice of form. Similarly, the preferences of decision-makers at the government level are reflected in policies directly or indirectly affecting the choice. These external forces play an especially important role in East–West relations; and they may be left to the following section for elaboration.

INTERNAL FORCES

Internal forces are those deriving from the nature of the object of cooperation – the product, service or technology involved. The organisation of the potential partner firms, and the subjective perceptions of decision-makers within these firms, are other important variables upon which choice depends.

Richardson argues persuasively that the boundaries of the firm are determined by the similarity of capabilities among producers.[13] The firm is organised on the basis of a common comparative advantage shared in a particular set of activities by producers who find it advantageous to concentrate on these and to leave dissimilar activities to other, separate firms.

Another line of explanation for the existence of firms focuses on imperfections in the market mechanism.[14] It argues that certain organisational costs ('transactions costs') attached to the market may be avoided, or reduced, if interaction is coordinated through the firm. The marginal benefits to be derived from circumventing the imperfections of the external market through the firm are compared with the marginal costs of 'internalising' relations within the firm, to establish its boundaries.

These arguments may be combined to explain cooperation. Relations among dissimilar firms are based on the mutual complementarity of capabilities. The matching of capabilities between firms, then, may be regarded as a necessary condition for cooperation. Complementarities in technical capabilities, in installed plant capacities, in access to factor and product markets, in the nature of demand in respective market areas, all underlie the cooperative association of firms.

Complementarity, however, is not a sufficient condition for cooperation. As trade theory emphasises, such complementarities are in principle exploitable through the market. Here the second approach may be brought into play. In a world of 'frictions', the search for means to reduce them may lead to the choice of the firm *or of cooperation* rather than the market. Market imperfections thus give rise to cooperation between firms possessing complementary capabilities and objectives.

What does this imply for the organisation of particular types of activity? The theoretical conditions for a competitively efficient and stable market (large numbers of buyers and sellers of divisible products, homogeneous products subject to standard valuation easily communicated and enforced) are not met in many sectors of a modern economy. Where interaction cannot be effectively accounted for by the market mechanism, market failure is customarily analysed in terms of externalities. These create strong incentives for coordination through cooperation – that is, through the internalisation of interdependencies which are external to the market within the framework of a cooperative association.

In sectors whose oligopolistic structure produces unstable demand and supply conditions, firms may seek to reduce uncertainty and attendant risk by exploiting complementarities through cooperation rather than the market. Where products and services are not standardized, the costs of valuation, communication and enforcement through the market are high. Thus differentiated products not only extend the scope for inter-firm complementarities, but also evoke market-sharing and product-specialisation agreements. Similarly, orders for intermediate products and services tailor-made to the customer's requirements may tend to evolve into commercial harmonisation, and ultimately into co-production, agreements.

Such considerations may help to explain why agricultural products are rarely the object of cooperation. Or why, in the case of development and supply of those raw materials where the scale of activities and limited number of purchasers and suppliers tend to dictate extra-market coordination, near-market forms of harmonisation are chosen. On the other hand, they may suggest why harmonisation tends to be inadequate for manufacturing industries characterised by highly differentiated products and information-intensive activities. These require more direct coordination of production operations through the chain of communications established under collaboration. Where, however, the technology precludes, or renders extremely costly, the temporal and spatial separation of production processes which collaboration entails, institutional integration may be the optimal cooperative alternative.

It is scarcely accidental that the transfer of technology is a common element of cooperative arrangements, or that cooperation is observed to be concentrated in high technology industries.[15] When technology (especially process technology) is the object, limitations on effective transfer through the market have led to the development of alternative avenues for joint international commercialisation. In these circumstances there are important incentives on both sides to incorporate the transfer element in a cooperative arrangement.

On the receiving side, the arms-length acquisition of patent rights through the market does not ensure the technical and marketing know-how necessary to render the technology fully operative and commercially viable in a new setting. Nor does it enable the development of 'in-house' capability to duplicate, much less to extend, the technology. Simple licensing in fact has been seen to reinforce technological dependence.[16] There are therefore strong motives for the acquiring firm to seek the cooperation of the innovating firm in the transfer process, through a 'package' arrangement which provides not only the basic production and marketing rights, but specialised equipment and components, continuing technical and managerial assistance, training of personnel, up-dating of technology, marketing assistance and the possibility of collaboration in further R&D.

On the other hand the market transfer process may afford the innovating firm inadequate protection of its investment in the technology. The commercial value of the technology may be difficult to assess; the further dissemination of information transferred may be difficult to control; the terms on which the technology is to be exploited in the market may be difficult to enforce. All raise the cost to the transferring firm of coordination through the market.[17] In these circumstances, an alternative to arms-length transfer is some form of cooperation: the harmonisation of policies in regard to the application of transferred technology, collaboration in production based on shared technology, or, if the partner possesses the potential for innovation, the coordination of R&D programmes and the joint commercialisation of their results.

Why should such considerations not dictate the innovator's exploitation of a technological advantage directly through the mechanism of the extended firm rather than indirectly through cooperation? The outcome may be determined by external constraints on direct investment. But internal considerations, in the form of complementarities with the potential partner, may be important. If, for example, the partner offers convenient productive capacity and attractive market access, then the innovating firm may decide that it is in its interest to concentrate its efforts on the development of new processes and products in which its comparative advantage appears to lie and to exploit the resulting potential commercial advantage indirectly via cooperation.[18]

These considerations also suggest that the nature of the technology involved in the transfer may determine the form of cooperation chosen. In general, the simpler and more stable the technology, the more amenable to market transfer and near-market harmonisation of related commercial aspects; the more complex and volatile the technology, the more likely it is to require joint exploitation through production collaboration or institutional integration. The most advanced and rapidly changing technologies appear to necessitate unilateral exploitation, through direct export or through foreign subsidiaries.

Cooperation may also be partially determined by the organisational nature of the partner firms themselves. A cooperative arrangement (involving a package of coordinated activities) may be the most effective way to take advantage of the geographic or functional diversity offered by a multinational conglomerate. Similarly the degree of vertical or horizontal integration already achieved by the partners will necessarily influence the nature of the inter-firm arrangement. Is a decentralised, multinational firm, which already by definition engages in a substantial degree of intra-firm cooperation among affiliates, a more likely candidate for cooperation with other firms? Perhaps, but it is not uncommon for the subsidiary of a vertically organised multinational to be designated as the partner in an external cooperation arrangement based on the subsidiary's specialisation within the multinational framework.

The determinants discussed above are all 'objective' in character, linked to the nature of the object of coordination or of the parties involved. They indicate in a preliminary fashion in what activities and between what kinds of partners cooperation may tend to be concentrated. On the other hand, subjective considerations may also play an important role in the choice of form. One observes firms in the same industry, of generally similar capabilities, pursuing markedly different strategies with regard to the organisation of their international activities. The evidence suggests that individual preferences influence the outcome, corporate policies significantly reflecting the 'tastes' of key decision-makers in the participating firms.

V DETERMINANTS IN THE EAST—WEST CONTEXT

In the East—West case the institutional choice has inevitably been influenced by the inter-systemic nature of the relationships. The determinants of the preceding section must be modified and supplemented accordingly.

These special factors are of three sorts:

(1) The legal and policy environment has significantly constrained the choice.
(2) Differences in system have created unique complementarities.
(3) The relative costs of different alternatives have been affected by the inter-systemic character of relations.

ENVIRONMENT

None of the socialist countries allow direct foreign control of economic assets within their boundaries, and foreign equity investment not entailing a controlling interest is permitted in only a few cases and under limited conditions.[19] Moreover, a number of Eastern countries have been reluctant to engage in cooperation involving direct foreign participation in the management of their enterprises. Thus significant portions of the right end of the institutional spectrum (Table 13) are ruled out, although this varies from country to country.[20] These constraints reflect fundamental systemic obstacles. Foreign equity investment (and even significant foreign participation in management) raises serious problems in a socialist planned economy, not only of a legal and organisational, but also of a fundamental socio-political, nature since it involves employment of workers in a socialist state by foreign capitalist firms.[21]

Within these constraints, policy preferences play a direct role in the choice of forms; most importantly on the Eastern side where the choice is made, or at least approved, at a relatively high, governmental level. Eastern governments, in particular, have made clear that they consider some forms to be more desirable than others. The Eastern policy preference for cooperation over the market may be interpreted as an appeal to a higher rationality than that of micro benefits and costs. Eastern macroeconomic objectives have been much stressed in the literature on East–West cooperation,[22] but Eastern policy-makers may find cooperation more appealing than trade on political and ideological grounds also, and view its extra-market character as more consonant with a controlled economy.

Cooperation generally, and often particular sub-categories, are promoted in the East as 'higher' forms,[23] and these policy preferences are signalled in bilateral intergovernmental agreements, thus gaining Western governmental concurrence and support. Western firms, made well aware of these preferences, necessarily weight them heavily in making their own decisions. The benefits to be derived may be more tangible than good-will, when tariff and other financial incentives are attached to the cooperation alternative.

Priorities established by Eastern national development plans determine the sectors in which foreign trade and cooperation may occur. Given the links I have sought to draw between the activities to be coordinated and the form of coordination, such plan priorities may be regarded as indirectly, but importantly, influencing the institutional pattern of relations. These sectoral priorities are also jointly designated in bilateral agreements, so that Western government policy also plays an indirect, if weaker, influencing role in this respect.

COMPLEMENTARITIES

Complementarities which provide scope and incentive for cooperation may be created by systemic differences. They serve to supplement the kinds of complementarities discussed in the preceding section, which are found in East—West relations as elsewhere. Two examples may serve to demonstrate the point.

East—West market-sharing arrangements are frequently based on differences in access to third markets which are linked to systematic factors. The Eastern partner affords improved access not only to the CMEA planned economies through special regional mechanisms, but also to certain Third World countries via special East—South bilateral trade and clearing arrangements. Special Eastern-partner access to Third World markets often supplements technical and factor complementarities in joint East—West development projects in the developing countries.

Another example is the complementarity between an Eastern comparative advantage in basic research and a Western developmental capability, which tends to underlie East—West R&D cooperation. The Eastern partner provides access to state laboratories and experimental facilities, as well as to the services of a large pool of highly trained mathematicians and scientists. The Western partner provides access to a flexible supply system and experience in commercialising technology on world markets. On this basis, innovative ideas emanating from a jointly planned research programme in the East are developed in the West for ultimate industrial and commercial use by both partners.

SYSTEM-RELATED COSTS

The category of system-determined forces which requires the most extensive elaboration here is that which covers the relative costs of coordination and enforcement offered by the two major options in East—West relations: trade and cooperation. In the East—West setting, choice is vitally affected by the special nature of the trade alternative. While East—West trade is conducted within a general market-price framework, on one side the state is a trader and domestic and international inter-firm relations are planned. This inevitably affects the functioning of the market mechanism and the costs associated with the trade alternative.

We have already stressed the important role which technology and the requirements of its transfer play generally in determining the choice of extra-market forms. In the East—West setting, however, there are special attractions in the indirect exercise of proprietary rights through cooperation.

The East—West market for patents and trade marks has been relatively underdeveloped, and many of the laws and institutions facilitating East—West trade in technology are quite recent. Socialist traditions and institutions for the domestic and regional commercialisation of, and trade in, technology have also been limited. In these circumstances, the Western partner, as the supplier of the technology in the majority of cases, views cooperation as an avenue through which it can share in any locational or production-cost advantage enjoyed by the Eastern partner, while exercising greater control over the use to which the transferred technology is put. The Western firm sees its interests better protected by licensing agreements extended to include mechanisms for quality control and arrangements by which it absorbs or markets any exports to the West.

On the receiving (for the most part Eastern) side, cooperation has also been viewed as affording improved guarantees in the uncertain circumstances of East–West relations. By combining in the transfer process a variety of mutually reinforcing elements, cooperation raises the prospects that the technology will be effectively absorbed and successfully commercialised. Furthermore, in cooperation the receiving partner plays a more active role in the implementation of the technology than under simpler forms of transfer. For example, it will customarily assume increasing responsibility for the supply of required components. The shared responsibilities inherent in cooperation improve the probabilities that the recipient firm will not only absorb, but 'assimilate' the technology (gaining the capability to reproduce it independently), and that it will ultimately attain a level at which it can contribute significantly to further development. Reduction of the technical gap between the partners increases the viability and the potential of the arrangement and is therefore in the longer-term interest of both.

Firms may seek to increase the stability of their relations through cooperation agreements. The uncertainties of imperfect markets are heightened in the East–West case by the degree to which, in these relations, administrative decisions supersede market forces. These uncertainties are further compounded by the political atmosphere in which East–West relations are conducted. The possibility of disruption of trade relations by arbitrary administrative intervention raises the costs associated with the market alternative and the incentives to attempt to reduce them, and diversify the associated risk, through direct, long-term, contractual commitments negotiated with foreign partners.

Instability also results from the bilateral nature of bargaining characteristic of a large proportion of East–West trade transactions, where a monopsonistic (monopolistic) Eastern foreign trade enterprise frequently faces a monopolistic (monopsonistic) Western corporation. For both parties the coordination of their relationship within, say, a joint venture or a co-production agreement offers the possibility of circumscribing, if by no means eliminating, this source of instability. While the provisions of a cooperation agreement are established and implemented through a bargaining process, the agreement can be viewed as an effort by the parties to accommodate their bilateral relationship and to regulate their interdependence to mutual advantage.

The separation of foreign and domestic economies under the traditional central planning system dominant in the East also serves to raise the costs of coordinating inter-firm relations in a traditional trade framework. Even in countries where the monopoly of specialised foreign trade enterprises is strictly enforced, and the latter are therefore the formal partners to all cooperation agreements, cooperation inevitably results in direct contacts between Western and Eastern producers and end-users. This direct link is an important benefit to be derived from the cooperation alternative.

Imperfections in capital markets obstruct efficient allocation of funds to the most profitable international uses. It is axiomatic that large Western international firms are favoured borrowers, enjoying both greater access to capital and preferential terms. Cooperation agreements may provide a vehicle for circumventing capital market imperfections by channelling funds to profitable uses in the East through Western partner firms. The financial advantage is therefore a 'firm-specific' factor which the Western firm may exploit through the arrangement, and which makes the cooperation alternative attractive to both parties.

Cooperation, like direct investment, affords the opportunity to circumvent obstacles to trade through operations which yield direct access to national or regional markets. The Western firm wishing to sell or buy in the East faces the barrier inherent in the foreign trade plan – to be realised the transaction must be approved by the planning authority. Eastern firms, on the other hand, face discriminatory tariffs and quotas on Western markets. These factors inevitably raise the cost of conducting trade via traditional channels Through cooperation, a firm gains an advocate within the other system; for example, cooperation brings the Western firm a partner who participates in the planning process. Such advocacy is advantageous not only in terms of operations within the other system but also in terms of any external sales or purchases which may be a component of the arrangements. Moreover, products resulting from cooperation may enjoy special treatment under tariff and currency regulations.

While internalisation of market relations within a cooperation agreement does not proceed so far as it does in the direct investment alternative, it does give scope for departure from the price terms of the market. Thus, the transfer prices of an inter-firm cooperation arrangement, like those within a multinational firm, may diverge from the prices of similar transactions on the market. This is because the packaging of a number of two-way transactions within a single cooperation arrangement allows the parties to distribute profits and losses among them under the terms of their agreement in a manner which would be impossible if these transactions were conducted separately through the market. This flexibility may offer a number of advantages to the parties. They may be thus able to engage in profitable price discrimination to an extent impossible through the market, or they may be able to raise profits through avoidance of tax differentials.

Balance of payments pressures and the inconvertibility of currencies have made payment in kind a common feature of East–West trade. For the same reasons, there is a tendency to render cooperation agreements of all types 'self-liquidating'; that is, to ensure that their convertible currency earnings are sufficient over time to offset their 'hard-currency' expenditures.

Even simple harmonisation in the form of 'compensation' agreements offers distinct benefits to both sides, however, in comparison with barter trade. The Western partner gains more control over the nature and quality of the goods he receives in return for his contributions, typically of capital goods and technology. Payment is either in the product resulting from cooperation or in related products, which may be used directly by the Western partner, or marketed directly by him, without recourse to special barter agents. Because the arrangement does not impose on the Western firm the costs of barter trade, the Eastern enterprise may also obtain more advantageous terms.[24] East–West cooperation agreements have frequently evolved from trade relations on the basis of cost comparisons of this sort.

The limitations on competition imposed by the inter-systemic nature of East–West commerce weakens the enforcement mechanism of the market alternative. This is not to argue that it is inoperative; the record of socialist foreign trade enterprises for scrupulous fulfilment of commitments testifies to the discipline imposed by East–West market relations at least on one side. Nevertheless, inter-firm agreements give greater scope for the stipulation of penalties and the establishment of special enforcement procedures. Such provisions alone are insufficient, as complaints from both sides about failures to fulfil obligations under cooperation agreements attest. The most effective instrument of enforcement which the cooperation alternative holds is the interdependence which is ideally established between the partners by the scope and variety of the activities packaged in the agreement.

Against these potential benefits must be weighed the organisational costs specifically associated with cooperation. Certainly the organisational costs of establishing, administering and monitoring a complex international agreement are substantial. The average time required to negotiate a basic agreement is apparently in excess of two years, with at least another two years usually required to resolve 'shake-down' problems.[25] An important component is the communications costs involved; these are the greater in the East–West case owing to the systemic distance which separates the partners and adds to the geographic and cultural distances to be spanned.

Our knowledge of the organisational costs of cooperation remains limited, but the slow growth of East–West cooperation suggests that they act as important disincentives to both Western firms and Eastern enterprises. Uncertainties of supply created by the centralised nature and ambitious tempo of planning are cited by Western firms as raising the costs of operating within the Eastern economies. The costs of accounting are also high, and are again raised by systemic factors — the separation of domestic and foreign prices in the socialist countries, the inconvertibility of socialist currencies and the lack of an operational exchange rate. Maintaining accounts in hard currencies does not resolve the basic problem posed by these conditions. Currency restrictions also raise the cost of operating within the CMEA region through cooperation agreements. The attraction of regional market access is substantially offset when the Western partner's opportunities for profitable regional activities through cooperation are limited by the requirement that hard-currency balance be maintained under the arrangement.

We should remind ourselves that relative costs are at issue, and that the costs imposed by the conditions in which East−West trade is conducted are especially high. Many of these costs have been cited in this discussion of the comparative benefits to be derived from cooperation. As one illustration, recall the absence of a direct link between end-users and producers and the communications costs this separation imposes on trade transactions. The savings from avoiding the costs of market relations may increasingly outweigh the high costs directly associated with cooperation. These latter costs will perhaps depend most upon how well the interests of the partners are balanced in the arrangement.

This discussion of the benefits and costs of cooperation, as contrasted with market relations, between Eastern and Western partners has been necessarily general. It has for the most part neglected the ways in which benefits and costs will vary according to the form of cooperation, the nature of the cooperative activities and the industry in which the cooperation takes place, as well as the broader national conditions on both sides. It has been intended to convey the general range of choice and to indicate its more fundamental determinants, in the East−West context.

VI CONCLUDING REMARKS

Sound governmental policies require much greater knowledge and understanding of cooperative relations among firms. Theory and research in this area has lagged far behind that devoted to the organisation of the international market and the multinational firm. Yet delineation of the rich intermediate range of the organisational spectrum reveals the extent of possible alternatives not only to the market but to direct foreign investment. Increasing concern over the perceived negative features of the multinational firm lends special significance to these possibilities. The widespread importance attached to the extension of inter-firm cooperation to East−West relations adds further to the need for a theory to explain and interpret these phenomena.

This paper has sketched a possible analytical approach. In view of the need for more theoretical and empirical research in this area, I may conclude by indicating what appear to be some of the more urgent questions to be explored.

Is cooperation an adequate and viable functional substitute for direct foreign investment, and in what circumstances? The links between forms and activities require much more investigation, if we are to know to what extent and in what circumstances one form may substitute for another. Such information is essential to policy formulation, if governments are to continue to decide whether and how to regulate inter-firm activity. In the area of technology, these links imply the conditions for successful transfer, and yet they have only begun to be investigated.[26]

This paper has concentrated on the nature and determinants of cooperation.

What are its broader effects on the participating firms and more generally on their national economies? Does cooperation provide to 'host' countries relief from the negative behavioural effects associated with the multinational firm, and if so, at what real cost? Or does the cooperative alternative offer little effective protection, unless an approximate balance of economic power between the partners is achieved under the arrangement? More generally, what are the welfare implications in terms of the gains from international specialisation and the distribution of these gains?[27]

The dynamics of inter-firm relations have only occasionally been alluded to in the preceding pages. Is there a general tendency for progression through the spectrum of relationships? In the absence of external constraints, are cooperative forms not only intermediate, but transitional, forms — half-way stations towards the consolidation of relations within the framework of the multinational firm? Are some forms of cooperation less stable in this sense than others?

Other conceptual approaches might be fruitfully applied. In East—West relations, for example, the organisational decision may be regarded as the outcome of bilateral bargaining between the Western firm, pursuing global commercial policies, and the Eastern state, seeking to further complex foreign and domestic objectives. The process might then be analysed in terms of the goals, strategies and relative bargaining power of the participants. A game-theoretic approach[28] could be of potential explanatory value.

Limitations on equity-forms and impediments to the functioning of the market mechanism in East—West relations would appear *a priori* to dictate that cooperation play an especially important role. The East—West setting would appear on these grounds to offer a rich 'laboratory' in which to study cooperation. The treatment of East—West cooperation as a sub-case of a general phenomenon has been deliberately intended to demonstrate that what appear to be new forms in East—West relations are not essentially different from organisational responses elsewhere.[29] Nevertheless the responses of firms in the East—West case are specially conditioned by systemic factors, and the way in which these have limited and shaped cooperation in the East—West case can only be separated from other determinants if comparisons can be drawn with inter-firm cooperation in other contexts. Much more comparative work needs to be done on the pattern of inter-firm relations in different contexts (including the organisation of inter-enterprise relations within the CMEA) before the East—West experience can be properly evaluated.

NOTES

1 Gerth (1971), Novikov and Shishkov (1972) and Richardson (1972), among others, have analysed these relationships.
2 A recent *Economist* survey portrays the complexities of these links in the computer industry (*The Economist*, 13 September 1975). 'Inter-firm cooperation' appears preferable to the extensively used 'industrial cooperation', because the relationships in question are not limited to industry, but occur also in agriculture, mining, construc-

tion and various services. Moreover, the adjective 'inter-firm' stresses that the relationships occur at the enterprise, as opposed to the governmental, level.

3 *Cf.* UN Economic Commission for Europe (1973) and St Charles (1974).

4 While in trade a contract between the parties may 'govern' a transaction, it does so in a passive way, reflecting the conditions set by market forces, so that the market remains the real governing mechanism. A cooperation agreement, on the other hand, is the instrument through which the partner firms actively administer the conditions of their continuing relationship.

5 *Cf.* Migue (1971). Domestic cooperative variants adopted by producers in agriculture are strikingly similar to those adopted internationally by firms in commerce and industry.

6 A good deal of attention has been paid in the recent economic literature to the concept of 'ownership' as composed of a 'bundle' of property rights, which are separable and therefore can be allocated in a number of ways. Legal title need not entail operational control over the use and disposal of assets, or exclusive rights to the returns from them. This is familiar in the case of the leasing of assets. It is also characteristic of arrangements where the rental features are implicit, as in the cases of corporate firms or state enterprises, where use, income and disposal rights are variously distributed among the 'absentee' private or public 'owners' and the management and personnel of the firms and enterprises. See Furubotn and Pejovich (1972).

7 *Ibid.*, p. 1139.

8 As noted in Note 6 above, some separation of property rights is also possible here, as in the case of the corporate firm.

9 The formal agreement for an arrangement of this type has been published in Bundestelle für Aussenhandels-information und Ungarische Handelskammer (1975) pp. 239—52.

10 Substantial functional integration is already achieved under collaboration.

11 The formula for foreign investment in Yugoslavia provides an example of the contractual joint venture approach. See Friedmann (1972), Sukijasovic (1973) and McMillan and St Charles (1974). Wilczynski (1975) also discusses this option.

12 The equity joint venture allocates property rights in a further variant. In this case, the partners customarily transfer title, together with other property rights to the assets invested, to a mixed enterprise which they establish for the purposes of the venture. However, the rights granted tend to be more attenuated by the terms of the agreement than they are in the case of the firm. Thus the enterprise may be established for a limited term, with disposal rights restricted during that term, and upon dissolution of the venture further restrictions on them prescribed (partner right of first refusal or veto over sale to a third party, for example). While the partners usually share in the joint income from the venture in proportion to their equity, these rights may be contractually attenuated, with provisions for obligatory reinvestment, special formulas for deriving profit shares, etc. Finally, use rights to the joint assets are also assigned by the provisions of the contract, and are shared in ways similar to those described for the joint management of the contractual joint venture. The Romanian conditions for mixed enterprises illustrate many of these points. See McMillan and St Charles (1974, Chapter 5 and Appendix A) and also Burgess (1974) for details. For the application of joint venture models to a different setting, see Tomlinson (1970).

13 Richardson, pp. 887—9.

14 This approach was originally expounded by Coase (1937) and most recently by McManus (1975); the latter's bibliography contains further references to this literature.

15 Certainly this is true in the East—West case. The author's research has shown the transfer of technology to be a major component of a large majority of the cooperation arrangements surveyed. See also Lodgaard (1973).

16 Crookell (1973).

17 These problems have been analysed in the literature on the multinational firm, with

regard to the decision to invest abroad on the basis of a 'firm-specific' technological advantage. See Caves (1971).
18 *Cf.* Richardson (1972) p. 893.
19 See McMillan and St Charles (1974) for details. Only recently have Western representative offices been allowed in all Eastern countries.
20 *Ibid.*, Chapter 2.
21 Eastern investment in the West does not face the same restrictions, although regulations governing Eastern personnel resident in Western countries have been an impeding factor. More important has been the scarcity of Eastern capital for such investment and reluctance on ideological and political grounds to invest in the West. The obstacles to the movement of capital in both directions, while still severe, are gradually diminishing.
22 Especially the role of cooperation in the strategy of intensive growth and in improvement of the balance of hard-currency payments. See the references on East–West cooperation in the bibliography for further discussion of these macroeconomic aspects.
23 Examples are the Soviet Union's encouragement of 'compensation' agreements (which fall into our 'harmonisation' sub-category) and Romania's promotion of equity joint ventures.
24 A measure of the costs which barter arrangements impose (ultimately on both parties) is the margin at which barter goods are discounted by the specialised Western agencies which undertake to market them.
25 Based on interviews conducted by the author.
26 The need for further research in this area was emphasised in the meeting of the ECE Seminar on the Management of Technology within Industrial Cooperation held in Geneva in July 1975.
27 See Schenk (undated) for a preliminary discussion of some of these issues.
28 An abstract model of domestic inter-firm cooperation has been developed along these lines by Harms (1973).
29 For a different view, see Holzman and Legvold (1975, pp. 290–2), who regard East–West cooperative arrangements as *ad hoc* solutions and imperfect substitutes for economic reform in the East. By implication they view East–West cooperation as primarily system-determined.

BIBLIOGRAPHY

K. Bolz, and P. Plötz, *Erfahrungen aus der Ost-West-Kooperation* (Hamburg, 1974).
Bundestelle für Aussenhandels-information, Koln, Ungarische Handelskammer, Budapest, Institut für Konjunktur – und Marktforschung, Budapest, *Handbuch der Kooperation zwischen Unternehmen in der Bundesrepublik Deutschland und in der Volksrepublik Ungarn* (Cologne/Budapest, 1975).
J. A. Burgess, *Romanian–US Joint Ventures* (Washington, DC: Chamber of Commerce of the United States, 1974).
M. Casson, *A Long-Run Theory of the Multinational Enterprise,* University of Reading Discussion Papers in International Investment and Business Studies, No. 22 (April 1975).
R. E. Caves, 'International Corporations: The Industrial Economics of Foreign Investment, *Economica,* XXXVIII (February 1971).
CEPES/RKW, *Grenzuberschreitende Unternehmenskooperation in der EWG* (Stuttgart, 1968).
R. H. Coase, 'The Nature of the Firm', in G. Stigler and K. Boulding, eds, *Readings in Price Theory* (Chicago, 1952). (Originally published in *Economica,* IV[1937].)
H. Crookell, 'The Transmission of Technology Across National Boundaries', *Business Quarterly,* V, 38 (August 1973).

Wolfgang Friedmann, 'The Contractual Joint Venture', *Columbia Journal of World Business* (January–February 1972).

E. G. Furubotn, and S. Pejovich, 'Property Rights and Economic Theory: A Survey of Recent Literature', *Journal of Economic Literature*, X, 4 (December 1972).

E. Gerth, *Zwischenbetriebliche Kooperation* (Stuttgart, 1971).

V. Harms, *Interessenlagen und Interessenkonflikte bei der zwischenbetrieblichen Kooperation* (Würzburg, 1973).

S. Hirsch, *An International Trade and Investment Theory of the Firm,* University of Reading Discussion Papers in International Investment and Business Studies, No. 17 (September 1974).

F. D. Holzman and R. Legvold, 'The Economics and Politics of East–West Relations', *International Organization*, 29, 1 (Winter 1975).

S. Lodgaard, 'Industrial Cooperation, Consumption Patterns, and Division of Labor in the East–West Setting', *Journal of Peace Research*, 10 (1973).

J. C. McManus, 'The Costs of Alternative Economic Organizations', *Canadian Journal of Economics,* VIII, 3 (August 1975).

C. H. McMillan and D. P. St Charles, *Joint Ventures in Eastern Europe: A Three-Country Comparison* (C. D. Howe Research Institute, Montreal, 1974).

Jean-Luc Migué, 'La participation, l'éfficacité et la théorie économique de la coopérative', *Economies et Societés*, V, 12 (December 1971).

J. Nötzold, *Die Bedeutung des Technologietransfers in der Wirtschaftlichen Ost–West Kooperation,* Eggenberg: Stiftung Wissenschaft und Politik, Forschungsinstitut für Internationale Politik und Sicherheit (February 1974).

P. A. Novikov, and Iu. V. Shishkov, *Mezhdunarodnaia kooperatsiia kapitalisticheskikh firm,* (Moscow, 1972).

OECD, Committee for Invisible Transactions, *Foreign Investment in Yugoslavia* (Paris, 1974).

Revue de l'Est, 5, 2 (April 1974). Issue devoted to East–West European Industrial and Commercial Cooperation.

G. B. Richardson, 'The Organisation of Industry', *Economic Journal,* 82, 327 (September 1972).

K-E. Schenk, *Wirkungen der industriellen Ost-West–Kooperation auf Faktorallokation und Wettbewerb,* Forschungsbericht Nr. 3, Institut für Aussenhandel und Übersee-wirtschaft der Universität Hamburg.

D. P. St. Charles, 'East–West Business Arrangements: A Typology', in C. H. McMillan, ed., *Changing Perspectives in East–West Commerce* (Lexington, Mass., 1974).

M. Sukijasovic, *Joint Business Ventures in Yugoslavia between Domestic and Foreign Firms: Developments in Law and Practice* (Institute of International Politics and Economics, Belgrade, 1973).

J. W. C. Tomlinson, *The Joint Venture Process in International Business* (Cambridge, Mass., 1970).

UN Economic Commission for Europe, *Analytical Report on Industrial Cooperation among ECE Countries* (Geneva, 1973).

J. Wilczynski, *Joint East–West Ventures and Rights of Ownership,* Working Paper No. 6, East–West Commercial Relations Series, Institute of Soviet and East European Studies (Carleton University, Ottawa, October 1975).

12 The Microeconomic Aspect of East–West Cooperation: The Hungarian Experience

Béla Csikós-Nagy
PRESIDENT OF THE BOARD OF PRICES AND MATERIALS, HUNGARY

I THE BACKGROUND

This study is concerned with East–West cooperation in its microeconomic aspect, which it analyses in the light of the Hungarian experience. With Hungary, we focus on a socialist country whose economy is highly foreign-trade sensitive and marked by a substantial trade with the West. In 1975, Hungary's exports accounted for over 40 per cent of her national income, and her foreign-trade turnover was divided between CMEA and non-CMEA countries in the proportion of 66:34.

In an economy with a high degree of foreign-trade sensitivity practically all productive investments serve import substitution or export promotion. In such an economy, *efficiency* can be quantified only by a comparison of input costs and the foreign-trade price. But both the foreign-trade price and production costs are variable magnitudes and, in addition, only the enterprise in question can have a clear picture of the price ensuring an adequate return to capital as a function of the utilisation of capacity. Therefore, the determination of the sectoral pattern of investments, the product mix and the material structure of products must all be capable of *flexible adaptation to the changing conditions of international division of labour*.

This recognition induced Hungary to carry out the 1968 economic reform. The Hungarian system of economic control and management, now in force for almost a decade, is marked by two important features:

(1) the economically-determined price system, which provides an appropriate orientation for economic decisions;
(2) enterprise independence, based on responsibility and risk-taking, to which deliberate limits are set by the economic regulators and statutes which are the instruments of the state plan.

Hungary's trade with countries outside the CMEA is not based on foundations of long-term cooperation. Her exports to the world market, apart from a few traditional products, are fragmented, and the picture of export turnover is that of a sort of industrial bazaar. Deliveries based on cooperation agreements, even as late as 1974, represented only around 4 per cent of the total, despite the fact that other measures designed to intensify East—West trade had already been in force for several years. But Hungary is nevertheless most interested in developing her trade with the West so as to bring an ever-increasing proportion within the framework of cooperation agreements concluded for a long enough period of time and covering also technological development and marketing.

Two questions thus require to be answered:

(1) To what extent can our trade with the West be based on cooperation agreements?
(2) What explains the fact that the up-to-date forms of cooperation have as yet been applied to such a low proportion of trade?

Neither question is easy to answer, because a great many difficulties, ranging from semantic to political problems, complicate a 'purely' economic approach. The factual question of primary importance to us is: what potentialities exist for intensive cooperation between countries with different socio-economic systems? Or, to put it another way, what limits are set to such cooperation by differences in the socio-economic systems?

Historically, international cooperation in production came into being under *capitalism*, and was organically tied to the free flow of capital and commodities. Looking at it in this context, we see a typical microeconomic phenomenon, whose appearance was made possible — at least in part — by the surplus capital of individual countries, or was motivated by an allocation policy aiming to ensure the most favourable return to capital. This has to be borne in mind when reference is made to the fact that 65 per cent of the trade between Common Market countries is based on cooperation agreements.

When investigating the microeconomic aspect of East—West economic relations, therefore, we must make our point of departure the fact that *in the socialist countries foreign trade is a state monopoly, and capital is in social ownership.* It follows that certain forms of cooperation existing in capitalist countries cannot be applied in East—West economic relations — those forms which presuppose the private ownership of capital or the free flow of capital and commodities in world trade. Consequently, it would be absolutely unrealistic to expect that the greater part of East—West trade could ever be based on cooperation agreements.

A Hungarian enterprise can conclude a cooperation agreement on the basis of a government permit; the government authorises the enterprise to carry on agreed activities with the capitalist firm within the limits and in the way specified in the permit. Such cooperation may be authorised in the fields of intellectual activity (research and development, planning and organization, transfer of licences and know-how, etc.), production (transfer of technology or of products, etc.), as well as in that of marketing; and it may assume any of the following forms:

(a) *Simple cooperation*, when the participating firms do not create a new

legal entity, but lay down their agreed activities in a cooperation
contract.

(b) *Cooperation with Western 'finance' capital*, in which, therefore, the
socialist enterprise appears from outside as the only legal entity, and
cooperation is embodied in a contract concluded on a debtor-creditor
basis.

(c) *Cooperation with Western 'active' capital*, in which a new legal entity,
a joint venture, is created on the basis of profit participation by each
partner.

The state monopoly of foreign trade means that such cooperation activity
can be undertaken only in an organised way, under the policy guidance of the
Minister of Foreign Trade. Foreign trade is carried on overwhelmingly by
specialised foreign-trade enterprises founded with the conduct of this trade as
their specific function. But the Minister of Foreign Trade — as the depository
of the foreign-trade monopoly — may grant the right to engage in foreign
trade to producing enterprises also. In 1974, 5—6 per cent of total foreign
trade and about 4 per cent of East—West trade were transacted by such
enterprises. In most cases, specialised foreign-trade enterprises act only as
commission agencies for the enterprise manufacturing the export product or
using the import product. About 90 per cent of their total turnover in 1974
was transacted on a commission basis, and only about 10 per cent was own
transactions.

This institutional system of foreign trade makes it possible for Western
firms to conclude cooperation agreements both with Hungarian foreign-trade
enterprises and with Hungarian producing enterprises. The number of East—
West cooperation agreements concluded up to the end of 1974 was almost
400; and most of them were concluded with Western firms jointly by
Hungarian specialised foreign-trade enterprises and producing enterprises.

The socialisation of capital does not mean, of course, a ban on capital
relations with capitalist countries. The socialist countries take up Western
credits (finance capital), and there exist in capitalist countries a large number
of enterprises which are either in socialist ownership or are joint ventures
founded with some socialist capital contribution. The latter partly undertake
financing activities and are partly engaged in promoting East—West trade.

In addition, since 1972, Western 'active' capital can be domiciled in
Hungary (as in Yugoslavia and Romania) or can participate in founding joint
ventures. For this it is necessary to obtain the permit of the Hungarian
Minister of Finance, and to meet the conditions specified by him. The
participation of the foreign partner in a joint venture can usually not exceed
49 per cent. In other words, *a Western firm can cooperate in a joint venture
only on a minority basis.* Moreover, an economic partnership with a Western
firm can be established only with the aim of raising the level of technical and
economic efficiency and of carrying on trading and servicing activities. *No
Western firm can acquire proprietary rights in any economic unit where*

production activity is carried on. The limitations of minority holding and only indirect participation in the sphere of material production have served to obviate potential political and social problems. A solution had to be found which would exclude the possibility for any firm in Western majority ownership to operate in a socialist country, or for a socialist production unit to come, even partly, under the management of a Western firm.

II CONTROL OVER A JOINT VENTURE

If a joint venture is built into the institutional system of a socialist economy, then complementary new elements have to be introduced into the state system of economic control and management. This is because it is impossible to apply to a joint venture all elements of the mechanism on which the state relies for controlling the national microeconomy – a mechanism which presupposes only economic units operating as autonomous bodies of the *national* economy. Obviously, it is not sufficient merely to declare the possibility of founding joint ventures. Conditions must also be created which ensure the material interest of the capitalist firm participating in the cooperation and make it possible for the socialist enterprise to undertake long-term commitments.

In implementing the plan for the national economy, the Hungarian government applies a system of normative regulation based on the use (subject to specified exceptions) mainly of economic instruments, applied with modifications – preferential or the reverse – for certain enterprises or possibly sectors. Thus, the socialist planned economy, as such, does not set any obstacles in the way of founding joint ventures. The special nature of preferences and commitments relating to joint ventures consists in the fact that they tend to intensify East–West economic cooperation, which implies that political considerations play a pronounced role in determining such commitments. If, however, political considerations deem the forms of East–West cooperation based on joint ventures to be possible and necessary, there will be no major difficulties in making such adjustments in the economic mechanism as may be necessary to make Western firms materially interested in, and Eastern socialist countries suitable areas for, participation in joint ventures.

Problems connected with the economic mechanism differ with the different types of cooperation. In the case of simple cooperation, especially if the compensation for the services of the Western firm (transfer of licences and know-how, leasing of productive equipment, etc.) is made by the delivery of products manufactured by means of these services, the commitment undertaken by the Hungarian enterprise is essentially confined to the obligation to see that these products are available to the Western firm in the volume and the manner specified in the agreement. This is, after all, a commitment towards state planning also, and it does not differ in the least from the obligations that follow from the cooperation agreements on production, specialisation, etc., within the CMEA.

But a joint venture raises microeconomic problems which do affect the normative regulation of a socialist planned economy. Thus, first of all, the question must be answered: What justifies the joint-venture type of cooperation, given the availability of other forms more compatible with the systems of economic control and management established in the socialist countries?

Looked upon from a socialist point of view, an undertaking based on joint risk-taking and profit participation can, under certain circumstance, offer the best chance to reach the objective set for technical progress. A joint venture offers the better alternative for a socialist enterprise if it is unable to produce with its own resources, within a reasonable time and economically, some machine or piece of equipment — whether because of its high technological level or for other reasons. If technological development is continuous, buying a licence involves the risk that by the time the capacity has been built or modernised the product manufactured under the licence will no longer be saleable on the world market at a price assuring an adequate profit. Thus the time factor plays an important role when the alternatives are weighed.

Looked upon from a Western point of view, joint ventures are to be preferred if the advantage to be derived from this type of cooperation is tied to clearly defined commitments. A Western firm which has attained and maintained goodwill in the world market by the consistently high technical quality of its products will undertake obligations to accept in payment, or to sell, the products manufactured in cooperation (especially if they are machines) only if the research and development activity of the partner enterprise is of high quality and effective. But the firm will see the future effectiveness of cooperation as ensured if it is allowed to provide technical and organisational assistance and given the right to intervene in the productive processes. Rights of this nature can of course be included even in a simple cooperation contract; but when a constant, continuous contribution — or interference — is necessary a joint venture seems to be the appropriate form.

I will therefore examine the microeconomic implications of East—West cooperation in relation specifically to joint ventures. This narrowing down of the investigation seems to be desirable, because it makes it possible to give a complete answer to the question whether there exist limitations stemming from differing socio-economic systems which hamper the intensification of East—West trade and, if such limitations do exist, whether they can or cannot be overcome.

All countries with international partnerships operating in them regulate capital transfer, and specify the guarantees they offer for the safety of capital investments. In Hungary, such regulation is particularly important for economic partnerships created with the cooperation of Western participants. The Hungarian forint is inconvertible and the country pursues a restrictive foreign-exchange policy. Without a specific regulation it would not be possible to provide for continuous transfer of profits, etc., or, in case of liquidation, for repatriation of fixed capital. Moreover, the Hungarian government changes the instruments of economic policy from time to time. The Western firm investing its capital in a joint venture might justly fear that the modification of certain regulators could create a situation detrimental to its interests, making its participation in the joint venture undesirable.

It was for these reasons that the Minister of Finance issued in 1972 a statute which contains the following regulations, among others:

(a) The National Bank of Hungary will transfer abroad, in the currency stipulated in the contract, the profits and other benefits accruing to the foreign partner to the extent of the payments made to his credit at the Bank.

(b) If asked by the foreign partner at the time of the approval of the association contract, the Bank may undertake to pay compensation, to the extent of the partner's contribution to the assets of the joint venture, for any losses sustained by him as a result of future state-policy measures.

(c) Under the usual banking conditions, the National Bank of Hungary, or the Hungarian Foreign-Trade Bank Ltd, may guarantee to the foreign partner the fulfilment of the Hungarian partner's commitments under the partnership relationship.

(d) In case of the foreign partner's withdrawal, the Bank will transfer abroad, in the currency specified in the agreement, the share of assets due to him in proportion to his contribution and to the extent of his payments made at the Bank.

(e) In applying international agreements on the exclusion of double taxation, reciprocity is the determining factor, and the Minister of Finance's decision determines practice in each case.

The Minister of Finance authorises the setting up of an economic partnership with foreign participation if it is the type of cooperation best promoting the social interest; and, if this is so, it is justifiable to make a joint venture attractive by granting it preferential treatment. The general preferences may be summed up as follows:

(a) The Hungarian enterprise pays into the state budget an annual capital charge amounting to 5 per cent of its assets. The joint venture is freed from the obligation to pay that capital charge.

(b) The Hungarian enterprise pays into the state budget, as a rule, 40 per cent of the amount of money set aside as depreciation. The joint venture is not obliged to make this payment.

(c) A joint venture enjoys preferential profit-taxation. If the economic association uses its after-tax profit to expand its assets, then part of the profits tax may be refunded.

(d) On official approval of the contract, care is taken to see that, within its framework, the wages paid to the employees of the partnership are in line with the wage relations prevailing in Hungary. But it must also be taken into account, of course, that there are foreign nationals in the employment of the joint venture who live far away from their domicile; and their wages while working abroad are determined in relation to the wages usual within their parent company.

Hungarian enterprises operate under a mechanism of selective, or preferential, regulation. A Hungarian enterprise is authorised to take up foreign credits subject to the approval of the National Bank; and this may also be granted to the foreign partner participating in a joint venture, provided that favourable conditions can be ensured. The Minister of Foreign Trade may grant the right to conduct foreign-trade activities to any Hungarian producing enterprise; and a joint venture may also apply for such right. Obviously, it will be interested in obtaining it if it regards the charge for the services of a Hungarian foreign-trade enterprise as a superfluous additional cost.

The Hungarian forint is not convertible, yet it has a few of the essential characteristics of a convertible currency. Thus:

(a) The Ministry of Foreign Trade cannot refuse to grant export or import licences to enterprises applying for them unless this would contravene statutory regulations concerning commodity trade or the administrative limitations published annually by the government when approving the plan for the national economy.

(b) In order to create an organic relationship between foreign-trade and domestic prices, the so-called 'foreign-trade price multiplier' was introduced in 1968 and, until 1976, performed the function of a *currency* conversion coefficient. Since 1976, the price multiplier has been acting as a *trading* conversion rate, which implies that its price-regulating role has been strengthened.

It means that export products do not, as a rule, have administratively fixed prices. The government extends to the enterprises no guaranteed prices for products exported even if the domestic marketing of the product in question is subject to administrative pricing. The underlying principle is that, in the case of exported products, enterprise earnings are regulated by the price realised in foreign trade.

The state may extend financial support to exporters, however, and this mainly takes the form of the 'export refund'. In taking this action, Hungary is influenced by the consideration that countries with which she has to compete in the world market also support exports — e.g. by granting export products exemption from taxes which are imposed on their sales in the domestic market. The Hungarian government takes a similar action when it extends export refunds, of a magnitude specified in advance, to certain productive branches (enterprises or products); and the gradual diminishing of the scale of this support is the economic-policy measure chosen to enforce an efficiency-oriented structural transformation at the microeconomic level.

(c) With inflation ever-sharpening in the world market, Hungary can maintain a relative price stability only by, from time to time, granting subsidies from budgetary resources to imports. Therefore it appeared justifiable to introduce the 'price-differential levy on imported materials'. It is paid, since its introduction in 1975, by enterprises which produce export articles by processing imported basic materials subsidised from the state budget.

The financial and price mechanism presented here in its broad outlines regulates both price formation and also the profit earned by joint ventures. However, attention must be drawn to a peculiar circumstance; since a joint venture is different in its legal status from a producing enterprise, the prices at which transactions will enter into its accounts must be clarified contractually. We may consider two basic formulas:

(1) The producing enterprise places the product at the disposal of the joint venture at its cost price. That is to say, profit accrues to the producing enterprise only through the joint venture. In the case of such a price clause, the foreign partner cannot, of course, claim a separate profit on sales; the whole excess of income over cost is subject to accounting within the joint venture.

(2) The joint venture, in agreement with the producing enterprise, fixes the delivery price in a contract, together with the conditions on which that price may be changed. Given such a price clause, the profit of the producing enterprise is divorced from that of the joint venture, and the profit included in the delivery price, including any additional profit resulting from cost reductions attained by technical organisational measures, accrues to the producing enterprise. The profit of the joint venture results from the difference between the fixed delivery price and the sales price. The members of the association will share the profit between them in proportion to their contributions. When such a price clause is preferred by the partners, they may also stipulate, in particular cases, disproportionate shares in the profits of the joint venture.

III EXPERIENCE WITH JOINT VENTURES

In 1975, three joint ventures were in operation in Hungary, and deliveries effected on the basis of cooperation agreements represented about 4 per cent of total trade with Western countries. In accounting for these low figures, reference is generally made to the small weight of machinery and equipment in Hungary's exports to non-CMEA countries – their share in Western exports amounting to only 12 per cent even as late as 1975. But this does not relieve us from the need to pay more attention to this unimpressive experience with joint ventures. Hungary attaches great importance to this form of cooperation precisely because she is interested in transforming the commodity structure of her exports and particularly in increasing appreciably the share of engineering exports in the total.

It may be pointed out that the statutory regulations making possible the organisation of joint ventures were not elaborated until 1972, and the preparation and approval of the first association contract took a rather long time, for reasons including, *inter alia*, lack of experience. It may also be mentioned that shortly after settling the statutory status of joint ventures, a recession developed in the capitalist countries; and recession, of course, weakens the willingness of capital to participate in an undertaking which involves the obligation to accept products in payment for its services.

The recent absence of any further intensification of East—West trade has also raised the question whether there still exist difficulties arising out of the economic mechanism which impede, or even make impossible, the expansion of cooperation. Such questions always come to the fore whenever the causes of an unsatisfactory development in some aspect of the economy are to be sought; and it may be of some importance to note the prevailing views currently held on the most important questions raised in this particular economic debate.

Attention has been focused mainly on the *minority right of the foreign partner* (a maximum 49 per cent share of ownership) and with the *exclusion of the foreign partner from interfering directly in the production process.* But the prevailing view is that these limitations do not impede the effective pursuit of the objectives laid down in the cooperation contracts.

Minority rights are under the protection of the law, which contains provision for a unanimity vote on decisions on vital issues. Economic relations between joint ventures and Hungarian producing enterprises are regulated by contracts. Thus, for example, they may conclude partnership contracts, production contracts, joint-sales contracts, in which the rights and obligations, the rules of procedure and behaviour, are laid down in detail. In these contracts the foreign firm may indicate what it regards as significant, and it can ensure the right of veto on all decisions which it deems to be important in relation to risk-taking and efficiency.

Technological advance must be embodied in production: and this fact raises the question whether it is compatible with the idea of joint ventures, established with a view to promoting production and marketing, if limitations are set on the direct, *'capital' cooperation* of the Western firm in the Hungarian producing enterprise. Views on this question are widely divided. It is true that, in the three joint ventures already operating in Hungary, *contracts* concluded with the producing enterprises provide in fact for the direct intervention of foreign firms in the production processes — notably in all technical and organisational questions which are important in relation to the technical qualities of the product and the conditions of production and marketing. In the case of default or delay in performing the mutual commitments undertaken in the contract, the parties can apply sanctions (e.g. stipulated penalties) and the contracts also clarify the course of action to be taken in cases of *vis major.*

But still looking at East–West cooperation from a microeconomic aspect, I think it expedient to stress the following points. The joint-venture form can play only a supplementary role in East–West cooperation. Joint venture as a form of cooperation cannot by itself release East–West trade relations from the deadlock they have fallen into, which is highly harmful as it diminishes the prospects of general socio-economic development. This conclusion is based on a double hypothesis:

(1) it is unrealistic to assume that, Western capital, in the form of 'active' (as distinct from 'finance') capital, will flow to the socialist countries in such volume as would be necessary if we were to regard the joint venture as the main form of future cooperation;

(2) the difference between proprietory rights and the rights stemming from contractual relations does *not* constitute an objective obstacle to production cooperation and to the material interest in such cooperation of the Western firm.

Consequently, in the intensification of East–West Trade primary importance must be attached to simple cooperation and cooperation based on the participation of Western 'finance' capital. But this does not mean that we should underestimate the possibilities offered by joint-venture-type cooperation. Technical progress follows in the wake of millions of critical decisions. It is not the commodity turnover that will be achieved by a joint venture that determines whether or not this is the appropriate form of cooperation, but rather the answer to the question whether the venture will perform its most important function in promoting technical progress – including in this the saving of time. Hungarian experience offers evidence that a generally high level of production is a significant common characteristic of the 'efficient' and 'progressive' branches of production. A selective industrial development which realises an 'efficient' concentration of capital by delaying the development of the so-called 'non-progressive' branches may be self-defeating. From this point of view, a joint venture may improve the balance and 'quality' of the process of industrialisation. Recognition of this played a role in shaping the legislation making possible the creation of joint ventures; and we can only hope that the foundation of joint ventures will experience an upswing in the second half of the 1970s.

Looking at the broader field of East–West production cooperation, and still its microeconomic aspects, attention has been focused lately on *some questions of calculations affecting economic rationality.*

In Hungary, the system of normative calculation has been adopted. Norms regulate, directly and indirectly, the type and scale of costs that can be taken into calculation in price fixing. There are norms to be applied item by item – e.g. to the depreciation of fixed assets. Under the relevant regulation, the value of fixed assets is written off, as part of prime costs, in instalments evenly spread over eight to fifteen years. There are norms which indicate the limit to certain costs that can be calculated tax-free — for example allocations to the fund assigned to technical development. And, finally, there are costs that cannot be included at all as production costs in accounting. These are usually the kind of costs incurred when, owing to deficient organisation at the producing enterprise, the development and/or the production cycle are lengthened or marketing meets with difficulties — thus causing additional costs (e.g. excess interest payments) — or penalties or charges have to be paid for the violation of specific regulations (concerning, e.g., environmental protection, the unloading of railway waggons, etc.).

In Hungary, the margin of profit over admitted costs is regulated by statutory provisions only in the field of administrative prices. But in the case of free-price products, too, the circumstance under which the earnings have accrued are considered when assessing realised profits. A government statute specifies the cases when part of an enterprises income must be regarded as 'unfair profit', and will attract sanctions. This regulation is similar in its nature and purpose to the measures relating to 'restrictive' or 'unfair' practices applied in the market-economy countries.

Foreign companies participating in production cooperation are of course interested in these various regulations, and have to consider them in relation to the principles of calculation applied within their own companies; and the Hungarian enterprise, also, must be concerned with these differences of practice since they have a direct bearing on the profitability of exports and on competitiveness in general.

Among these differences, it appears that major importance is attached to the ways of *writing-off fixed capital*. In the market-economy countries, taxation provisions permit accelerated depreciation which takes obsolescence into account. Let us assume, first, that the product manufactured in cooperation commands a constant price over time in the world market. The profit gained from its cooperative production will then be greater in the first three years than it could be if the plant were domiciled in the West; but from the fourth year on profits will rise more slowly. The foreign partner will obviously not object to this. However, the situation is different if cooperation is realised in branches where technical development is continuous. Then the write-off method which takes account of the life cycle of the product offers a greater chance of justifying a relatively high initial price, rather than maintaining the same price both before and after the fourth year. In other words, a different depreciation practice involves a different price policy and, under certain circumstances, the Western practice offers the possibility of pursuing a better, more flexible price policy.

In Hungary, the *separation of 'investments' from 'renewals'* differs from the practice adopted in the capitalist countries. 'Investment' means installing capital goods, irrespective of whether they serve for replacement or for expansion of capacity. That is to say, the 'renewal' category is significantly narrowed. From this fact several problems arise for the foreign partners. They regard the rates of depreciation as too low; they consider the practice of amortisation evenly spread over time as too rigid; they deem it detrimental to technical progress that the producing enterprise may charge in its accounts as production cost practically any expenses incurred in maintaining existing machines; at the same time they hold that the limitation on accounting the replacement of machinery to cost is too strict. Hungarian provisions make it possible for enterprises – and thus for joint ventures also – to apply to the Minister of Finance, exceptionally, for accelerated depreciation; and there have been cases in which a 20 per cent accelerated depreciation allowance has been granted in recognition of obsolescence.

Finally, it is also general practice in the West that international companies enjoy the advantage that *deliveries made under cooperation agreements are free from import duties.* Hungarian customs regulations make it possible, in certain cases, to grant exemption from import duties; but this, too, is rather an exception to the rule.

Depreciation, renewal and import duties are undoubtedly questions which, in the interest of the intensification of East–West trade, but also independently of it, deserve to be reviewed in the light of the general social interest in the speeding up of technical progress and the expansion of economic relations.

IV CONFLICT OF OBJECTIVES

The further development of production cooperation, and thus of joint ventures is also hampered by the conflict of objectives. Inter-firm associations (with each contributing capital) in market-economy countries constitute homogeneous economic units in which the partners have one common aim, i.e. profit maximisation. It would not be fruitful to start debating what is in reality the significance of the profit motive, or what are the parameters of capitalist business policy which restrict profit orientation. What I wish to emphasise is the uniform business policy. And even when capitalist firms create agreements based on the coordination of disparate interests, the aim is the stabilisation or improvement of the already established state of affairs. Even if the agreement changes this state so that one firm is adversely affected, it will still be interested in the agreement if the alternative is to face the danger of being ousted from the market.

Production cooperation in East–West trade serves a different aim in so far as profit is merely a precondition for the association. Viewed from an Eastern angle, a joint venture appears as a means by which technological advance and the improvement of economic efficiency can be accelerated, the commodity structure of trade can be transformed and import restrictions, now necessitated by balance of payments difficulties, can be removed. Seen from a Western angle, however, production cooperation is a direct or indirect means of market expansion. In other words, cooperation in East–West relations reflects a problem arising from the fact that the inclination to sell commodities is greater than the propensity to buy them. To put the point in other words again: no country wants to be indebted beyond the limit determined by a rationally acceptable burden of debt service, nor to become a creditor country beyond the limit determined by policy.

If it is possible at all to draw conclusions from the Hungarian experience, they may be summed up as follows:

(1) The readiness to participate in production cooperation is greater on the part of Western firms if the consequent export expansion is directed to a rouble rather than to a convertible-currency area.

(2) Western firms are interested in production cooperation which will provide its return in the form of the end-product primarily — apart from a few exceptions — in the case of such scarce items as energy resources and raw materials. Their degree of interest in the transfer of more labour-intensive production processes to the partner country is always a function of employment conditions.

International comparative analysis would perhaps provide proof that the relative share of the individual socialist countries in East—West production cooperation is determined not so much by the extent to which certain elements of their economic mechanism are adjusted to the requirements of that cooperation as by their economic endowments (production structure, development possibilities, etc.). If so, the obvious deduction is that East—West cooperation *can* be intensified through central organisation.

Both under capitalism and under socialism it is possible to develop those mechanisms which promote intensive economic relations by means both of plan- and market-conformity. If this hypothesis can be accepted, we are entitled to draw some important conclusions for economic analysis which are relevant to the question of how we account for the following unsatisfactory developments:

— the share of East—West trade in world trade is only about 30 per cent of the weight of the partner countries in the world economy;
— the commodity pattern of East—West trade is distorted in relation to the production structure of the socialist countries;
— the trade is one-sided; the volume of exports from the West to the East is substantially larger than that of exports in the opposite direction.

The accusations brought against the socialist planned economies — couched in such catchwords as dumping, discrimination, exclusion of competition and the like — are only too well known. Also well known are the views on the slowness of public administration, the deficiencies of information, and the sometimes rather frequent changes in policies affecting development and production. But we, too, are aware of the history of East—West trade. The real problem is not of recent origin and it was debated when capitalism was still the only ruling system in the world economy. Already before the First World War, in the days of the Austro-Hungarian monarchy, Hungarian economists had criticised in the so-called customs-union debates the economic policy which hampered industrialisation in Hungary; but since that time two new elements have entered the scene: a homogeneous world economy has ceased to exist; and industrially highly, or at least moderately, advanced countries have come into being in the East.

If we set out from the fact that no political obstacles stand in the way of intensifying East–West trade, then the problem we are really faced with is how to lift the barriers that currently impede the flow of capital goods and consumer goods from the socialist to the market-economy countries. The investigation of this problem is still, largely, an outstanding debt owed by economic research.

The factor overwhelmingly determining the volume of East–West trade today, and for the foreseeable future, is still the simple exchange of goods and services. Thus, joint ventures, while constituting a specific problem for economic research, are merely a minor issue within the general problem of East–West trade. More general economic questions arising in this context are dealt with in the other studies prepared for this Conference. Nevertheless, it has seemed appropriate to refer to these more general problems in this paper, too, in order to indicate the relative significance of microeconomic questions and, within this area the question of joint ventures.

Discussion of the Papers by Professor McMillan and Professor Csikós-Nagy

For too long, said *Professor Wolf*, discussion of the subject of these two papers had consisted, for the most part, of relatively superficial analyses of motives for industrial cooperation (technology gaps, Eastern balance-of-payments pressures, etc.) and lists of different types of cooperation. A major step forward in analysis had been made in the ECE's 1973 report (see McMillan's list of references); but a serious analytical and empirical gap in this field had remained, although it was now significantly narrowed by the two papers before the Conference. He was grateful for Professor McMillan's effort to establish a general analytical framework for the examination of international cooperation at the enterprise level before proceeding to examination of specific East–West cooperation issues.

After summarising the main points of the analysis, Professor Wolf raised several questions. First, McMillan (p. 184) had suggested that firms might seek to increase the stability of their relations through cooperation agreements and had portrayed much of East–West trade as taking place in conditions of bilateral monopoly and, thus, inherent instability. But was either party really likely to be more than an 'oligopolist' or possessed of some degree of 'monopoly power' in the world market? It would be interesting to investigate whether in fact most cooperation agreements involved firms in oligopolistic industries. Secondly, McMillan suggested (p. 187) that the high communications costs of arms-length trade relations, in the absence of direct links between end-users and producers, might outweigh the costs of industrial cooperation. This could be interpreted as suggesting that industrial cooperation agreements would be most prevalent with socialist countries having the least direct linkage between domestic and foreign-trade prices. Yet Hungary and Poland, which of all the CMEA countries had the closest linkage, seemed to lead in terms of the number of such agreements. Here again was a hypothesis that could usefully be subjected to empirical testing. Professor Csikós-Nagy had suggested that the different economic endowments of the socialist countries might be a more important determinant of their interests in cooperation agreements than differences in economic mechanisms.

Professor Wolf particularly appreciated in Professor Csikós-Nagy's paper (a) the setting of industrial cooperation agreements within the planning framework of a socialist country, (b) the relating of the systemic and economic implications of joint ventures to the Hungarian economic mechanism, (c) the examination of the impact of macroeconomic fluctuations in the West on the microeconomic calculus of joint ventures in Hungary and (d) that without belittling the role of joint ventures or of other forms of industrial cooperation, the paper made clear the small quantitative significance — actual and potential in the near future — of such activities in relation to Hungary's total trade with the West.

In connection with the changes in Hungarian regulations made in order to accommodate joint ventures (pp. 197–9), Professor Wolf asked whether the still limited number of joint ventures in Hungary reflected a Hungarian attempt to minimise the reverberations of these special measures on the rest of the economy, or unwillingness of Western partners to settle for only minority ownership, or other factors – such as differences regarding depreciation practices or investment policies, the impact of import duties, etc. He was also interested in the impact on joint ventures or other industrial cooperation arrangements of fiscal and other measures recently taken in Hungary to restrain the import of Western inflation and protect the balance of payments. Was not import licensing now more selective than stated in the paper (p. 198)? Was it still the case that export prices were not 'administered' (pp. 198–9) given (a) the revaluation (but not floating) of the forint as a counter inflationary measure, (b) the introduction of the 'price-differential levy on imported materials'? Had such measures affected the profitability of joint ventures?

Finally, Professor Wolf suggested that Western recession might have increased the interest of the socialist countries in industrial cooperation agreements, because of the Western partner's committment to accept the product or to sell on Western markets. On the other hand, Professor Csikós-Nagy had noted that recession was discouraging to Western capital when repayment had to be accepted in the form of the product (p. 200); and he had also suggested that Western firms were more interested if the product was to be sold in the rouble area (p. 204). This last observation raised an interesting question of the impact of East–West industrial cooperation on the integration processes of the CMEA.

Professor McMillan accepted Professor Wolf's points. He agreed that the 'monopoly' character of the Western partner could be exaggerated; his own research had shown that out of 200 East–West cooperation contracts only about half involved multinational firms (having subsidiaries or affiliates in at least one foreign country); but the proportion varied considerably from one Western country to another. On the costs of market relations versus those of cooperation, he suspected that both might be lower in Hungary than else-where; in any case, other factors reviewed in his paper would also influence the extent of cooperative activity in Hungary.

He then added some elaboration of his paper. First, it struck him that he had arranged it in such a way as to suggest a theme that had since emerged in the course of the Conference – that East–West relations reflect general world economic conditions but require adjustment to the special factor of inter-action of two different economic systems. Secondly, he had approached the analysis of forms of cooperation in terms of alternative distributions of separable property rights. The formula on pp. 177–8 circumvented the problem of Western ownership of property in a socialist country, but there remained formidable problems – ideological and practical – of joint-use rights. Thirdly, he could now add that since writing the paper additional evidence had become available of a very strong element of technology transfer in the majority of cooperative arrangements;* this was relevant to his paper's stress on technology transfer as a determinant of the choice of cooperative form.

* C. H. McMillan 'Forms and Dimensions of East–West Inter-firm Cooperation', paper for Second Workshop on East–West European Economic Interaction (Tbilisi, USSR, June 1976).

Professor Csikós-Nagy wished to reply to Professor Wolf's questions about recent adjustments to the Hungarian Economic Mechanism. After the world oil-price explosion in 1973, Hungary had been compelled to introduce certain restrictions. They were, in the main, designed to economise natural resources and more selective import licensing was one of these measures. It had, similarly, been necessary to counterbalance the impact of inflation in world markets. But most of the temporary restrictions imposed for these purposes had by now been abolished.

Professor Lavigne saw the interest taken in the distinction between 'trade' and 'industrial cooperation' in East—West economic relations as an example of the general underdevelopment of these relations; in West—West relations the latter term was not used and it was simply accepted that this was the modern form of trade, necessarily developed with growing international division of labour. She wondered why in intra-CMEA relations, 'joint ventures' — unhampered by systemic obstacles — were even less significant than in East—West relations. Though foreseen in the CMEA's *Comprehensive Programme*, there seemed to be very few CMEA international enterprises or associations as yet, and none with Western links also.

The answer, said *Professor Mateev*, was not a less developed international division of labour within the CMEA; Bulgaria's export/GNP ratio of 35 per cent proved that. Coordination of national plans had so far promoted branch-wise, and indeed sub-sub-branch-wise specialisation, leading to ordinary trade exchanges on a large scale. But the time had now come to develop intra-CMEA industrial cooperation and international enterprises, and he expected to see this in the near future. *Professor Holzman* observed that trade/GNP ratios were not a good indication of a country's degree of integration into world, or regional, trade if the size of the country was ignored; capitalist countries similar to Bulgaria in size had higher (comparably defined) trade/GNP ratios.

Considering incentives for, or obstacles to, industrial cooperation, *Dr Hardt* suggested that Western corporations looked to consolidation of a very strong competitive position as compensation for the heavy costs of entering into such East—West arrangements; we might see a consequent increasing tendency to concentration in the West. They also often hoped for improved access to other CMEA countries; but where one CMEA enterprise benefited from a transfer of technology as a result of Western cooperation, why should not it then, itself alone, enter into a joint enterprise in another CMEA country? He also raised the question whether cooperation agreements based on labour-intensive production in the ĆMEA partner country were really to the advantage of that partner, now that industrial labour reserves — especially of skilled workers — were everywhere said to be low or exhausted. *Dr Jacobsen* contrasted the nearly 5 per cent of total transactions currently taking place under cooperation agreements with the insistence of most members of the Conference on the benefits to be derived from them. What were the obstacles, as seen by a socialist economist — political, technical, economic or systemic?

Dr Hanson raised the question whether the relationship of East—West industrial cooperation and technology transfer was not more complicated than was suggested by Professor McMillan's paper (pp. 183—4). Cost and price differences – ultimately reflecting differing factor endowments – were likely strongly to influence the content of cooperation agreements, and thus to limit the scope of any related transfer of technology. This could be important where the attraction for the Western partner was the relative cheapness of Eastern labour. Empirical evidence suggested, moreover, that a simple sub-contracting role for the Eastern partner was quite common, as was 'vertical' specialisation, giving the Eastern partner a role in manufacture but not in design, development work or marketing. In such cases transfer of technology of a given vintage might be facilitated and might immediately benefit the Eastern partner; but the agreement might also have the effect of 'locking' the Eastern partner into the less sophisticated role (rather than transferring the crucial capacity for independent technical adaptation and innovation or for successful marketing) and thus doing nothing to reduce a technology gap in a world of continuing technical change.

Information on conditions for industrial cooperation in Romania was given by *Professor Constantinescu*, who said that trade under specialisation and cooperation agreements now constituted 25 per cent of the total. While continuing to attach great importance to reduction of trade barriers, to the conclusion of long-term agreements on economic, technical and scientific cooperation and to efforts to establish a new world monetary system and a new world economic order, Romania also saw joint ventures, in both production and trade, as a most promising new technical form of cooperation. He listed mixed Romanian-foreign companies – Rifil, with an Italian partner producing and marketing acrylic fibres; Romcontrol Data, American partner, parts for electronic calculators; Resita-Renk, West German partner, mechanical engineering; Roniprot, Japanese partner, certain proteins; Elarom, French partner, electronic medical equipment; Romelite, Austrian partner, mechanical engineering; mixed banks in London and Paris. Mixed companies were required to have 51 per cent Romanian participation; the Romanian government guaranteed the transfer of the foreign post-tax profit share as defined in the contract establishing the company; annual profit after a 5 per cent provision for reserves was taxed at 30 per cent, but tax relief could be given on the first three years' operations and any profit reinvested paid only a 20 per cent tax. Provisions for the partners' representation in management, powers of appointment, etc., were covered in each contract. Altogether, 109 foreign firms had their own representatives in Romania.

Replying to the discussion, *Professor McMillan* agreed with Dr Hanson that it remained an *a priori* hypothesis that industrial cooperation tended to narrow the technology gap. Subcontracting arrangements were least likely to do this – being based more on lower labour costs in the Eastern country – but they were not widespread, except in Hungary. He also sounded a warning against measuring the significance of cooperation arrangements in terms of the share of trade covered; in many cases such arrangements tended to replace trade between the partners.

Professor Csikós-Nagy wished to stress that the forms of cooperation described in his paper were not exclusive; they represented Hungarian experience so far, but any proposal would be examined. Moreover, the case for Hungarian investment in foreign enterprises operating outside Hungary was currently under discussion. The three joint ventures already operating in

Hungary represented the acceptable proposals out of about 100 offered by foreign firms, the rest being still under negotiation or rejected. Some of those rejected had contemplated only production for the Hungarian market, whereas Hungary was concerned to increase export capacity. On the question of industrial labour reserves, it could not be said that there was yet labour shortage in Hungary; many enterprises were over-manned and suitable cooperative projects could provide welcome opportunities for redeployment of labour or conversion of inefficient enterprises to new lines of production. The question of intra-CMEA industrial cooperation had been raised: there were plenty of examples in the energy and raw materials fields but these did not take the form of joint ownership of enterprises. The foreign contribution normally took the form of fixed-interest credit, often combined with the supply of some physical capital input.

13 Scope for Industrial, Scientific and Technical Cooperation between East and West

N. P. Shmelyov

INSTITUTE OF ECONOMICS OF THE WORLD SOCIALIST SYSTEM, ACADEMY OF SCIENCES OF THE USSR

As the international political climate and the technical and economic potentialities of our time improve, special importance attaches to the question of the prospects for long-term East—West cooperation in the industrial, scientific and technical fields. The interconnection of vital economic interests of the countries involved as partners in cooperation, and the complementarity of their national economic structures, constitute the material foundation for international détente and a major factor in growing confidence and good-neighbour relations among states with different social systems. The Final Act of the Helsinki Conference, which was signed by the leaders of thirty-five states from East and West, explicitly points to the existence of a number of important areas in which tangible, positive contributions to the economic and social progress of all the countries concerned could result from a pooling of efforts on an international basis, whether bilateral or multilateral.

The substantial changes that have occurred in techniques and technology under the scientific and technical revolution have modified the criteria for efficient investment and for optimisation of the structure of production, not only within the framework of individual economies or regions but also in interregional terms. Today, the criteria of efficiency in production, whether macroeconomic or microeconomic, must take account of the alternatives latent in the possible further development of the international division of labour, including the division of labour among states with different social systems.

Technical progress has caused, on the one hand, the emergence of a spate of new and independent lines of production turning out not only finished products, but also components, parts and assemblies and, on the other hand, the need to bring together large numbers of quasi-independent enterprises into technologically integrated complexes, within which the partners are held together by a thick network of stable, long-term cooperative relations. Within the framework of such technological complexes the ties between the producers and the buyers of their products acquire the character of relations between associates in the same production process, so that the disruption of these relations is equally undesirable for both parties. With the advance of technical progress, this process tends to transcend national boundaries and increasingly to acquire international dimensions.

One of the most characteristic expressions of this tendency is the growing role of multinational industrial corporations in the economy of the capitalist world: it is estimated that intrafirm and cooperation deliveries already account for 25–30 per cent of the trade turnover between the leading industrial countries in the West. In the CMEA countries, also, the growth of industrial cooperation is one of the main lines of development of their mutual economic relations and the integration of their economic structures.

The deepening of industrial specialisation and cooperation in production between the countries of East and West is still in its initial stages. The economic (primarily investment) foundations for this process have hardly yet been developed. So far, the foreign-trade approach to East–West cooperation has tended to prevail. This approach has, on the one hand, attracted most thought and, on the other, is a method which has been tested in practice and which the partners fully trust, whereas close production ties are attended with some risk. But, without in any way minimising the importance of mutually advantageous foreign trade, I must stress that in present-day conditions stable and long-term production ties offer considerably greater, and as yet unrealised, possibilities of national economic benefit than does traditional trade. Today, there is need, both in the East and in the West, for a new structural approach to the problems of mutual cooperation.

For historical reasons, national industrial complexes have emerged in many countries of Europe which exhibit excessively high degrees of self-sufficiency in most of the manufacturing industries. One obvious negative aspect of this development is the existence of a number of parallel, duplicating and relatively small-scale production facilities in the individual countries. The urge to develop a full-range industrial complex has saddled some industrial countries with a heavy burden of investments of relatively low efficiency. But it would hardly be right to see this kind of national economic structure in some of the highly developed countries as historically inevitable; it is, rather, a consequence of the protracted political tension in relations between socialist and capitalist countries.

In the long run, the European economy could be both much more complex and better balanced if based on *complementary* structures in the individual national economies. In my view, it is time to consider the important, practical questions of the need, and the possibility, to develop some means for coordinating long-term programmes for the economic, scientific and technical development of countries both in the East and the West of Europe and, primarily, for coordinating their investment programmes which will create tomorrow's economy.

At present, the productive potential of the CMEA countries tends to double roughly every ten years; and Western Europe also has a high rate of capital investment. In principle, within ten or fifteen years a new productive potential, equal to the present one, could be built up in Europe, but on the basis of much greater interstate specialisation. Coordination of long-term investment programmes could become an important factor in optimising national economic structures in the East and the West of the continent. It would ensure more favourable conditions for developing modern large-scale production in national enterprises and close international-cooperation ties between them.

Today, it is quite realistic to consider, not only in theory but also in practice, the possibility and advisability of jointly formulating large-scale, long-term programmes for cooperation among socialist and capitalist countries in vital areas of the economy. The long-term approach best meets not only the economic, but also the political interests of the partners, helping to consolidate material guarantees of lasting peace and security. Large-scale joint projects have either already been started or are realistic prospects in several fields – automobiles, fertilisers, the extraction and transport of oil, gas and coking coal, metal ores and forest resources, and some services. In some countries, some of these projects will remain of economic importance beyond the end of the twentieth century. Such projects help to create a stable and lasting division of labour among the states of East and West. Large-scale mutual deliveries become a reliable, long-term element in the national economic programmes and expand the range of the partners' common economic interests.

Finally, it is becoming ever more obvious that some economic problems have already become of far more than national or regional importance, acquiring at least a continental or even a global character. Their most efficient solution – and perhaps any solution at all – is possible only through a pooling of efforts and resources on an international scale. Problems increasingly accepted as being of this nature include the growing energy and raw material shortages, the need to modernise international transport networks and communications systems, the dangers of an irreversible destruction of the environment.

I feel that, over the long term, East–West industrial, scientific and technical cooperation could develop successfully along the main lines which I will now indicate.

I DIRECT INDUSTRIAL COOPERATION

Up to now, socialist enterprises' interest in cooperation with capitalist firms has largely reflected their need to raise the technical efficiency of some lines of production, although there are instances even today of enterprises in the CMEA countries operating as the leaders, and makers of the end product, with Western firms acting as minor partners in the process.

The interest of the CMEA countries in cooperation with Western firms does not spring from any short-term considerations, and it is bound to grow with the acceleration of technical progress and the more active involvement of the socialist countries in the international division of labour. According to the UN Economic Commission for Europe, agreements on the sharing of production programmes and exchange of components, and providing also for the extension of technical assistance, tend to reduce by fourteen to twenty months the time it takes to bring new types of goods into full-scale production, as compared with the time needed with the conventional transfer of technical documentation, etc.; to reduce the 'learning cost' by 50–70 per cent; to attain 93–99 per cent of the partners' standards of quality, and to increase the profits of the enterprise by 60–70 per cent.[1] In addition, deliveries of cooperatively produced products are among the most effective ways of finding new marketing outlets, and of improving the structure and increasing the volume of the socialist countries' exports.

The Western partners' interest in developing cooperation with socialist enterprises is also undoubtedly of a long-term character. Cooperation assures Western firms of the required level of profits, helps to expand production and use productive capacity more fully, and to consolidate their positions in new and steadily growing markets. Cooperation enables Western firms to resolve manpower problems more efficiently and to reduce the energy-intensiveness and material-intensiveness of production. With the general worsening of the economic situation in the West, considerable importance also attaches to the stability and reliability of cooperative ties with enterprises in the socialist countries, whose planned economies have a high degree of protection from short-term fluctuations of world demand.

Enterprises in the CMEA countries and Western firms are estimated to have concluded more than 1000 agreements on industrial cooperation. Under these agreements, the production and marketing facilities of the partners are tied in with each other in a variety of ways. Among these are agreements on

(1) the granting of licences and know-how on a product-pay-back basis;
(2) deliveries of complete plant for enterprises or for output of some high-technology product on a product-pay-back basis;
(3) joint production and specialisation;
(4) co-production;
(5) joint enterprises;
(6) joint research, or design or construction of installations, including those in third countries.

The most intense form of cooperation is co-production, providing for stable, long-term exchanges of parts and completed products but so far it has been an insignificant element of East–West industrial cooperation, accounting for only about 10 per cent of all cooperation agreements.[2]

The various branches of engineering, electronics and the chemicals industry account for the overwhelming majority of cooperation agreements; and cooperation is embryonic in key industries like metallurgy or light industry, each of which accounts for only about 5 per cent of the total number of agreements on industrial cooperation. The present-day structure of cooperative ties shows that so far this process has penetrated only the surface of the available pool of potentialities, and this is true both of the intensity of the East–West economic relations established, and of the range of industries in which cooperation would be advisable and advantageous for both sides.

Among the CMEA countries, Hungary and Poland have done most in developing relations of industrial cooperation with the West: cooperation deliveries already constitute something like 20 per cent of their engineering exports to the West. But nevertheless, all cooperation deliveries still account for no more than 3·5–4 per cent of their total exports to the West. I think that the further deepening of East–West industrial cooperation could eventually result in a marked increase of the share of cooperation deliveries in the exports of most CMEA countries. Yugoslavia's experience, with cooperation deliveries running at over 20 per cent of total exports to the West, gives some idea of the still unrealised potential.

In the past few years, Soviet industry has also begun to take a more active part in this development. The Soviet Union has concluded a number of agreements on cooperation deliveries in various areas of machine-tool building. Soviet machine-tools, fitted with French and Swedish-made automated control systems, are already finding acceptance in Western markets. The Soviet Union has been expanding deliveries of component plant for ships being built under Soviet contracts in Finland. Some positive experience has been gained in cooperation with Japanese firms manufacturing coal-mining equipment, excavators and other engineering products to Soviet specifications.

It would, of course, be unwise to ignore the subjective and objective difficulties which tend, at present, to slow down East–West industrial cooperation. Some of these difficulties spring from preconceptions left over from the Cold War, while others are connected with the specific characteristics of the economic systems of the socialist and the capitalist countries.

Thus, our Western partners are frequently still poorly informed about the production potential of the socialist countries and their unquestionable achievements in a number of leading areas of modern technical and techno-logical advance. In practice, one finds now and again a clear desire to transfer to socialist enterprises by way of cooperation mainly labour-intensive and material-intensive lines of production, outdated technological processes and ancillary operations which cannot be of much importance in promoting technical progress. The cause of mutual cooperation is also quite obviously being considerably harmed by various propaganda campaigns in the Western press, notably the widespread warnings about the hazards of excessively close industrial ties with the socialist countries. But a closer look will show that the risk involved in long-term cooperation is a two-way street, and that both parties are equally concerned to have effective guarantees against risk. The deepening of détente indicates that mutual guarantees are now being gradually, and on the whole successfully, created.

There is also the question of insufficient flexibility in relations between the partners involved in cooperation, above all on a microeconomic level. The

further improvement of the mechanism of economic management in the
CMEA countries – for example, the extension of the economic functions of
production associations and scientific-production associations in the Soviet
Union – is bound to improve the basis for efficient cooperation not only with
each other but also with their partners in the capitalist countries. Monetary
and financial problems are also of great importance in relation to the
possibilities of cooperation; and such problems include the question of the
convertibility of the socialist countries' currencies. I feel that the progress
made in this area over the past few years is bound to lead eventually to the
elimination of many of the obstacles in the monetary sphere which now tend
to limit the scale of cooperation ties between East and West.

II PRODUCT-PAY-BACK AGREEMENTS

This is the main form of industrial cooperation with Western firms now
practised by the Soviet Union. Large-scale product-pay-back deals signify not
only a quantitative advance in East–West economic ties, but also an
impressive qualitative change, the transition from lump export-import transactions to cooperation on a stable, long-term basis. Product-pay-back deals
help to enhance the efficiency of economic and financial cooperation with
other countries which are also interested in long-term benefits, and to ensure
a comprehensive approach to the solution of urgent problems of importance
to both parties.

Product-pay-back agreements, which have recently shown a dynamic
development, provide for the extension of long-term credit by the foreign
partner and delivery to the USSR under that credit of licences, equipment,
machinery and materials for the construction of large-scale industrial
facilities, to be followed by the purchase in the USSR on a long-term basis
(as a rule, ten to fifteen years) of a part of the output produced by these
facilities, so as fully to cover repayment of the credit with interest. Let us
note that the facilities so constructed remain entirely the property of the
Soviet side. As a rule, the share of the annual production exported by way of
compensation, under such agreements, comes to 20–30 per cent. By now, a
number of agreements and contracts have been signed for delivery to the
USSR on a product-pay-back basis of equipment and materials for more than
fifty industrial projects – in the chemical and petrochemical, oil and gas,
forest and pulp and paper, ferrous metallurgy and coal industries – totalling
several billion roubles.

The opportunities for cooperation with the CMEA countries on a product-
pay-back basis in the future could clearly become a more important factor in
tackling the West's energy and materials problems, providing not only the
immediate commercial benefits accruing from such projects but also
diversifying sources of supply. At the very least, there are no purely economic
grounds for ignoring the potentialities of this form of cooperation when long-
term programmes are formulated in the West to tackle the problems whose

acuteness has been so strikingly revealed over the past few years.

But in their present form, product-pay-back agreements also have some weaknesses which limit their sphere of application. The foreign partner, receiving by way of compensation the agreed quantity of products at a fixed price, has little interest in seeing the enterprise boost its output or enhance its efficiency; specifically, he is not interested in the steady improvement of production techniques. The fact that product-pay-back deals are concluded for the production and export of goods whose qualitative characteristics remain virtually unchanged over the whole period of the agreement tends to limit their sphere of application mainly to raw materials. Thus while making the utmost use of the already proven mutual advantages of the product-pay-back form of cooperation, it is advisable to probe for new and more promising forms of cooperation, better adapted to the tendencies of present-day scientific and technical progress.

Analysing the general problems of the development of economic relations between the USSR and the capitalist world, General Secretary of the CPSU Central Committee, L. I. Brezhnev, in his Report to the XXVth Congress of the Communist Party of the Soviet Union, emphasised:

> One major question is the development of new forms of external economic ties which go beyond the framework of conventional trade, which greatly expand our potentialities and, as a rule, yield the greatest effect. What I have in mind, in particular, are compensation agreements, under which new enterprises, fully owned by our state, are built up in cooperation with foreign firms. For the time being, such agreements mainly involve branches turning out raw materials and semi-finished products. But the time has perhaps come to extend the area of their operation, and to include in it manufacturing industry, and to seek new approaches to industrial cooperation.

As time goes on, new steps can clearly be taken to tackle the economic and organisational problems arising from cooperation on a compensation basis, and to seek mutually acceptable forms of participation by the partners in determining policies for future technical development in the newly erected enterprise – which would help to extend the practice of compensation agreements to the manufacturing sector.

III JOINT ENTERPRISES

So far, the legal conditions for setting up joint enterprises on the territory of socialist countries – to operate with share-participation by foreign partners – have been created only in Yugoslavia and in two CMEA countries, Romania and Hungary. In Romania, the number of such enterprises – in operation and now being tooled up – comes to at least ten. The experience gained by joint enterprises is still too scanty to warrant any firm judgement about the prospects for their efficient operation within a socialist planned economy. It will take some time for the planning agencies of the CMEA countries and the potentially interested Western investors to obtain a clear picture of their economic viability.

At the same time, it is obvious that the joint sharing of the capital of the enterprise is not the only possible way of establishing closer ties between the long-term interests and responsibilities of the cooperating partners. In the opinion of such a financial specialist as David Rockefeller, the main purpose of investors is ultimately to have a share in the profits of the foreign enterprise, so that for many companies the question of property ownership is not of much importance, provided their share of the profits is guaranteed.[3] I think that in the future practical forms of cooperation will be devised providing a mutually acceptable basis for guaranteeing a share of the profits of the enterprise being set up with the assistance of a foreign investor and for determining the latter's say in the technical and commercial policy of the enterprise, representation of his interests in management, and so on.

Let us note the successful experience gained from the establishment in the West of joint marketing companies, bringing together the capital of foreign-trade organisations from the socialist countries and their Western partners. In recent years, such companies have helped to promote the sale of goods from the socialist countries on Western markets and have demonstrated their viability and high degree of commercial efficiency. Thus, in Western Europe there are now operating nearly fifty mixed companies in which Soviet foreign-trade organisations are taking part. If current tendencies are maintained, one could expect such enterprises quite naturally to extend the field of their operations to more and more of the operations leading from the producer to the consumer. Here, the experience of the Hungarian company Medicor, which has set up two joint enterprises in Britain for the manufacture and sale of certain instruments, is worth attention. The Hungarian share in the capital of the joint enterprises has been contributed in the form of the provision of a licence, deliveries of equipment and transfer of the trading right. I think that this form of East—West cooperation has a definite future before it.

IV MULTILATERAL PROJECTS

For the time being, international projects involving partners from several socialist and capitalist countries remain a rarity in East—West relations.

The first important precedent was created by the construction of the motorworks at Togliatti with the assistance of Fiat of Italy. Today, a number of CMEA countries are contributing components to the finished product at that plant, on the basis of cooperation agreements. However, from the stand-point of East—West relations, the plant at Togliatti is perhaps an example of a large-scale lump deal rather than of a stable cooperation agreement. More characteristic of the true multilateral cooperation project is the construction, with the participation of most of the CMEA countries and France, of the pulp and paper mill at Ust Ilim, whose products will subsequently be delivered to all the participants in the project over a long period. Another important step in developing multilateral East–West cooperation is the construction of the trans-European gas pipeline with terminals in Austria, the Federal Republic of Germany, France and Italy. Finally, the proposed construction of a system of gas pipelines between Iran and Western Europe, to run across the territory of a number of East European countries, will undoubtedly do much to strengthen confidence and extend multilateral cooperation among the European countries.

Multilateral cooperation in the leading industries and the infrastructure opens up fresh opportunities for economic and social progress in the countries concerned. It makes for large-scale business operations and best meets the demands of the current scientific and technical revolution, with all its positive and negative consequences. It has already become clear that in the construction of such engineering giants as the Kama Motor Works multilateral cooperation in one form or another is inevitable; and in the future one must expect that projects of this kind will provide the basis for increasing multilateral industrial cooperation between East and West.

But multilateral cooperation will have an even greater role to play in tackling problems of continental importance. Just now, for instance, there are the questions of the advisability, and also of the real possibility, of linking up the power grids of East and West in Europe, of an accelerated development of a continental network of atomic power stations, of a link-up of inland waterways across the continent and modernisation of other transport systems, and of a pooling of efforts by various countries in space exploration, development of the world's oceans and protection of the environment.

Solution of these problems calls for a fundamentally new approach to various aspects of long-term cooperation among states belonging to the two social systems. The difficulties in organising such cooperation spring above all from the lack of adequate experience in planning and concerting action, by countries from East and West, in joint undertakings extending beyond national or regional boundaries. The finding of sources of finance for large-scale multilateral projects is also a problem in its own right.

A positive role in tackling these problems could, I think, be played by closer business relations between the two European integration groupings. For all the specific characteristics and differences of their regional interests, the integration groupings in the two parts of the continent should be, not an alternative to, but rather an important stimulus for, developing cooperation on an all-European basis. The economic and organisational potentialities of the CMEA and the EEC could be extensively used not only for solving regional problems, but also in the interests of Europe as a whole. It would also be logical to expect new initiatives in this sphere from other authoritative international bodies, notably the United Nations Economic Commission for Europe. It is a source of satisfaction to note, for instance, the attention given by the ECE to the Soviet Union's proposal that European congresses be convened on problems of cooperation in the fields of energy, transport and protection of the environment.

V *SCIENTIFIC AND TECHNICAL COOPERATION*

The exchange of scientific and technical achievements becomes an ever more important aspect of East—West economic relations, and is a component part of virtually all agreements on industrial cooperation. At present, licensing arrangements account for nearly 40 per cent of all cooperation agreements, and agreements on transfer of technology for another 20 per cent. Moreover, scientific and technical exchanges have recently been increasing, and developing into an independent type of cooperation.

The scientific potentials of the socialist and capitalist countries, and notably those of Eastern and Western Europe, are largely complementary in structure. The CMEA countries hold leading positions in areas of modern scientific and technological development, such as nuclear research and new sources of energy, space exploration, laser techniques, solid-state physics, improvement of metallurgical processes, and new lines of development in mathematics, cybernetics, chemistry and biology. If we look at the key indicators of scientific and technical development (personnel involved, growth of appropriations for scientific work, network of research establishments, number of inventions registered), the CMEA countries have a significant edge over other countries and regions. But at the same time, fundamental research in the CMEA countries is not always duly backed up with applied research or, especially, with industrial development. Meanwhile, many developed capitalist countries, with powerful experimental and production facilities, frequently face shortages of new ideas and projects needing further development or just approaching the point of practical industrial application. According to some sources, for instance, firms in the Federal Republic of Germany have been studying the possibility of buying more than 500 Soviet licences in various fields of science and technology.[4]

Long-term bilateral and multilateral cooperation can open up fresh opportunities for efficiently pooling the scientific and technical potential of various countries and for a deepening international division of labour in fundamental and applied research. The Soviet Union, for instance, now has agreements on economic, scientific and technical cooperation with fourteen Western countries. These are ten-year agreements covering nearly 160 areas of science and technology.

Let us note the successful experience in scientific and technical cooperation between the USSR and France. Among its distinctive features are not only the large scale of some of the projects, but also the diversity of the problems being tackled, the broad range of participants, and the adjustment of the organisational mechanisms of cooperation to the needs of different projects. Alongside fundamental research in fields like high-energy physics, atomic energy, space exploration, the chemistry of high-molecular compounds and medicine, Soviet-French cooperation has yielded substantial results in various technical and technological fields; and some of these have led to the linking of the partners' patent rights and the commercial sale of joint licences for new technological processes.

Scientific and technical exchanges and joint research create the basis for long-term cooperation ties covering the spheres of science, technology, and the production and marketing of new manufactured goods. Even in the rare instances when both sides have already accumulated considerable scientific and technical stock in one and the same field, the exchange of information and experience can substantially accelerate the solution of problems. This applies both to industrial projects and to that research which, for the time being, has no everyday, practical importance. Evidence is provided by the successful experience of the Soviet—American Soyuz-Apollo space programme, which also indicates that the main condition for major success in East—West scientific and technical cooperation is the agreed-programme approach and the firm determination by the partners to meet all their mutual commitments.

In conclusion, I should like to emphasise that in the sphere of East—West economic, scientific and technical cooperation, as in many other spheres, one is acutely conscious of a characteristic feature of our age — the lack or inadequacy of purposeful information, within the chaotic diversity of data sweeping across the modern world. The point is that long-term planning of cooperation, and the selection of the most promising firms and projects, cannot be successful in the absence of sufficiently full and reliable information on the requirements and potentialities in a given field. In this context, it would perhaps be advisable to set up an international coordination centre for problems in East—West industrial, scientific and technical cooperation, with the tasks of collecting the relevant information and making it available to the countries and firms concerned, exploring the appropriate legal forms and the most promising lines of cooperation, providing a forum for consultations on the available opportunities, and so on. Such a centre would undoubtedly have a definite and positive role to play in further advancing equitable and business-like cooperation among states belonging to the two social systems.

NOTES

1 Doc. E/ECE/730 Add. 1, p. 8. (The results of a sample survey to discover the benefits Yugoslav firms had derived from the types of cooperation mentioned.)
2 Doc. E/ECE/844, p. 8.
3 *U.S. News and World Report* (13 August 1973).
4 *World Economics and International Relations*, No. 9 (1974) p. 97.

14 The Scope for Industrial and Technological Cooperation on a Larger Scale

N. Scott

GRADUATE INSTITUTE FOR INTERNATIONAL STUI
GENEVA

I INTRODUCTORY

It is tempting to affirm that the scope for expanding any type of economic
(or, for that matter, non-economic) relationship for which 'cooperation' is an
accurate description should be boundless. Admittedly, the wish is the father
of the thought in such an affirmation, because economics is largely the study
of constraints on the possible and/or the desirable. This communication takes
up two questions relevant to policy. Is the scope for East—West industrial and
technological cooperation already subject to or approaching, identifiable
constraints? If so, what type of action could be taken to ease or remove them;
and what kind of benefits might be expected to result?

These questions have to be considered in the light of the experience of new
forms of economic relationships which have developed in an East—West
context over the past decade. The constraints on East—West trade, in the
conventional — narrowly defined — sense of the term, had kept it through the
first two post-war decades at a volume well — indeed, notoriously — below its
potential level. Many of these constraints — of a policy, institutional or
structural nature — still depress the volume of trade and account for the
peculiarities of its structure and financing. None the less, since the mid-1960s
there has been an active search, by governments and enterprises, for means
both of circumventing 'traditional' and long-established trade barriers and of
concluding longer-term, more complex agreements which often take new
contractual forms, ranging from licence *plus* buy-back contracts to joint
ventures. Besides this 'innovative' willingness to experiment which has
characterised the governmental *and* business approach to East—West economic
relations, there have been far-reaching changes in the economic setting. The
'internationalisation' of production and marketing, partly reflected in the
growing role of transnational enterprises, both West and East, has changed
industrial organisation, with numerous (and in some ways incalculable)

* The full text of Mr Scott's contribution was not available to participants in the
Conference (Ed.).

consequences for trade, economic interdependence and the transfer of technology. Sub-regional economic integration, and long-range 'perspective' economic planning or programming have reflected shifting governmental priorities while at the same time rewriting many of the rules by which trade is conducted and within which new opportunities arise. The radical realignment in recent years of the relative prices of basic materials and manufactures has also added to opportunities for more extensive cooperation.

Not all of these factors lend themselves to quantification, and several have not yet attracted the empirical research on which measurement of the relative contributions to the diversification and growth of East–West economic cooperation would have to be based. This communication is confined to a discussion of what would appear to be the principal economic constraints and opportunities determining the scope for the further development of East–West industrial and technological cooperation. On balance, the opportunities considerably outweigh the constraints. The conclusion is therefore that the 'economic' scope is large enough to justify energetic action by governments to create favourable policy conditions for initiative at the operational level of trading organisations and enterprises. The Conference on Security and Cooperation in Europe codified *inter alia* collective (i.e. multilateral) progress towards defining the shared objectives of commercial, industrial and technological cooperation. The translation of the relevant provisions of the Helsinki Final Act* into a wider community of economic interest is a task that commands the attention of economists as well as of policy makers.

II UNEXPLOITED OPPORTUNITIES

The following headings can be considered as defining the scope for industrial cooperation which could be developed over the next decade, provided certain conditions – some of which are the subject of comments later – are satisfied:

(a) Development of matching, or complementary, industrial structures.
(b) Development of a neo-classical international division of labour in the sense of an interlocking structure of exchanges of technology-intensive consumers' manufactures from the West against technology-intensive basic materials and investment goods from the East.
(c) New mechanisms of financial recycling, to ease the strains caused by leads and lags in West–East investment and repayment in kind, under conditions of convertibility.
(d) Extension of existing forms of industrial cooperation to new sectors and branches.
(e) Extension of existing forms of industrial cooperation to medium and small-sized enterprises.

* All references are to the English text, *Conference on Security and Cooperation in Europe, Final Act*, Cmnd. 6198 (London: HMSO, 1975).

(f) Development of new forms of industrial cooperation.
(g) Realisation of 'projects of common interest' referred to, but not
     identified, in the Final Act of the Helsinki Conference.

As regards complementary industrial structures, there is no evident
economic reason why East—West trade should not follow the traditional path
of trade amongst highly industrialised countries by becoming increasingly
specialised in the exchange of manufactures (and, in particular, of intermediate
manufactured products, component parts and sub-assemblies). True, a considerable 'historical' back-log exists, in the sense that the present volume and
composition of East—West trade is far from corresponding to the present
industrial maturity of the socialist economies. There are well-known reasons
of an economic policy and 'systemic' nature to explain this situation —
chiefly an unwillingness at the governmental level, in earlier years, to allow or
a fortiori encourage a heavy level of dependence on the other partner.
Reluctance to accept high degrees of East—West trade dependence slowed
down the development of economic and technological *interdependence*. (By
the same token, there has been a strong tendency to intensify trade with
neighbours or allies, within sub-regional economic groupings. These groupings,
instead of being considered merely as instruments of deliberate trade-diversion
from East—West to intra-trade-bloc channels should be seen to have been to
some degree alternative channels.)
   If this reasoning is valid, it suggests the following points of departure for
further discussion and research:

  (i)   intra-Western and intra-Eastern industrial and trading patterns have
        developed in conditions of organic separation largely (though not
        exclusively) as a result of non-economic policy objectives and
        systemic constraints.
  (ii) Over the past eight to ten years there has been a widespread
        recognition (at both the government and enterprise levels) of the
        implicitly high opportunity cost of a continuation of this separate
        and parallel development. The main elements of this opportunity
        cost are the failure to exploit potential gains from trade available
        from a region-wide pattern of specialisation — not merely in terms
        of production, but also in R & D, innovation, and expertise in
        marketing and enterprise management and industrial organisation.
        Other potential advantages forgone include (from the Western side)
        the greater stability of export demand and of prices obtaining on
        Eastern markets; and, from the Eastern side, a higher rate of technical
        progress, export diversification and an improvement in mass-
        consumption goods' quality and assortment that would probably
        have been possible in conditions of a deeper East—West division of
        labour.
  (iii) This unsatisfactory situation is now being corrected, at the govern-
        mental level, by the very marked progress in the number and coverage

of bilateral intergovernmental agreements on commercial, economic, industrial and technological cooperation, together with the whole apparatus of joint commissions, technical seminars and fairs with government sponsorship, etc., and, on a multilateral level, by the efforts being made to implement 'Basket 2' of the Final Act of the Helsinki Conference. At the enterprise or trade-organisation level, there has also been a welcome readiness to enter into medium- to long-term industrial cooperation contracts, and to explore a variety of forms of such contracts, tailored to the requirements and legislation of the partner enterprises and countries.

(iv) Judging by the ECE secretariat Register which now lists over 400 such contracts, on a fairly restrictive definition, there seems to have been, in the past two or three years, a discernible slowing down in the number of new industrial cooperation contracts concluded. This tendency — while not yet alarming — suggests that the initial momentum to enter into enterprise-to-enterprise specialisation and coproduction contracts may now be losing strength. The explanation may lie in faulty collection or interpretation of the statistics. It may also be associated with the combined effects of recession and inflation in the West. Perhaps the initial novelty has worn off for some enterprises, and certainly the heavy pre-investment or 'entry' costs of locating and negotiating with promising partners for industrial cooperation has acted as a disincentive to many Western enterprises. In the past year or two, the insistence by many potential Eastern partners on very high buy-back proportions — from 80 to 100 per cent — (while understandable, given the difficulties they have been experiencing in placing their products on Western markets during the recession) has added to the difficulties of Western enterprises in financing such transactions and has discouraged new entrants into the 'industrial cooperation market'.

(v) In summary, the existing complementarities between Eastern and Western resource, industrial, technological and managerial capacities would justify a much higher degree of interregional specialisation, and a much higher volume of trade. Industrial cooperation agreements offer a promising contractual form through which a community of interests can be realised. It is promising both for the well-known advantages for both sides and because it is an organisational type of association intermediate between what has been called 'arms-length' trade, or 'one-shot deals' and the types of organic association or fusion (with majority ownership rights) towards which Western industrial organisation has been tending — most conspicuously in the economic and trading power of the transnational enterprises (cf. MacMillan's paper). While recognising these advantages (some of which are macroeconomic, some microeconomic and therefore operating with varying strength at the governmental

and enterprise levels in the West) we should note (1) a certain
vulnerability of industrial cooperation to the effects of the present
inflation-recession and (2) the costs imposed on Western partners
by lack of information about partners and plan priorities, etc. — costs
which bear particularly heavily on medium- and small-scale
enterprises.

III INNOVATIVE POLICY OPTIONS

What could be done to reduce these difficulties? The following approaches
could be considered:

(a) *Policy-oriented research.* Economic research — conducted by
participants in Round Tables such as this — directed to providing
governments with guidance on what the option profile of intra-branch
(or product-) specialisation between the two groups of countries might
be. No mean task, admittedly, in the present state of the art. But the
type of study that Hal Lary, Jan Tindbergen or Wassily Leontieff have
conducted into the capital, labour, technology- and resource-intensities
of trade in manufactures in South—North flows could possibly
illuminate some of the East—West options. It is easy — though not
supported by adequate empirical evidence — to envisage an interlocking
structure of exchanges of technology-intensive consumers' manufactures
from the West against technology-intensive basic industrial materials
and investment goods from the East, supplemented, of course, by a
broader exchange of intermediate manufactures — component parts
and sub-assemblies — moving in both directions, as already happens in
many industrial cooperation contracts.

(b) *New mechanisms of financial recycling.* A distinguishing feature of
industrial cooperation contracts is their long-range nature: five years to
ten years. Moreover, many of them provide for the creation of new
technological or extracting capacities in Eastern Europe. In the nature
of the case, a sometimes considerable time-lag occurs between the
initial Western input and the resultant Eastern output, part of which
constitutes the 'pay-back'. Financing this gap has put pressure both
on Western partners (especially the medium-sized and smaller enterprises) and on Eastern resources of convertible currency. Large-scale
recourse to the Eurocurrency markets, inter-bank loans and government-guaranteed credits have made it possible to bridge the gap, but
in conditions of hard-currency scarcity and often without the benefit
of governmental export credit guarantees, which do not as a rule
accept repayment in kind as adequate collateral. A new mechanism
for bridging the gap, specialised in East—West industrial cooperation,
would therefore provide a service which would 'lubricate the wheels'
of this form of East—West trade. The case for setting up a joint-equity
bank — an East—West Industrial Development and Cooperative Bank —

in which Eastern and Western governments would be the principal shareholders and guarantors (possibly in association with both Western and Eastern transnational enterprises and banking consortia) deserves serious consideration. The ECE secretariat is now preparing a detailed proposal of this kind, for examination by the Committee on the Development of Trade.

(c) *Extension of existing forms of industrial cooperation to new branches and products.* Although the relevant statistics are scarce, and often difficult to interpret, by common consent industrial cooperation still accounts for a small share of East–West trade (not more than 10 per cent) and is heavily concentrated in the engineering (especially transport) and electrical industries. There are, of course, good reasons for this state of affairs – notably the strong priority attributed to the machine-building branch in East European plans, and the fact that product and component specialisation is characteristic of production processes in that branch. By contrast, bulk chemicals manufacture or the agricultural sector use far fewer processes which lend themselves to technological disaggregation and geographical separation. None the less, there are many other branches where the scope for industrial cooperation would appear, *prima facie*, to be large. This is particularly true of the consumer-manufactures and automobile industries. There seems every prospect that these sectors will attract higher priority in future East-European plans and given the fairly long gestation period of industrial cooperation contracts, from the original search for partners to the commissioning of cooperation capacities, contracts negotiated now could contribute significantly to the volume, quality and assortment targets of eastern Europe in the 1981–5 quinquennium. When we also bear in mind the medium-term prospect of excess capacity for automobile production in the West, this would seem to be a branch *par excellence* where there is a basis for a long-term community of interest (viable complementarities of capacities and requirements) between East and West.

These are obvious examples: there are others in the extraction and processing of basic industrial materials, chiefly in the Soviet Union, with its great untapped reserves of oil and metals; and electric energy generation (including – even – nuclear engineering, where the US and USSR already have active bilateral cooperation in research and development on fusion) and electronics.

It would not, however, be enough to identify – by means of the empirical research referred to earlier – those branches in which the scope for extending industrial cooperation would seem to be greatest. Another prerequisite is that the authorities in the socialist countries decide (and also publish) at an early stage of plan formulation, which projects they will open up for international tender. The Helsinki Final Act states quite explicitly that there is a recognised need for more,

and more detailed, information.* Western enterprises would then be
better placed to adapt their own long-range investment and R & D
strategies accordingly.

(d) *Extension of industrial cooperation to medium- and small-sized
    enterprises.* The information gap affects medium- and small-scale
    enterprises particularly severely. Given the importance of such
    enterprises — with a labour force of up to, say, 500 — in both intra-
    Western and intra-Eastern trade (especially in sub-contracting), their
    sparse participation in East—West industrial cooperation means the
    loss of a large catchment area of potential industrial cooperation
    partners. True, in many large-scale East—West contracts, such as
    Togliattegrad or Kama, the principal Western contracter has engaged
    thousands of such enterprises as sub-contractors. One can understand
    why an economy of the Soviet Union's scale prefers to deal with large
    Western enterprises. This does not apply in the same way to the other
    East European countries, but none the less the medium- and small-
    scale enterprises are not particularly active in industrial cooperation
    there either, because of the information problem, high entry costs and
    limited financing capacity.

    An industrial cooperation centre, or equivalent mechanism, with an
    information exchange and partner-matching 'bourse' function, and a
    specialised East—West industrial cooperation bank could remove some
    of these difficulties.

(e) *Development of new forms of industrial cooperation.* Much discussion
    has centred on the appropriateness of joint ventures for the two
    partners — that is, the guarantees for venture-capital, repatriation of
    assets and profits and managerial control for the Western partner: and,
    on the Eastern side, of the compatibility of this type of arrangement
    with socialist principles and planning. The compromise type of
    legislation which has now been in force in Yugoslavia for several years,
    and in Hungary and Romania more recently, has resulted in the
    establishment of so few joint ventures that there must be some doubt
    about how successful the present formulae will prove to be. Recent
    changes in such legislation in Hungary and Poland are implicit
    recognition of the need to find more satisfactory arrangements.

    A more active search for other contractual forms of industrial
    cooperation seems therefore necessary. Two directions worth exploring
    are:

    (i) the establishment of international, i.e. East—West holding
        companies, with equal equity shares, which would *lease* their
        installations, management and consultancy services to Eastern
        or Western enterprises, as the case may be. Alternatively, the
        Eastern enterprise could lease its assets to the holding company,

* See p. 240 below (Ed.).

thus retaining ownership but surrendering operational control.

(ii) the creation of East–West transnational enterprises or consortia, possibly drawing their constituents from existing intra-Western and intra-CMEA transnationals. Such 'joint-transnationals' would have at least two advantages:

- they would bring to East–West industrial cooperation a multilateral dimension *in both systems*, thereby increasing the scope for economies of scale
- they would be better placed than individual enterprises or ministerial departments to undertake large-scale projects on a continuing basis, as opposed to the *ad hoc* consortia now formed in the West.

(f) *Large scale projects of common interest.* This brings me to the subject, explicitly referred to but not defined in the Helsinki Final Act, of 'projects of common interest'. The absence of definition in the Final Act probably reflects the difficulty of identifying, in a multilateral diplomatic conference, projects which could command the support of all participants. Yet the fact remains that virtually all industrial cooperation within Europe is at present conducted through *bilateral* channels. There are some triangular arrangements, e.g. the Iranian– Soviet-FRG gas pipeline (and, of course, the tripartite cooperation with developing countries described in Mr Davydov's paper).

In order to give some substance to the Helsinki provisions on projects of common interest, I believe that multilateral intergovern- mental bodies such as the ECE, or *ad hoc* high-level conferences in such fields as energy, transport or environment, as proposed by the Soviet Union, should begin to draw up a list of major schemes that could and should be undertaken on a pan-regional basis over the next fifteen to twenty years. Transport infrastructure and equipment, from the Soviet Far East to the Channel Ports, or from the Baltic to the Adriatic and Aegean is obsolescent by reference to today's require- ments and *a fortiori* to those of tomorrow. Yet the scale of resources necessary to renew road, rail and inland waterway capacities exceeds by far the resources of most countries of the region taken individually. If East–West trade continues to grow rapidly in volume, or even more if it accelerates, North Central Europe could easily find itself in the same position of sudden over-congestion as the roads of Turkey or the ports of Iran and the Gulf when there was an upsurge in trade between the Middle East and Western Europe. Other sectors, such as those mentioned in the papers by Senin and Shmelyov also merit study from this point of view.

One way of starting would be to build on the experience of CERN (the most successful multilateral scientific and technological cooperation scheme); and to launch one or two multilateral cooperation

research projects of common interest: examples from transport have
been mentioned — non-waste technologies is another possibility, as is
Arctic research.

IV TECHNOLOGICAL COOPEARTION AND TECHNOLOGY TRANSFER

The discussion of technology transfer and cooperation in this Round Table has
been so wide-ranging that in order to avoid repetition some very brief
additional remarks are offered here.

There is a strong and rising demand in the socialist countries for Western
technology: the sources of this demand — in intensive growth policies, the
desires to avoid duplicating R & D expenses and to improve the technical
quality and competitiveness of exports — are well known: the demand for
technology is reflected in plan priorities and the very active acquisition of
licences, and in technology transfer provisions in industrial cooperation and
scientific and technological cooperation agreements at the governmental and
enterprise level. It makes sense for the Western supplier to respond to this
demand — because (a) it usually widens the market for its next to latest
technology (e.g. Fiat 124 and Zhiguli) and (b) because it can expect a
cumulative effect which can be described as continuing technological interdependence — the first round of transfer guaranteeing a second round of
demand for improved-process technology. We should note also the reverse
flow: technology transfer is not necessarily a one-way street.

It is not necessary to rehearse all the familiar 'peculiarities' of East—West
trade as a preface to considering what the scope for future development and
diversification of technology-transfer transactions may be. Awareness of these
peculiarities (or inter-systemic differences) does, however, affect the international discussion of East—West prospects. For example, the economic
rationality of Western enterprises transferring technology to the developing
countries of, say, Latin America is never challenged in the technology-
exporting countries. (The methods and terms by which the transfer takes
place are, of course, contested by many developing countries, which are
insisting on an internationally agreed code of conduct to redress their weaker
bargaining power; but that is another story.) Why then should so many
doubts be raised about the transfer of technology from West to East? The
answer is part political and part economic — and in both cases consists in an
anxiety that technology transfer may strengthen a potential competitor. This
attitude has never been predominant in Western policy towards other
technology-importing areas — not even towards Japan, which no longer has
any significant technological lag *vis-à-vis* North America or Western Europe.

One is drawn to the conclusion that political and security anxieties still
exert a decisive influence on the nature of East—West economic relations.
That is why any genuine progress towards removing or reducing such
anxieties — the process of détente and the follow-up to the Helsinki
Conference — is a *sine qua non* for economic cooperation to reach its true
potential.

15 UNCTAD and Tripartite Industrial Cooperation*

M. Davydov
UNTAD SECRETARIAT

I INTRODUCTION

Tripartite industrial cooperation, which refers to cooperation between enterprises from the socialist countries of Eastern Europe, the developing countries and the developed market-economy countries, though a fairly recent phenomenon, has quickly become of interest to business circles, governments and international organisations. The need to ensure that this form of cooperation benefits the developing countries seems to be generally accepted, as is attested by the attention accorded to it in a recent United Nations resolution 3362 (S-VII) and in policy documents issued by other international bodies.

Within the United Nations family, UNCTAD took the initiative in promoting trade-creating international industrial cooperation, in accordance with its mandate to deal with issues of trade and related problems of economic development which might lead, *inter alia*, to an amelioration of the developing countries' position in the world economy. Thus, UNCTAD deals with all types of industrial cooperation – bilateral, multilateral or tripartite – between developing and other countries which contribute to the industrialisation of the developing countries and which influence, directly or indirectly, their trade-flows so as to create new exports from them, diminish their imports, change the commodity structure of trade or its geographical pattern, etc.

UNCTAD's work on tripartite cooperation is organised within its assignment to promote trade and economic relations between countries having different economic and social systems. By now UNCTAD's activities in this field have developed in several directions: a number of studies have been prepared, information has been gathered and an expert seminar on various aspects of tripartite cooperation was convened in December 1975 by the Secretary-General of UNCTAD in the context of trade relations among countries having different economic and social systems.

UNCTAD's work on tripartite industrial cooperation has been guided and

---

* The views expressed in this paper do not necessarily reflect those of the UNCTAD secretariat. The designations employed and the presentation of the material in this document do not imply the expression of any opinion whatsoever on the part of the secretariat concerning the legal status of any country or territory or of its authorities, or concerning the delimitation of its frontiers.

inspired by recently accentuated developments on the international economic
and political scene.

The international community has generally become more aware of the
need to establish a new international division of labour more equitable for
the developing countries and based on new patterns of complementarity with
other countries. The role of international cooperation, in creating favourable
external conditions and in assisting the developing countries in their efforts to
industrialise their economies and achieve new patterns of international
specialisation, has been specifically underlined. The developing countries
themselves have recently been undergoing considerable changes. The emergence
of a group among them with rich resources, both material and financial, the
attempts to create integrated areas among countries of the developing world
and the progress of industrialisation in some developing countries, have substantially affected international economic relations. At the same time, the
socialist countries of Eastern Europe have been involving themselves more
deeply in international trade and economic cooperation. The dynamic
expansion of their productive capacities and the progressive integration of
the CMEA area have created conditions for an extended specialisation on a
world-wide basis, offering a new range of opportunities to other groups of
countries.

The normalisation of political relations between the socialist countries of
Eastern Europe and the developed market-economy countries, and the
parallel intensification of East—West economic links, could not fail to have a
beneficial effect on the developing countries. This expansion of East—West
trade and cooperation, along with the progress made in détente, seem to be
major explanatory factors for the recent acceleration in the development of
tripartite industrial cooperation. There appear to be greater opportunities for
the developing countries to join in East—West cooperation arrangements, and
in other new forms of international cooperation. The developing countries'
support for such arrangements is an expression of their wish to profit from
détente and the expansion of East—West relations. Both in the socialist
countries and in the developed market-economy countries tripartite industrial
cooperation is seen as a way of answering the demands of the developing
countries that their interests be safeguarded when countries in the former
groups embark upon their own projects and programmes.

II SUBSTANTIAL ISSUES LINKED WITH TRIPARTITE
INDUSTRIAL COOPERATION

The work and studies undertaken in UNCTAD so far have highlighted several
substantial issues of interest for a realistic assessment of the prospects for, and
likely scope of, tripartite cooperation. In view of the fact that the interested
governments (or international organisations) might wish to undertake some
legislative or other regulatory action, or to harmonise their respective
prescriptions, it seems necessary to devote some attention to the meaning of

tripartite (or multilateral in general) industrial cooperation, in order to delineate the field of application of eventual measures. There is as yet no generally accepted definition of the term 'industrial cooperation'. In the countries which have most experience of this form of international cooperation the term is used in a broad and flexible manner, as can be seen from the provisions concerning industrial cooperation in their national legislation. The UNCTAD secretariat has evolved a working definition, broad in scope, which defines this type of industrial arrangement as cooperation at the enterprise/organisation level between the industrial sectors of developing, socialist and developed market-economy countries; and it has concentrated its studies on cooperation arrangements located in developing countries.

Several different types of contractual arrangements were identified by the secretariat and discussed by the participants in the December seminar. It appears that the developing country may sign:

(a) a single contract with a consortium leader who bears the responsibility for the participation of the other partners;
(b) one contract with each of the foreign partners acting jointly;
(c) a single contract with the two foreign enterprises, these being co-signatories; and
(d) two separate contracts with each foreign partner.

There has been no general consensus as to which form of tripartite industrial cooperation is the ideal one from the point of view of all three partners involved. UNCTAD's interest is in determining the forms of tripartite cooperation which could promote the economic development of developing countries. Some of the development goals on which tripartite industrial cooperation could have an effect are:

(i) the desire for economic independence – i.e. the desire of developing countries to attain greater control over their economies and their development process;
(ii) strengthening the industrial capacity of developing countries; creating a competitive and viable industrial sector;
(iii) increasing and diversifying the exports of developing countries, especially the export of non-traditional goods such as manufactures and semi-manufactures; the creation of competitive industries could contribute to the achievement of this goal;
(iv) increasing the flow of advanced, though relevant, technologies and managerial skills to the developing countries;
(v) increasing the flow of financial resources to the developing countries.

The analysis of actual cases of tripartite industrial cooperation permits their classification according to the criteria often utilised by UNCTAD – i.e. their trade effects.

(i) The majority of cases identified so far have concerned firms from the socialist countries and from the developed market-economy countries combining to execute a defined project in a developing country, sometimes with only minimal participation by firms from the developing country. In most cases the participation by developing-country enterprises has consisted in erection and construction work. This kind of cooperation has trade effects, in that it results in exports from the developed and/or the socialist countries of Eastern Europe for the duration of the project. Frequently, it has produced longer-lasting exports to the developing country, although of a changing composition. An increase in the exports of the developing country could also result, whether directly as a result of the project or indirectly; but this has not been the reason for the establishment of the cooperation arrangement, enterprises from other countries undertaking no obligation to import the newly produced goods. A number of such cooperation agreements have been achieved in the field of heavy industry (iron and steel), machine-building (tractors, heavy machinery, vehicles), energy-producing industries (electricity, coal, petroleum for home consumption), food processing, and infrastructure (communications, transport facilities, etc.), which were all primarily directed to meeting the needs and demands of the developing country.

(ii)   In some cases a more or less durable flow-back of goods from the developing countries was ensured by the socialist countries' stipulating repayment in kind of their credits utilised for the execution of the project. (But repayment in kind is a practice rarely adopted by creditors from Western countries.) This kind of trade effect has been widespread in cases of cooperation in mining or in primary production in the developing countries; but the socialist countries have increasingly been adopting repayment in kind in other industrial fields, such as machine-building, production of vehicles and parts, chemicals and pharmaceuticals.

(iii) Only a few cases have been identified of tripartite industrial cooperation directly creating exports to the partners of the developing country within the same scheme (e.g. cooperation in car production between Italy, Poland, the USSR, Yugoslavia, Egypt; fertiliser production between Poland, Morocco and the Federal Republic of Germany, and some others).

The classification according to trade effects is important for the developing countries, which attach different priorities to each type of effect. The financial resources available to a developing country also influence the form of tripartite cooperation which it favours. Thirdly, a clause on assistance in marketing the goods produced — in the developing countries or in other markets — is very often requested by the developing countries. In this respect, the socialist countries of Eastern Europe have proved very valuable partners — accepting long-term deliveries, helping the suppliers in the developing countries to adapt their production to the standards and requirements of the importing markets and lending an element of stability and security to the developing countries' foreign trade.

Tripartite industrial cooperation can also be studied from the point of view of its effect on the industrialisation process in developing countries. Thus it may be that such a form of cooperation enhances the ability of developing-country enterprises to obtain advanced technologies and managerial and marketing skills from socialist and developed market-economy countries. It has been argued that the choice and control of the developing-country partner is enhanced with an increase in the number of its partners in a cooperation project.

UNCTAD has investigated also the motivations for tripartite cooperation (the reasons enterprises enter into such arrangements) in order to be able to suggest answers to several questions: Where could tripartite cooperation be expected to emerge? How might it be promoted? Who might initiate such combinations?

Among numerous reasons which have induced enterprises to cooperate in the execution of tripartite projects, several were recurrently observed in the factual information available to UNCTAD, so that certain generalisations are possible.

The initiative may be taken by any one of the three partners. Often an enterprise chose to seek the collaboration of an Eastern or Western partner with which it had already worked in some other cooperation project. In several cases general inter-enterprise/organisation cooperation agreements providing for joint exploration of possibilities, joint bidding, planning and construction led to the establishment of specific tripartite projects. Most of the identified cases of tripartite industrial cooperation stemmed from an assessment by the responsible authorities or firms in the developing country of the comparative strengths of the foreign firms, as reflected in competitive bidding.

One factor which has motivated firms to participate in tripartite cooperation arrangements has been the desire to seek new marketing outlets, or to expand old ones. Often one enterprise will seek out a partner from the East or West that has already established a firm marketing base in the developing country involved. The desire to take advantage of economic complementarities (such as special resources or technologies possessed by a certain partner), thus expanding the international division of labour, can also be a motive. The Western partner may possess certain technologies or managerial skills which could lead to a successful project. The socialist-country enterprise may be more ready to adapt to host-country requirements. Many Western enterprises have been motivated by a desire to reduce costs of the resulting products, marketed in the host country or in third countries. The socialist-country enterprises can offer more competitive conditions in certain cases, and are also not as affected by short-term cyclical fluctuations and inflation as are the enterprises of developed market-economy countries.

The latter have increasingly sought cooperation with other enterprises on a long-term stable basis in order to assure better planning of their operations. The socialist countries have always stressed the value of stable and durable economic links.

The demands of some large-scale projects may be too great for one particular enterprise; thus it may seek the cooperation of a partner in implementing a project in a developing country.

The desire to ensure a stable source of supplies may motivate some tripartite arrangements, though this applies mainly to the socialist countries, who are more apt to establish buy-back arrangements. Examples are such materials as crude oil and phosphates (from the Middle Eastern countries), some steel products, pharmaceuticals and chemicals (from India, Yugoslavia, Egypt and some Latin American countries), but also consumer goods such as textiles, leatherware and the like, which satisfy a constantly growing demand in the socialist countries.

Financial considerations have also been an important factor in establishing tripartite links. The socialist partner may be interested in joining its financing facilities with those of a Western partner, such as intergovernmental credits, export guarantees and, to a lesser extent, bank credits. The socialist partner can often offer credit to the developing-country partner through the bilateral clearing facilities existing between the socialist and the developing country and, as has been mentioned, the socialist partner is often willing to accept payment in kind for the services and goods it delivers.

There may be political reasons behind the desire to cooperate with a third partner in a developing country. Thus, one partner may seek an Eastern or a Western partner because it may not be welcomed alone in a particular developing country.

The secretariat has found that intergovernmental action was one of the main factors influencing the development of tripartite industrial cooperation. Such action includes the negotiation of bilateral intergovernmental agreements designed to establish a framework for the development of international trade and industrial cooperation and to influence decision-makers at the production level. Autonomous policy measures normalising international trade and economic relations between countries having different economic and social systems could also encourage tripartite industrial cooperation.

It seems obvious that the developing countries welcome any kind of international cooperation which permits them to increase or transform their productive and exporting capacities. The tripartite form may have considerable advantages for the developing countries, in that such cooperation widens the scope and opportunities for industrialisation beyond those offered by purely bilateral combinations. In particular the developing country, having a wider choice and possibilities of combining techniques from many partners, may be able to obtain a higher quality technology than it could in purely bilateral relations.

Several other questions have been considered in UNCTAD, with the purpose of discovering the advantages to the partners from the tripartite forms of cooperation as compared with those attainable through bilateral cooperation arrangements. In this connection, among other topics, the financial component of such relations was analysed, as well as the payments and currency problems involved. It was found that tripartite combinations offered the advantage that the financing abilities of the different partners could be combined in a project, perhaps allowing the implementation of a project by the three partners which would not have been possible had only two partners attempted a cooperation agreement. Nevertheless the question of financing, which is one of the decisive factors influencing progress in tripartite industrial cooperation, in fact often hinders such progress. It has been frequently noticed that socialist countries of Eastern Europe have been prepared to assume the role of accommodating and bringing into harmony the interests of the other two partners.

III MEASURES TO PROMOTE TRIPARTITE COOPERATION

In view of the general consensus that tripartite industrial cooperation can contribute to trade expansion among its member states, UNCTAD has explored ways and means which would contribute to the futher development of such cooperation. It has tried to identify measures which could be suggested to governments wishing to promote tripartite industrial cooperation. While respecting the interests and initiatives of individual enterprises, these measures should at the same time facilitate the emergence of these interests and their implementation through concrete deals. The relevant authorities in individual countries could take two roads to reach the same objective – see to it that such obstacles as exist to cooperation are removed and/or take direct measures to facilitate enterprises' activities under cooperation arrangements. While measures abolishing obstacles to cooperation seem to be recommendable in all cases, measures creating exceptionally favourable, and thus differential, conditions for enterprises involved in cooperation are more debatable. In general, the right balance has to be found of measures to stimulate the setting up and initial functioning of industrial enterprises in the developing countries.

One possibility in the field of government action is the inclusion of provisions dealing with tripartite (or multilateral) cooperation in the laws and regulations which, in each country, govern foreign trade and economic relations. At the moment very few countries have such legislative instruments. It also seems opportune to ask for international consistency in formulating regulations which might facilitate multilateral cooperation. This is particularly important in tripartite deals encompassing subjects from different legal systems. The multinational fora – UNCTAD, UNIDO or others – could undertake initiatives in this respect. The status of joint-ventures in the different national legal systems seems to require urgent attention, as was proved by legal acts recently adopted in some socialist countries of Eastern

Europe (Bulgaria, Hungary, Poland, etc.) in which the attempt was made to bring into closer concordance prescriptions (and definitions) from various legal systems.

Several UN bodies (among others the UNIDO and the ECE) have dealt at length with the problem of international action in the field of contractual arrangements, between enterprises from various countries. Admittedly, enterprises are reluctant to accept recommendations which would encroach upon their freedom of action or decision, but it has been proved that such activities as the drafting of model contracts, setting up of arbitration rules, offering technical assistance to the weaker and more inexperienced partners, are accepted without much opposition by all interested parties.

Tripartite cooperation could be promoted indirectly by international endeavours to identify areas where a future coincidence of interests might be expected. UNCTAD is only at the beginning of such research work. Taking into account reports from several typical countries whose enterprises have acquired experience in tripartite cooperation (India, Egypt, Iraq, Morocco, from the developing world; Poland, Hungary, Czechoslovakia and the USSR from the socialist countries of Eastern Europe; France, the Federal Republic of Germany, Austria and Italy from the developed market-economy countries) as well as the results of its independent investigations, UNCTAD has roughly delineated in its recent publications broad economic areas or industrial fields where enterprises from the three groups of countries might find possibilities to cooperate. However, more detailed studies are needed and UNCTAD plans to continue its activities in this field.

Discussion of the Papers by Professor Shmelyov, Mr Scott and Dr Davydov

Dr Hernandez introduced the first two papers, summarising Mr Scott's text, which had not been generally circulated. He agreed with Professor Shmelyov's stress on lack of information as a hindrance to mutually beneficial cooperation (p. 221) and was inclined to give even more weight to suspicions and misinformation reflecting outdated Cold-War attitudes. Mr Scott's paper was a valuable indication of the range both of unrealised opportunities and also of the technical and economic constraints and the policies which could possibly relax them.

Professor Lavigne drew attention to a report to the Council of Europe* which stressed the high technological and scientific potential of the socialist countries, analysed the obstacles to East—West technological exchanges and ways to remove them, and contained information on exchanges of patents and licences and scientific and technical agreements concluded between Eastern and Western countries. A subsequent directive by the Council had called for study of the problems and for action to promote East—West scientific, and general academic, contacts.

Examining the question why there was not more East—West cooperation in the fields covered by Shmelyov's — in his view excellent — paper, *Professor Kirschen* suggested reasons common to East and West: national pride; risk-aversion by industrialists or planners (greater risk if part of the production on which you depend takes place abroad); reluctance of managers to accept less cosy lives; reluctance of workers to move, especially to less developed regions of a country; reluctance to kill off old industries and to force workers to change jobs; the wish to preserve the benefit of innovations or the birth of new industries (often involving high research and development costs partly government-financed) for the national tax-payer. Multinational companies had a bad name, but they did spread research efforts internationally and could in many ways overcome bureaucratic constraints on cooperation. In the EEC the idea was being considered of encouraging 'EEC' multinationals, subject to EEC-agreed controls, tax obligations, etc. Could not the CMEA usefully develop similar organisations, producing the benefits through not the disadvantages of Western multinationals?

Professor Wolf contrasted Shmelyov's assertion that both Eastern and Western firms wanted long-term, stable supply and marketing arrangements with Csikós-Nagy's views that uncertainty about prices and demand conditions in the West made Western firms less interested in cooperation arrangements involving their acceptance of Eastern products and that, in general, the more popular product-pay-back deals were those involving energy or raw materials, while other cooperation arrangements were most attractive to the West where the resulting export was destined for CMEA

* Rapport sur la coopération scientifique et technique entre les pays européens (Rapporteur, M. Boucheny) (Conseil de l'Europe, Assemblée Parlementaire, 27 avril 1976). Doc. 3772.

markets (p. 204). Given (a) the uncertainty (*pace* Hardt p. 103) whether the
West really could now expect resumption of smooth growth without
inflation or worsening terms of trade and (b) the stimulus to rationalisation
of Western enterprises given by the recent recession, he wondered whether
traditional forms of East—West inter-enterprise relations (the market-end of
McMillan's spectrum, p. 175) might not be the fastest-growing element in
East—West relations in the future — despite Scott's persuasive argument on
the structural bases for cooperation agreements. Even if this were so, no
doubt energy or raw material product-pay-back agreements and some very
large projects of the kind mentioned by Shmelyov and Scott would still be
important. *Professor Rothschild* doubted, however, whether the slowing
down in the rate at which new cooperation agreements were reported
(mentioned by Scott) could be taken as evidence of any such trend; some
hiatus was to be expected once the most obvious and easiest opportunities
had been exploited. He thought that a register of agreements, describing their
exact terms, could be very helpful.

Dr Rogge and others stressed the more general need for information if
opportunities for trade or cooperation were to be exploited as efficiently as
possible, or national planners and industrialists to be able to undertake major
new developments without risking wasteful duplication of some other
country's project. Dr Rogge stressed, *inter alia*, the need for market research
and projections of the growth of the markets for different products in the
socialist countries, as well as *detailed* national development plans. *Dr Hardt*
asked that the relevant part of the Helsinki Final Act — which would require
improvements in the provision of data by both East and West to comply with
its demands — be reproduced in the Proceedings.* He saw a danger of trade
development being inhibited and competition restricted if, as often at present,
information was provided on a selective, privileged basis; Western multinationals might tend to acquire, selectively, special, non-competitive
relationships with Eastern monopolies.

Referring to Mr Scott's paper, *Dr Guzek* agreed that the process of
structural change in East and West was bound to open up possibilities of
beneficial cooperation; but he saw the Eastern interest as being in intra-
branch rather than inter-branch specialisation. The 'Leontieff approach' could
not guide the socialist countries' planning; they had to aim at developing in
selected, highly specialised areas of production high factor productivity
based on economies of scale and access to more than the national market.

Professor McMillan hoped that Professor Shmelyov would elaborate, in
the light of Soviet experience, on his statement that in the future practical
forms of cooperation will be devised 'for determining the [foreign investor's]
say in the technical and commercial policy of the enterprise, representation
of his interests in management and so on.' (p. 218). This he, McMillan,
had seen as a so far unresolved problem.

* The participating States . . . Considering that economic information should be of
such a nature as to allow adequate market analysis and to permit the preparation of
medium and long term forecasts, thus contributing to the establishment of a
continuing flow of trade and a better utilisation of commercial possibilities
. . .
Will promote the publication and dissemination of economic and commercial
information at regular intervals and as quickly as possible, in particular:

The interests and difficulties of the developing countries – considered in *Dr Davidov's* paper, which he introduced – were taken up by *Dr Medina*, who said that such countries did not have entirely happy experiences of cooperation with the industrialised world; satisfactory arrangements for stable, long-term cooperation were rare and choice of satisfactory partners was difficult. Possibly tripartite cooperation, including a socialist country, might offer better long-term prospects; but the developing countries generally had difficulty in discovering possibilities. *Dr Vaves* indicated some of the difficulties of economic relations between Latin America and the socialist countries: traditional trade was small and unbalanced, with the Latin American countries as the creditors; the latter countries' industries were generally equipped with Western machinery and this limited possible equipment imports from Eastern Europe. Yet in some sectors Eastern technology was probably more appropriate to Latin American conditions than that of Western industrialised countries (e.g. steel, urban infrastructure, medicaments). But lack of credit arrangements, and often too rigid conditions on the Eastern side (e.g. offers of complete plants, but not flexible supply of individual items of equipment), slowed down the transfer of technology and limited trade. *Professor Luu van Dat* drew attention to the existence of developing countries among those with socialist economic systems; his own country would welcome Eastern or Western investment and industrial cooperation with developed countries of either system. Professor Yamamoto's suggestions for some institution of Asian cooperation had been interesting, though economic integration of

---

statistics concerning production, national income, budget, consumption and productivity;

foreign trade statistics drawn up on the basis of comparable classification including breakdown by product with indication of volume and value, as well as country of origin or destination;

laws and regulations concerning foreign trade;

information allowing forecasts of development of the economy to assist in trade promotion, for example, information on the general orientation of national economic plans and programmes;

other information to help businessmen in commercial contacts, for example, periodic directories, lists, and where possible, organisational charts of firms, and organisations concerned with foreign trade;

Will in addition to the above encourage the development of the exchange of economic and commercial information through, where appropriate, joint commissions for economic, scientific and technical cooperation, national and joint chambers of commerce, and other suitable bodies;

Will support a study, in the framework of the United Nations Economic Commission for Europe, of the possibilities of creating a multilateral system of notification of laws and regulations concerning foreign trade and changes therein;

Will encourage international work on the harmonisation of statistical nomenclatures, notably in the United Nations Economic Commission for Europe.

. . .

Will encourage all forms of exchange of information and communication of experience relevant to industrial cooperation, including through contacts between potential partners and, where appropriate, through joint commissions for economic, industrial, scientific and technical cooperation, national and joint chambers of commerce, and other suitable bodies [Cmnd. 6198, pp. 15–17].

Asian countries of different economic and social systems was obviously out
of the question. *Professor Shmelyov*, replying to the discussion, reiterated his
belief that the problem seen by Professor McMillan would be solved, and
without the USSR's accepting foreign property-ownership. He agreed with
Dr Rogge about the desirability of further information on the likely future
development of markets, but thought that research and forecasting
techniques were as yet insufficiently developed, in East or West, to provide
data on which any foreign planner or enterprise could rely. What could be
said with certainty, and objectively, about the vast Soviet market was that
for no product could a foreign supplier expect to take over more than a
small corner of the market. The policy of an 'open door', in the classical
sense, was impossible in the actual conditions of the Soviet economy; the
USSR would always determine the form and content of industrial and other
cooperation in the light of its own planned development goals. He found
the idea of tripartite (East—West—developing country) industrial cooperation
entirely acceptable in principle; but it was too early to say whether generally
acceptable forms could be found.

   Mr Scott doubted Professor Wolf's prediction that industrial
cooperation might develop less rapidly in the future and traditional trade
become again the most dynamic element in East—West economic relations.
But the ambiguity of the two concepts made them difficult to contrast or
measure; many forms of cooperation showed their results in trade statistics.
He agreed with Professor Rothschild that the apparent slowing down in the
rate of registration of new contracts could reflect the exhaustion of the
easiest opportunities; it was also possible that the values implied in new
contracts were increasing faster than the numbers of them. Annual
fluctuations could, in any case, not be identified precisely; negotiations
were often protracted and first reports sometimes misleading. He agreed with
Dr Guzek that neither Leontieff's work nor any other could provide the
planner with a prescription for efficient specialisation; but he still thought
it drew attention to factors that the planners had to take into account.

Index

Entries in **bold** type under the names of participants in the Conference indicate their papers or discussions of their papers. Entries in *italics* indicate contributions by participants to the discussions.

Economic Relations Between East & West